THE
AMERICAN REINFORCEMENT
IN THE WORLD WAR

The
American Reinforcement
in the World War,

By
Thomas G. Frothingham

With an Introduction by
Newton D. Baker

BOOKS FOR LIBRARIES PRESS
FREEPORT, NEW YORK

First Published 1927
Reprinted 1971

INTERNATIONAL STANDARD BOOK NUMBER:
0-8369-5736-9

LIBRARY OF CONGRESS CATALOG CARD NUMBER:
70-152984

PRINTED IN THE UNITED STATES OF AMERICA

AMERICA IN THE WORLD WAR

by NEWTON D. BAKER

Secretary of War during the World War

CAPTAIN FROTHINGHAM, believing that certain views expressed to him in personal conversation and certain events and facts related to him would be of general interest in connection with this volume, has invited me to state them in a prefatory note. What follows, therefore, is in no sense an introduction to the book, which tells its own story, but is rather a response to an invitation to state the facts about two or three of the larger aspects of our organization for war as they appeared to me as Secretary of War at the time.

Ten years have gone by since the United States entered the World War, and, in this tenth anniversary year of 1927, it is possible to obtain the right perspective. Captain Frothingham's book is a serious effort to describe in their true relative proportions the great forces, industrial, military, and naval, which brought into being and sustained the American Army on the Western Front. The book also aims to show the use of this American military reinforcement, in its relation to the armies of the Entente Allies on the battlefields of Europe. Apart from the skill and detachment of its author, the book has the advantage of being far enough away, in time, from events and persons to rest upon

fuller evidence and calmer analysis than was possible
to books written in the high tension months of the war
itself or the several years of low tension which so
soon followed the Armistice.

It is to be hoped that monographs will follow, giving
the details of these many American activities, and personal narratives which will supplement this history of the
American effort in the World War. Three personal military narratives, in particular, are still to appear. We
are all eager to have them, the authoritative statements of the three American military leaders in their
respective spheres of duty. General Pershing's own
story will be necessary to satisfy the curiosity about
his problems which is aroused by our grateful pride in
his achievements. General Bliss, who represented us as
military adviser to the Supreme War Council at Versailles, should tell us of the coördination of fronts and
the coöperations of allies which finally succeeded against
another coalition, in which the masterful dominance
of the German General Staff imposed Germany's will
upon her allies as autocratically as it sought to impose
it upon her enemies. To complete the picture, we need
General March's account of the battle on the home
front—it was a battle—in which a stern and resolute
soldier refused to concede either to tradition or to sentiment the least point which delayed or hindered his
support of our forces overseas. When these stories are
told, others will follow, filling in details and adding il-
lustrative incidents and heroic episodes. It will be a help
to the study of these volumes that Captain Frothingham's narrative carries us into broader thinking and
gives us the basis for juster judgments than we have
been able so far to form.

One of the characteristics of advancing civilization is the progressive amelioration of the effects of force; war completely reverses the process. This, of course, has nothing to do with the objects or justification of any particular war, for it may be temporary or necessary, in search of a higher good or in self-preservation. But while war lasts, force reigns, and laws, human and divine, are silent. The last war was, in a very literal sense, a world war. Not only did its consequences affect the entire political and economic structure of modern society, but it drafted men from the desert and supplies from the recesses of dark continents to feed the fires which burned at the same time on a dozen widely scattered fronts. It stripped the human race of its variant civilizations and subjected all men everywhere simultaneously to the dominance of a single primitive passion. Within each nation the war interrupted all customary and familiar relations. Each nation started with "business as usual" as a slogan for its civil population and ended with its civilians almost as militarized as its soldiers.

The fact is that war requires a continuous improvisation. From the battle of the Marne on, even Germany was obliged to improvise. German preparedness sufficed up to the first major unforeseen obstacle, but after that Germany too had to dig in and take many fresh and different starts, with all the adaptations that that implies. To peoples democratically governed, so high a state of pre-war preparedness is unattainable. They can be prepared to parry, not to deliver, the first blow; thus improvisation comes earlier with them and is more confused, less positive. It is also more disconcerting, coming, as it does, as a part of the greater shock of discovering any preparation at all to be necessary. So it was that, when Germany declared war, her armies marched with confident banners, while when we entered the conflict there was deep searching of hearts and hurried exploration of resources to find a basis upon which to build confidence.

I have, as a souvenir, one of the several million post cards mailed by the French War Office when mobilization was ordered. They were all addressed and in readiness and told each man in France his immediate duty. When we went into the war, nobody knew what anybody's duty was to be apart from the regular, organized forces of the country. Thus, for days and weeks after our entrance into the war, as the country comprehended and sympathized, there surged in upon Washington, by telegram, by letter, and in person, literally tens of thousands of men and women of all ages and occupations, filled with devoted and loyal zeal, wanting merely to be told where they could help, where their duty led. But Washington had, and in the nature of the case could have, only a few answers ready. Certain steps had been taken which gave us a start, and they were invaluable, but they were few and inadequate. The genius of Secretary Root had given the army a General Staff, in place of the wrangling bureau system in the War Department, but Congress had imposed limitations upon the personnel of the General Staff which kept it barely sufficient in numbers to preserve the semblance of centralized administration and quite inadequate to its more important task of visualizing and preparing for a great and sudden mobilization. The service schools, notably at Leavenworth and Fort Sill, had for some years been successfully transforming our

officers from Indian fighters into modern soldiers, and
the officers trained in those schools proved in the war
the value of their post-graduate instruction—but they
were a handful as compared with the vast officer personnel required for the armies which gathered into the
cantonments and camps. The Plattsburg system of training camps for officers, established by Major General
Leonard Wood, was an invaluable model upon which
it was possible to build a great series of such camps.
The officers so trained were indispensable. Both the mobile part of the Regular Army and the National Guard
had been mobilized on the Mexican border for practically
a year and had there gotten both the experience of being
parts of large forces and those elementary initiations into hardship and coöperation which take time with
young soldiers and make "an army of a million men
between sunrise and sunset" an impossible exaggeration.
The value of this preparation can hardly be overestimat-
ed, and its results were shown in the ease with which
the new men acquired camp habits from the sprinkl-
ing of border men among them.

On the side of industrial mobilization we were singu-
larly fortunate. In the years prior to the World War,
the United States had developed a highly organized
industrial system. The abundance and variety of our
natural resources invited the ingenuity of our engineers,
and they, adopting the results of the researches of our
own scientists and of the advances of science elsewhere,
rapidly developed the industrial arts. At the same time,
our industrial progress was marked by changes and developments in business methods in the interest of
economy and efficiency. By 1914 we had learned to do
things on a vast scale. Standardizations of method and

product, mass production, and widespread and rapid distribution characterized our industry. Inevitably men of vision and power had come to preside over our great industrial establishments, and the whole country had caught the spirit of the industrial advance as a romantic adventure. To a greater extent than we or anybody else had realized, modern war is essentially an industrial art. Improved transportation facilities have rendered possible the collection and supplying of armies which would have starved under earlier conditions.

The demands of the modern fighting force for munitions are constant and all but insatiable. Perhaps the best illustration of this is that given by Colonel Leonard P. Ayres in his official summary on the war with Germany. Comparing the battle of the Wilderness in the Civil War with the battle of the Meuse-Argonne, he says: "The Meuse-Argonne lasted six times as long as the battle of the Wilderness; twelve times as many American troops were engaged as were on the Union side; they used in the action ten times as many guns and fired about one hundred times as many rounds of artillery ammunition. The actual weight of the ammunition fired was greater than that used by the Union forces during the entire Civil War." This comparison, however, deals only with artillery ammunition. The equipment of a modern army contains all of the old arms, improved with intricate mechanical devices, and, in addition to them, complicated mechanisms like tanks, motor transport, and airplanes. For the production of these the highest industrial organization is necessary. The pilot in his airplane has taken the place of the cavalryman on horseback as the eye of the army. Thus the soldier in the field rests for his efficiency and his safety upon the mechanic at home, and war is conducted under modern conditions by the joint effort of the soldiers in the trench and the workmen in the factory separated by thousands of miles, but each indispensable to success.

Prior to our entrance into the war, American industry had to some extent adapted itself to the production of war material, but in the vaster adaptation necessary to assure continuity of military supplies to the Allies and at the same time furnish and sustain our own great forces, the greatest masters of industry and business were necessary. The most immediate and pressing problem the War Department faced was to bring these men into complete and effective coöperation with our military men. My own life had been spent in an industrial city. I knew the spirit which animated American industry and the enthusiasm with which its leaders would coöperate in a national emergency. The legislative basis of such coöperation, however, was slight. Our national practice has always been to enact war-time legislation after war begins. The Act providing for the Council of National Defense was passed as a rider on the Army Appropriation Bill of 1916. Its donation of power, so far as the express language of the Act is concerned, was modest and tentative. As a matter of fact, the Council of National Defense was given no power, and the Advisory Committee was, from the point of view of the legislation, an academic and purely advisory body. Happily, however, a series of broad, if not bold, interpretations of the Act enabled us to set up an effective organization. The outstanding feature was the Advisory Committee, under the incisive and entirely practical leadership of Daniel Willard, which turned rapidly, as the possibility of our entrance into the war drew nearer from its early search for the best scheme of civilian and industrial organization to a series of recommendations to meet real and practical problems as they arose.

In this connection, a highly fortunate circumstance was the presence in Washington of Frank A. Scott. Mr. Scott, as president of a company manufacturing high-grade machine tools and certain instruments of precision for both the Army and the Navy, had been summoned to the War Department to help organize a board to standardize munitions and their manufacture. Thus coöperation between the Ordnance Department and civilian industrial agencies, which would be called upon for supplies in any emergency, was already established. Happily, Mr. Scott was a man of vision and resourcefulness and also a man of tact and sanity. Under his leadership, from the beginning, there were understanding, good will, and effective coöperation between the officers of the Army, Navy, and civilians. He saw approaching difficulties as they arose and brought them to me while they were small and easily overcome. He brought, too, thoughtful suggestions for the solution of industrial problems. The security and confidence with which I came to rely upon his judgment and foresight is a happy recollection of days very heavy with perplexities and responsibilities. Mr. Scott, Mr. Gifford of the Council of National Defense, General Palmer Pierce, and their associates laid the foundations of our industrial mobilization, both in the matter of organization and of policy, and the future organizations and policies were but developments along the lines laid down by them: expansions which came with the experience of new and larger needs.

At the very outset, the Munitions Standards Board subdivided the field of its activities. Separate sections of it had charge of artillery small arms, gauges, and dies, and other military equipment. The Board was organized in March, 1917, just before we entered the war; it rapidly extended the scope of its own activities, and, in a few weeks, April 3d, it became the General Munitions Board. On July 27th, of the same year it was transformed into the War Industries Board, Mr. Scott remaining chairman throughout these transitions until October, 1917, when he was succeeded by Mr. Willard, who acted until the reorganization of the War Industries Board in March, 1918. In effect the War Industries Board was a general staff on the industrial and procurement side. Through it the leaders of the industries in the country were mobilized about the War and Navy procurement sections, and the intimate knowledge of industrial possibilities and conditions which these leaders of industry in civil life brought with them enabled the Board to recommend policies of priority of access to raw materials, control of prices, forms of contract, and selections of plants and facilities to be adapted to war work, which were essential. Later, of course, these policies were extended, and some of the activities initiated by the War Industries Board were committed to separate agencies, such as the Food and Fuel Administrations. In the main, however, an orderly development of plans laid by Mr. Scott and his associates, civil and military, avoided friction between the military and naval people on the one side and the civilians on the other, and it was rarely necessary for us to go back and start over or create different agencies. The start having been right in principle, its evolution

was natural and adequate. Perhaps no small part of
this experience was due to the fact that Mr. Scott,
in addition to being a manufacturer with an intimate
acquaintance among the leading industrial engineers of
the country, was at the same time a student of history,
and particularly military history, so that to his military and naval associates he spoke with sympathetic
understanding of their problems and with a certainty
about industrial processes which inspired their confidence.

Another striking service was brought to us by Colonel Leonard P. Ayres. There had always been an
exact and adequate record system in the War Department, to fix responsibilities and protect the Government. But as we now faced a tremendous program
with speed as its essential element, we needed some
concise and graphic means of seeing at a glance, from
day to day, the progress, made in a thousand places,
in details of the program, for delay anywhere might mean
delay everywhere. Colonel Ayres brought us the modern
science of statistics, with his own mastery of it. Soon
we had daily production charts. It was no longer necessary to read columns of figures or to send for bureau
chiefs. A glance showed every detail which needed attention and the relation of each detail to the possible
progress of the whole vast program. Without this ac-
curate and ordered knowledge, the problems of the
War Department would have been too intricate for
solution. Nor was its value limited to those charged
with immediate responsibility. Senators, members of
Congress, and representatives of the press were kept
abreast of all we were doing. To the rumors, anxieties
and questionings, naturally current, the charts were

the answer, and they told their story without the need of explanation or argument. Later Colonel Ayres performed a like service for the army overseas, at Tours and Chaumont. Thus we had the benefit of statistics, almost the youngest of the exact sciences, perhaps even more highly developed than it had as yet been in our great industrial organizations.

But when all is said that can be said for these beginnings, they were but tentative approaches to unknown problems. What was our part in the war to be? Our knowledge of the war in Europe was fairly detailed, but no great army, in the modern sense, had ever been transported and supplied across three thousand miles of ocean, nor had any ocean before ever been infested with submarines. The world's tonnage of ships was, at that time, disappearing. The early months of unrestricted submarine warfare caused mounting losses far greater than the replacement capacity of all Allied shipbuilding plants. The collapse of Russia and the failure of the Allied offensives in 1916 raised the question whether the war must not necessarily end before purely military assistance from the United States could be developed and transported. As a matter of fact, the real objective of both the Balfour and Viviani missions was to secure immediate financial assistance. The naval and military missions which accompanied them expected rather the moral value of the use of such military and naval forces as we had, than that we should really arrive, in time, in sufficient force to give military preponderance. *Time* was then to them, as it was with us to the end, the controlling factor, and our success lies not wholly in what we did, but also that we did it in time—the margin was very narrow!

The military members of the English and French missions spent many days in conference with corresponding sections of our War Department staff, giving us, in detail, the nature of the conflict and its demands both upon men and in the matter of supplies. Many of these officers remained in America and were joined by others, sent by their respective governments, to aid us in training and with advice in the technical supply services. But the expectation of the missions was very modest so far as an American army in France was concerned. Marshal Joffre urged upon me the early dispatch of "a regiment or perhaps even a division which could appear on the front with the American flag and arouse afresh the enthusiasm of the Allied soldiers." He told me that we need not delay for artillery, in which he understood that we were deficient, as France could easily supply all the guns we could need. Further, he told me that his government had arranged to place the port of La Pallice exclusively at our disposal, and that it would suffice for our needs until "you are ready to send over your great army, perhaps 500,000 men," when he promised additional port facilities. When one compares little La Pallice with the vast port facilities we built and used at St. Nazaire, Bordeaux, Brest, and elsewhere in France, the contrast between the expectation and the accomplishment is eloquent. Particularly it is eloquent of the foresight and imagination of General Pershing, who from the day he landed in France. seemed to grasp the needs of the situation with surer and larger views than any other person, military or civil, with whom I came into contact either at home or in Europe. In this respect, General Pershing shared and reflected the opinion of the General Staff in Washington. Both General Hugh L. Scott and General Tasker H. Bliss, Chief of Staff and Assistant Chief of Staff, throughout 1917 looked forward to the ultimate development of a large American army.

After the suspension of diplomatic relations between the United States and Germany, General Scott, discussing with me the possbiility of our entrance into the war, raised the question of the method by which men should be called to the service. He told me that, in his own view, there should be a draft law at the very outset and that we should avoid the British experience of starting out with the volunteer system and being later obliged to come to the draft. In this discussion I became convinced of the soundness of the suggestion and at once laid it before the President, who discussed it with me earnestly and at length and in the end approved the suggestion saying, "Have the law drawn at once so that, if I should be obliged to go to the Congress, I can refer to it in my message as a law ready to be presented for their consideration." The main outlines of the act were settled in a series of conferences in my office attended by General Scott, General Bliss, General Crowder, the Adjutant General, General McCain, and perhaps one or two others. The detailed preparation of the law was committed to General Crowder, and its later execution was also entrusted to him as Provost Marshal General. As it was necessary to fill up the organizations of the Regular Army and National Guard to wartime strength immediately, volunteering was permitted until the Selective Service law could be put into operation. No doubt there was some disappointment on the part of eager and devoted men that they were not permitted to form volunteer organizations, but the soundness of General Scott's suggestion was abundantly demonstrated. Our drafted army never came to be looked upon as made up of men who had been reluctant to volunteer, but rather as men selected, by orderly methods, to perform the duty common to us all of serving our country as our country needs us.

We had also to remember that the industries of the United States were indispensable sources of supply to the Allies as well as to ourselves. The disorganization of our factories and farms might well have had disastrous consequences to the peoples overseas. They were holding the line until our soldiers could arrive. The Selective Service law enabled us to preserve the continuity of our industrial processes and to console those who would have gladly turned from the lathe and the plough to active military service by assurances that they were performing their highest duty to their country by continuing their industrial occupations until they were called to the colors.

Thus, from the beginning, America's plan was the production of a large army, but the problem of transportation was long unsolved. The energy and ingenuity of our navy furnished the early transports which carried overseas the bulk of the American troops to provide the first invaluable reinforcement for the Allied armies at the time of the crisis in the spring of 1918. But the final solution only came with the great German drive of March, 1918, when the necessity of the situation at last justified the diversion of Allied ships from every other use to build up the American Army in France. How great that necessity was is strikingly shown by the hazard which America then took. Never before in history has any country sent overseas an army larger than it was able to supply; yet that is exactly what America did. If the Germans had broken through, separating the French and British armies, our great forces in France would have been unable to subsist themselves. This hazard weighed heavily upon us all up to the very day of the Armistice. We had less cargo tonnage at our disposal than was necessary to feed and supply our overseas army, and we several times reached the point where the further transportation of soldiers without a corresponding increase of cargo tonnage for their support seemed impossible. Nevertheless, the army continued to be sent in increasing volume with the result that the war ended in 1918, and we escaped all that would have been implied in a prolongation of the conflict in 1919.

In October, 1918, when I was in France, a considerable part of my time was given to discussing with statesmen and soldiers of the Allied countries the plans for the 1919 campaign. In a little more than a month, the end had come and the daring of General Pershing in demanding and of General March in supplying a great American army was justified.

In the pages of Captain Frothingham's book, the parts played by General Pershing and General March, on the fighting front and the home front, are correlated. The method of their selection and their relations to the War Department, and through it to each other, justify description.

In France there is always kept in readiness a commander-in-chief designated to take command of the army in the next war. He has an office and a staff which is constantly working on the details of the first operations upon the outbreak of war. When war is declared, this commander sets out with his staff for the front and takes charge of the army as it mobilizes. The American Army has no commander-in-chief. The General Staff in Washington is an administrative agency, the Chief of Staff being in effect the military secretary of the President. The highest peace-time rank in our army is that of major general, and officers of the line of the army, in that rank, are in command of the corps areas into which the United States and its possessions are subdivided. Administratively, they are all under the direction of the Chief of the General Staff in Washington, but among them there is no priority of rank, and, of course, no one of them is ever designated in advance as a field commander in the unlikely exigency of war.

During the visit of the French and British missions immediately after our entrance into the war, it was determined to send at once an American contingent to France. This, of course, involved the selection of a commanding officer, and plainly the officer so selected might ultimately come to command great armies. When General Scott, as Chief of Staff, brought this matter to my attention, I asked him to have sent to my house the records of all the major generals and brigadier generals then on the active list of the army, and I spent evening and night hours on those records until I had ultimately made my own choice of General Pershing. Having decided the question in my own mind, I told General Scott, who at once replied, "You could not have made a better choice. General Pershing is a very able officer." I had never seen General Pershing, but his record showed him to be a man of robust health and energy. I, of course, had had direct and continuous oppor-

tunity to observe his conduct of the so-called Punitive
Expedition into Mexico. The force of about ten thousand men, constituting that expedition, was the largest
force which any American general officer at that time
in active service had ever commanded. The mission
with which General Pershing was entrusted in Mexico
required the highest qualities of the soldier and many
of the qualities of the statesman. Primarily, of course,
the expedition was organized to capture the bandit
Villa as a means of discouraging, if not preventing,
raids into the United States ، cross the Mexican border
by the partisan bands and bandit groups which were
harassing Mexico in the profoundly disturbed state
of that country. When Villa fled to the mountains, the
Punitive Expedition was retained in Mexico as a warning and to prevent other bands from undertaking to
repeat his raid. It was, therefore, important that General Pershing's expedition should remain as far south as
possible without straining to the breaking point the
reluctant tolerance of such authorities as there were
in Mexico of this seeming invasion of their country.
The Carranza Government was unable to guarantee our
border against violence. Nevertheless, it was sensitive
to the presence of any American forces on Mexican soil
and perhaps suspicious that the Government of the
United States had purposes other than the mere pursuit
of Villa. General Pershing's task in Mexico therefore
required tact, sympathy, and self-restraint. His force,
though small, was splendidly equipped and no doubt
was superior to any force which might have been
brought against it at that time by Mexico. The President, determined to protect the border, was nevertheless anxious that there should be no war between the

United States and Mexico. With the rest of the world in flames, peace in the Americas must be maintained. The administrations of President Taft and President Wilson both pursued the policy of patience with Mexico, in the hope that the forces of order would gradually solidify, and both administrations pursued a policy of friendship toward Mexico in her difficulties. General Pershing's loyalty to this policy and to these purposes throughout the whole period of the Punitive Expedition showed at once his tact, his self-restraint and his subordination of the purely military aspects of the problem to the political aspects which were in the hands of his civil chiefs.

My father was a Confederate soldier, a mere boy even at the close of the Civil War. Being a man of very robust common sense, he quickly readjusted himself to the results of the war, and became of all men the most thoroughly reconstructed, repeatedly saying to me, when I was a child, that it was a great blessing that the war had turned out as it did. While a very busy country doctor, he nevertheless read practically every book of importance which came out about the Civil War, and, as I grew up, he read them aloud to me or listened as I read them. Many times, during our reading and discussion, he remarked to me that the superior good fortune of the Confederate Army was undoubtedly due in substantial part to the free hand given General Lee, after a single effort on the part of Jefferson Davis to interfere with strictly military operations, and that the military meddling of Stanton and Halleck had been a serious handicap to the Union commanders. When General Pershing went overseas, I told him that story and told him that I would endeavour to do everything I could on this side to make his task easier, but that I would not myself interfere with his administration of military questions or permit them to be interfered with by my military associates on this side. General Pershing has often said that this relation between us was most helpful to him, and I have many times been interested to reflect that the lesson which my father had taught me when I was a mere child did prove helpful in great matters which neither he nor I, of course, could have foreseen.

With this lesson remaining in my mind, I found myself thinking, from the beginning, that, having selected General Pershing and sent him overseas, my duty was to give him power in proportion to his responsibility, to refrain from interfering with him, and to protect him from interference. Happily, the views of the chiefs of staff and of the General Staff in the War Department were in complete harmony with this theory of the relation between the commander in the field and the Department. How far we were able at all times to live up to this theory is of course a matter of official record and needs no comment here. The War Department and General Pershing's headquarters were connected by cable lines which carried, day and night without interruption, a continuous interchange of messages showing General Pershing's expanding needs and giving in detail his reports of the progress of his industrial and military operations; but I doubt whether in a single cabled message from the War Department to General Pershing, there will be found even a suggestion as to any purely military operations under his direction. He was in France and the War Department three thousand miles away from the place where his decisions had to be made and his actions taken. In this, of course, he differed from the Union Commanders, who were at the head of armies fighting around Washington, and were often, therefore, in contact with and always within immediate reach of Secretary Stanton and General Halleck. General Pershing's situation reminded me of that of General Kutuzof, who, while commanding the Russian armies around Moscow, received one day from the Czar an autographed letter giving in great detail a plan formed by the Czar for the rout and capture of Napoleon's army. Kutuzof, having read the communication, turned it over and wrote on the back, "Sire, plans formed at a great distance are often difficult of execution," and returned it to the Czar. The fact is that, while we thought and still think of the World War from the battle of the Marne to the March, 1918, offensive as a stabilized, if not stalemated, operation, nevertheless, the details of the situation were constantly changing and differing, and no helpful suggestions could have been expected from the General Staff in Washington upon situations which had to be solved with reference to their condition at the moment of action.

Of course, General Pershing's designation for the command in France was made by the President, to whom I reported my own recommendation. The President discussed with me both the size of the first expedition and the qualities which its commander would need. He inquired into the basis and method of my own selection and referred with constant approval to the difficult service of General Pershing in Mexico. He approved the choice, and from that day General Pershing had his unwavering confidence and full support. In return,

General Pershing gave devoted service and unquestioning loyalty, both personally and officially, to his Commander in chief.

The selection of General Peyton C. March, to be Chief of Staff in Washington in 1819, grew out of my contacts with him in 1916, when he was a colonel in the Adjutant General's office in Washington. At that time he was particularly charged with the duty of revising and cutting down the enormous amount of paper work involved in the army system of records. When I became Secretary of War, the Chief of Staff was General Hugh L. Scott, a man of exalted character, deeply steeped in the traditions of the old army, and having the confidence of the army in his disinterested and impersonal fairness. From April, 1916, on, General Scott and I were in intimate daily contact, and he undertook, with infinite patience and affectionate kindness, the task of acquainting me with the traditions of the military service and the qualities and characteristics of the army's personnel. From him I learned to understand and admire the completeness of Colonel March's grasp of the details of War Department business and the boldness and simplicity with which he reformed the intricate record system which had grown up in the course of years. Colonel March went to the Mexican border, when we mobilized the National Guard there, and finally went to France, where he became, by General Pershing's selection, Chief of Artillery in the Expeditionary Force. General Scott's term as Chief of Staff ended in October, 1917, with his compulsory retirement from the active service under the age limit fixed by Congress, but he was immediately recalled to the active service and placed in command at Camp

Dix. He was succeeded as Chief of Staff by General Tasker H. Bliss, a scholarly and sagacious counsellor, with a long record of foreign service both administrative and military. But General Bliss's retirement was also approaching, and his transfer to the Supreme War Council at Versailles, as our military representative there, was from all points of view the happiest possible selection. As this second vacancy in the office of Chief of Staff approached, it seemed to me that the time had come when we should have in Washington an energetic and effective administrator, who by actual experience in General Pershing's army knew the situation in France, was acquainted with General Pershing's plans, and so could more effectively direct our coöperation with the Expeditionary Force. I therefore wrote to General Pershing and requested that General March be permitted to return to the United States to become Chief of Staff. General Pershing approved the choice but regretted the loss of his Chief of Artillery. In the long run, the sacrifice in France was justified by the achievements of General March in Washington.

Throughout the entire period of our participation in the war there was constant discussion as to the wisdom and possibility of brigading American troops with the British and French armies. I do not know how early the suggestion from abroad was first made, but the American policy on that subject was settled before the first American soldier went overseas, and settled upon grounds so obviously right that no departure from it was at any time possible. After General Pershing had reported to the War Department and been notified of his selection, he remained in Washington some weeks and participated in frequent conferences with the

Chief of Staff and other members of the general staff, while he was selecting the officers who were to accompany him, and generally making his plans. In these conferences, the whole question as to the size and form of the American effort were thoroughly considered. As the scene of operations was to be in France, it was of course recognized that our army would have to conform its movements to the front as established in the years of the war which had already elapsed. Belgium and Great Britain had special objectives which dictated the part of the defensive line they should occupy, and for clear reasons the actual defence of Paris would have to rest upon the French Army. But even at that stage it was clear that the American Army should constitute an independent force and that we should all look forward to a time when it would operate independently, but in unison with the armies of the Allied and Associated Powers. The orders given to General Pershing when he went overseas were drawn by General Francis J. Kernan. They have always seemed to me to be a model in their breadth of view, their clarity and conciseness. It was never necessary to change or even to amplify a single sentence in those orders. The complete order was as follows:

From: THE SECRETARY OF WAR.
To: MAJ. GEN. J. J. PERSHING, United States Army..
Subject: Command, authority, and duties in Europe.
    The President directs me to communicate to you the following:
    1. The President designates you to command all the land forces of the United States operating in continental Europe and in the United Kingdom of Great Britain and Ireland, including any part of the Marine Corps which may be detached for service there with the Army. From your command are excepted the military attachés and others of the Army who may be on duty directly with our several embassies.

2. You will proceed with your staff to Europe. Upon arrival in Great Britain, France, or any other of the countries at war with the Imperial German Government, you will at once place yourself in communication with the American Embassy and through its agency with the authorities of any country to which forces of the United States may be sent.

3. You are invested with the authority and duties devolved by the laws, regulations, orders, and customs of the United States upon the commander of an army in the field in time of war and with the authority and duties in like manner devolved upon department commanders in peace and war, including the special authorities and duties assigned to the commander of the Philippine Department in so far as the same are applicable to the particular circumstances of your command.

4. You will establish, after consultation with the French War Office, all necessary bases, lines of communication, depots, etc., and make all the incidental arrangements essential to active participation at the front.

5. In military operations against the Imperial German Government you are directed to coöperate with the forces of the other countries employed against that enemy; but in so doing *the underlying idea must be kept in view that the forces of the United States are a separate and distinct component of the combined forces, the identity of which must be preserved.* This fundamental rule is subject to such minor exceptions in particular circumstances as your judgment may approve. The decision as to when your command, or any of its parts, is ready for action is confided to you, and you will exercise full discretion in determining the manner of coöperation. But, until the forces of the United States are in your judgment sufficiently strong to warrant operations as an independent command, it is understood that you will coöperate as a component of whatever army you may be assigned to by the French Government.

6. You will keep the department fully advised of all that concerns your command, and will communicate your recommendations freely and directly to the department. And, in general, you are vested with all necessary authority to carry on the war vigorously in harmony with the spirit of these instructions and toward a victorious conclusion.

I have underscored in paragraph five of the foregoing the sentence which it is here desired to emphasize. It imposed almost the only limitation upon the complete authority given to General Pershing, although it was a limitation with which he himself was in entire accord.

The reasons for this determination were many. The Allied and Associated Powers had a common object, which was the defeat of the armies of the Central Powers, but they had diverse objectives, and it was quite inconceivable that the American Army should ever be so merged under French and British command, that it could ever be used to carry out operations or further purposes with which the Government of the United States was not in complete sympathy. There was, of course, no such diversity of sympathy apparent, but many things change in the course of a war, and it was necessary at all times to preserve the independence and identity of the American forces so that they could never be anything but an instrument of a policy of the United States.

Public opinion would not have sustained and ought not to have sustained turning over American soldiers to be lost in British and French commands. Nor would American soldiers have been happy under any flag but their own. The whole theory of our Army differed from the theories of the French and British just as we as a people differ from them. Our habits of diet, discipline, training, and recreation all differ from theirs, and an immeasurable loss to the cause would have been sustained if the American spirit which sent our soldiers singing to the front had been lost and the pride of our soldiers in their country and its cause dulled by the men themselves being used as mere replacements in foreign armies.

One further, but important, consideration should be mentioned. General Pershing and General March in

Washington agreed in believing that the war was to be won on the Western Front, and that, in order to win it, military preponderance had to be established there for the Allied armies. This preponderance could be brought about only by maintaining the strength of the British and French armies at what they were when we entered the war, so that the American Army became a constantly added force rather than a mere replacement. France and Great Britain had been in the war long, devastating years. It would not have been unnatural for them to be willing to see their decimated divisions brought to war strength with fresh men from the United States, but that would merely have maintained the balance between the opposing forces while the critical and necessary thing was to secure preponderance. By maintaining the separation and independence of the American forces, it was possible at all times to be sure that the British and French manpower was being used to the full, and that the growing American Army assured that ultimate preponderance in rifle strength which was necessary to success. These reasons all seem so conclusive and obvious that it would not be worth while to recount them but for the fact that practically to the day of the Armistice, in London, in Paris, and in Washington, representatives of Great Britain and France continued to urge, with more or less fervor, the brigading of American troops into their respective armies. General Pershing, of course, refused to accede to these representations when they were made to him, and President Wilson refused to interfere, leaving the whole question to be determined by General Pershing under the responsibility committed to him, and in view of the exigencies of the situation as they

appeared in the actual field of battle. In October, 1918,
I called upon M. Clemenceau in Paris to discuss questions of horses, airplane engines, and other material for
the campaign of 1919. When we had finished the conference, M. Clemenceau said to me, half playfully, that
he thought the United States had produced the two
most stubborn men in the world. I told him I thought
the countries with which we were associated in the war
had eminent candidates for the distinction, but asked
him who his American favorites were. He replied,
"President Wilson and General Pershing," and sought
to prove his case by showing how obdurate they were
against the advice of statesmen and soldiers alike in the
matter of distributing American troops to French commands. Two weeks earlier, Mr. Lloyd George had as
earnestly pressed the same view upon me. Practically
up to the Armistice, this question continued to be debated, although, except in temporary emergencies and
under special circumstances, the policy, established by
America when we entered the war, was never departed
from and never was in any danger of being yielded.

In Chapter XVII of this book, Captain Frothingham
refers to the Commission on Training Camp Activities.
Work of this kind really began with the mobilization of
our National Guard on the Mexican border in 1916.
Many of the National Guard regiments were from cities
in which there had been effective acceptance of the
belief that the provision of wholesome recreational opportunity was both a part of the community's obligation to its citizens and also a very substantial part of the
community's insurance against the growth of crime and
vice among the young. As I had spent fifteen years in
the service of such a city I was thoroughly familiar with

the programs and activities of the so-called "social workers," I had long realized that the tendency of youth is spontaneously upward, and believed the encouragement of wholesome opportunity was far better social discipline than multiplied restraints upon the leisure activities of the young. General Hugh L. Scott, who was Chief of Staff when I became Secretary of War, had the highest idea of and ideals for the common soldier of any man with whom I ever came in contact. He had a certain sturdy ruggedness in dealing with "soldier men," which meant no pampering or coddling, but he believed soldiers to be men, expected manliness of them, and had a compassionate comprehension of their shortcomings which made him very eager in his sympathy with every suggested opportunity for them to have a broader chance for self-culture and a stimulus to self-discipline.

Almost as soon as the National Guard moved to the border, Mr. Raymond B. Fosdick, with whom I had long been associated in the study of police and other disciplinary and social questions, called on me in the War Department to say that he thought it unfair that the National Guard should be subjected to the temptations which inevitably tend to grow up about soldiers' camps in places remote from their homes. I therefore asked him to go to the border and make a comprehensive study of conditions for my information. This he did. When he made his report, I asked him to go back to the border and take up with General Funston and with General Pershing, who was then in Mexico, the question of a radical change in the surroundings of our camps. Mr. Fosdick found that General Funston had a formula to the effect that "Soldiers will be soldiers," and it took some persuasion from Mr. Fosdick and from me to convince General Funston that he had nothing to fear from the "uplifters" and "welfare workers," but he was finally convinced and became radical enough to satisfy both Mr. Fosdick and me, as he cleaned up the border. General Pershing at once accepted the point of view presented to him by Mr. Fosdick and, as a consequence, when General Pershing went overseas, he was determined from the outset that the army should be wholesome and that his men, far separated from their home and from the restraints of neighbourhood environment, should not be driven or drawn into the temptations which surround unoccupied leisure. Thus it was that at home and abroad there was both civilian and military sympathy for the aims of the Commission on Training Camp Activities.

Mr. André Tardieu, in a recent book, has commented upon the existence in America of social workers and welfare agencies as a distinctive characteristic of our civilization. There is apparently no analogue to these things in France, and Mr. Tardieu expresses admiring surprise at their zeal and effectiveness in the United States. In this observation he is clearly right. Every community in America near a cantonment or camp during the war organized itself around the camp and adopted the soldiers into their community and social life. As the organization and training of the army went on, therefore, it was natural that there should be built up around it social substitutes for the home influences which were being left behind. After the army went overseas, these institutions followed it, both in the extended activities of the great welfare organizations and in the direct provision for soldiers' welfare afforded by the Commission on Training Camp Activities.

Far up in the front lines in France, I one day visited a detached regiment of about twenty-five hundred men who were scattered about a village and its adjacent farms. There was presented to me there a fine, intelligent American girl, who was with the regiment as mother, sister, and confidant to the entire outfit. I asked her whether she did not feel lonely and afraid, in so remote and so dangerous a place, the only woman with a whole regiment of men. She replied smilingly that she was the safest woman in the world, that "her boys" to the last one would protect her with their lives, and that each evening a voluntary detail of four soldiers was placed by the men themselves to guard her quarters and to accompany her, if duty called her to make visits by night from one part to another of the regiment. Later, after the war was over, at a dinner table in Paris I told this incident. One of the dinner guests said, "Mr. Secretary, I have been in charge of all the women in France associated in any way with the army. I could parallel your story by a thousand others. Indeed, I have talked with every American woman in any way connected with the army, and so far from any one of them ever having had an unpleasant experience, the universal testimony is that no one of them has ever had an uncivil word from a soldier."

I trust some day the history of the social side of our army in the great war will be written. If Mr. Fosdick does not write it, it should be written around his splendid service. Should the story ever be fully told, it will picture the most distinctly American thing about our whole participation in the war. America's wealth, her industrial supremacy, her splendid detachment and unselfishness of purpose, and the inexhaustible stream of robust youth which we supplied in the war were all great contributions. The mobilization of the scientific forces of the country around the army in the matter of supplies and medical attention is also a great story. But never before in the history of war has the elevated atmosphere of home been taken into the soldiers' camp, and the social consequences of this fact to us in America are immeasurably important.

With each new book about our participation in the war some new touch is given and some wider view permitted of the vast and magnificent achievement. Captain Frothingham has cut a new path, particularly in his correlations of the various activities, industrial, social, military, and naval, which had to be brought about for the effective assertion of our national power. But I doubt whether all the histories that can be written will ever quite convey to the generations who must learn of the war by reading about it, the unity of purpose and the fineness of spirit which our great American democracy developed in that crisis. Only those who lived in its light and felt its strength about them can ever know the full intoxication of being an American when America is at her very best.[1]

[1]In the foregoing I have not undertaken to recall, much less to weigh, the services rendered by individuals to the War Department and through it to the country. Time, however long, would be too short to recall and adequately to describe those services. I have therefore rigidly kept within the limits of a prefatory note and have included the names of individuals only where they were essential to the description of the particular incidents or problems commented upon. As for the rest of the great company with whom I was privileged to serve, military, naval, and civilian, I can, as to their services, at the moment do nothing better than take refuge in the rule of evidence: *res ipsa loquiter.*

CONTENTS

                                                                    PAGE

Introductory Chapter   v
America In the World War.   Newton D. Baker

CHAPTER

    I.   The Entrance of the United States   1

   II. The Object of the United States in the
        World War   11

  III. The People of the United States . .   16

  IV. The Influence of our Industries . . .   22

   V. The Effect of the World War Upon the
        American People   27

  VI. The Council of National Defense . .   33

 VII. Finance and Manpower   43

VIII. The Creation of the General Munitions
        Board   51

  IX. The Nation at Work.   60

   X. The Beginnings of our Armed Forces   67

  XI. The Development of American Strategy   76

 XII. The First Transportation of American
        Troops Overseas   84

XIII. The American Transports   97

XIV. Cantonment Construction   111

CONTENTS

CHAPTER   PAGE

   XV. American Preparations Overseas   .   119

  XVI. The First Months of the Mobilization
        of Industries   126

 XVII. Training the American Soldiers.   .   143

XVIII. The Transports and the Convoy
        System   155

  XIX. The Spread of War Activities in 1917   163

   XX. The Warnings from Overseas   .   .   171

  XXI. The Foundations Laid in France   .   178

 XXII. The Foundations Laid in the United
        States   190

XXIII. The Situation at the Beginning of
        1918   197

 XXIV. The Problem of Transportation.   .   204

  XXV. The Development of American In-
        dustrial Forces   218

 XXVI. In France Before the German Offen-
        sive   229

XXVII. The First Assault of the Great Ger-
        man Offensive of 1918   .   .   .   240

XXVIII. The Emergency Caused by the
        First German Assault   247

 XXIX. Rushing American Troops to France   259

  XXX. The Crisis of the World War   .   .   270

 XXXI. The Turn of the Tide   281

CHAPTER PAGE
XXXII. The First American Army . . . 289
XXXIII. The Naval Forces Supporting the Army 300
XXXIV. The Continuation of the Offensive 309
XXXV. The Last Months on the Seas . . 315
XXXVI. The American Expeditionary Forces of 1918 327
XXXVII. The Meuse-Argonne Battle and Its Effect 341
XXXVIII. The Collapse of the German Imperial Government 352
Appendix 365

LIST OF DIAGRAMS

PAGE

Locations of Camps and Cantonments in the
United States 75

Construction Projects in the United States . . 128

American Divisions Sent to France (with table of
Organization and Sources of Divisions) . . 152

The Bridge to France 258

The Growth of the American Trans-Atlantic
Fleet 325

American S. O. S. in Relation to the Battle Front 335

LIST OF MAPS

FACING PAGE

The Situation at the Beginning of 1917 . . . 1

The American Expeditionary Forces "Based on the American Continent" 120

The Western Front 240

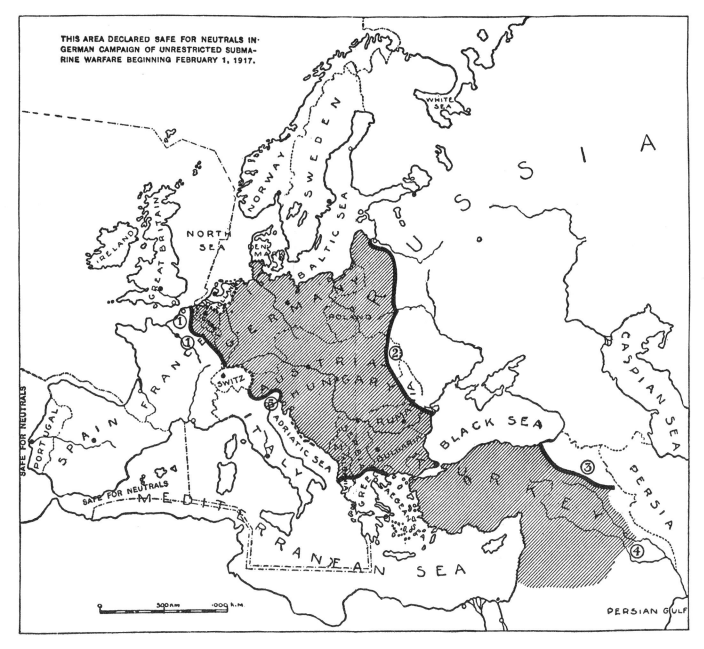

THE AREA DECLARED SAFE FOR NEUTRALS IN-
GERMAN CAMPAIGN OF UNRESTRICTED SUBMA-
RINE WARFARE BEGINNING FEBRUARY 1, 1917.

THE SITUATION AT THE BEGINNING OF 1917
(This map is diagrammatic only)

The shaded areas were controlled by the Central Powers.

——— Battle Fronts   ·············· Neutral Boundaries

The Central Powers had again improved their situation at the end of 1916. Rumania had been decisively defeated. The last effort of Russia had failed, and Russia had already been put out of the war, although the leaders of the Entente Allies did not realize the collapse of this great power.

With the whole Mittel Europa thus in their grasp, and the "Bridge to the East" consolidated, the Central Powers deliberately chose to defend their gains, and to make their whole offensive the campaign of unrestricted U-boat warfare on the seas. The broken lines indicate the prescribed areas and the areas proclaimed safe for neutrals.

In their ignorance of the decisive defeat of Russia, the Entente Allies were unduly optimistic at the first of 1917. They had a concerted scheme for early offensives on all fronts, and fully expected "to inflict a decisive defeat" in 1917.

Their plans comprised:

1 A double offensive by the British and French on the Western Front.

2 Renewed attacks by the Russians against the Austro-German armies.

3 Russian offensive in Asia Minor.

4 British attack on Bagdad.

5 Renewed Italian offensive.

These offensives were foredoomed to failure. On the Western Front the British and French armies only met heavy losses without being able to accomplish any results against the German armies. On the Eastern Front the Russian Revolution ended all hopes of success. On the Italian Front the Italian attacks failed, and the fall of Russia permitted a concentration of Austro-German armies which inflicted an overwhelming defeat upon the Italian armies in the fall of 1917.

In fact, this unfavorable situation at the first of 1917 held all the adverse factors which were destined to bring out the crisis of 1918, although this was unsuspected by the Entente Allies. With Russia out of the war, Italy no longer a factor for the offensive, and the British and French armies disabled for any offensive by the heavy losses of 1917, the Germans were to be able to concentrate superior forces on the Western Front. The assault of these overwhelming German armies was to become the actual crisis of the world war —and defeat was to be averted by the American Reinforcement.

The American Reinforcement in the World War

CHAPTER I

THE ENTRANCE OF THE UNITED STATES

THE attempt of the German Imperial Government to win the World War in 1917 by the unrestricted use of submarines must not be considered as a last desperate resort, but as a carefully calculated effort to gain victory by means which the German leaders thought infallible. The then existing German Imperial Government had been assured by the German Naval Staff that victory was a mathematical certainty. The German Army Command had assented to a military defensive, to hold what the Central Powers had already won in the World War, and had agreed that this U-boat campaign should be the offensive for 1917. The leaders of the German Imperial Government had thus decided that they could win by these means—and the result of their decision was upon their own heads.

It is a matter of record, and it should be stated to the credit of Bethmann-Hollweg, the German Chancellor, that he opposed this measure. Hindenburg has stated: "On January 9, 1917, our All-Highest War Lord decided in favor of the proposals of the naval and general staffs, and against the Imperial Chancellor." The responsibility is thus fixed—and it was another case of control by the militaristic régime which was the ruling element in the German Imperial Government of the World War. Again, as in 1914, a supposedly infallible plan of war was adopted, in spite of all other considerations.

It was a strange stroke of fate for the German Imperial Government that this provocative campaign of unrestricted U-boat warfare, which had been originally conceived in an unfavorable military situation, was eventually to be put into operation in a most favorable situation, when there were other means of victory actually in the grasp of the Central Powers. As a matter of fact, the last months of 1916 had seen the end of the fighting strength of Russia, although the German leaders had not realized it.[1] This powerful enemy was already on the verge of collapse and revolution, at the very time when the Central Powers began their ruthless U-boat campaign of 1917, which was destined to bring into the World War a still stronger enemy to take the place of Russia and turn German victory into defeat.[2]

The fateful die was cast for the then existing German Imperial Government when it was decreed that unrestricted U-boat warfare was to begin on February 1, 1917. A paragraph from the Memorandum of the Ger-

---

[1] "No intelligence had come through to us which revealed any striking indications of the disintegration of the Russian Army."—Hindenburg, *Out of My Life.*

[2] "Had we been able in Germany to foresee the Russian Revolution, we should perhaps not have needed to regard the submarine campaign of 1917 as a last resort. But in January, 1917, there was no visible sign of the Russian Revolution."—Hoffman, *The War of Lost Opportunities.*

man Naval Chief-of-Staff[1] showed the spirit in which this ruthless policy was undertaken: "A further condition is that the declaration and commencement of the unrestricted U-boat warfare should be simultaneous, so that there is no time for negotiations, especially between England and the neutrals. Only on these conditions will the enemy and neutrals be inspired alike with 'holy' terror."

Another paragraph in this same Memorandum made clear beyond any misunderstanding the confidence of the German leaders in their projected campaign: "I do not hesitate to declare that, under the prevailing conditions, we may force England into peace within five months through the unrestricted U-boat war. However, this can only be achieved by the unrestricted U-boat war, not by the U-boat cruising as practised at present, and not even if all armed vessels were free to be sunk." It was another example of the overconfidence of the German Imperial Government, derived from the habit of mind of basing all calculations on German formulas alone. This Memorandum also made the fatal error of positively asserting that "just as little effect can be ascribed to any extent to American troops, which, in the first place, cannot be brought over, through lack of tonnage."

But the German Imperial Government had adhered to its illegal program, and on February 1, 1917, the U-boats began to destroy ships, casting aside all international law on the seas. This U-boat campaign had

---

[1] To B 35840 I, Berlin, December 22, 1916 "(strictly secret)," given in full, Appendix A, *The Naval History of the World War*, *The United States in the War, 1917-1918*.

been carefully planned, and, in contrast to their former attempts, the Germans in 1917 had forces sufficient to carry out their undertaking. It at once became evident that the submarine, thus operated without regard for the lives of passengers and crews, was the most formidable destroyer of commerce in the world's history. The methods which had hitherto been used against the U-boats by the Allied navies, and which had been too hastily assumed sufficient to check their ravages, were found totally inadequate. Sinkings were recorded in the first weeks of this campaign which threatened a great decrease of the world's tonnage of shipping, and there is no question of the fact that the attack of this new weapon was a grave danger to the sea power of the Entente Allies.[1]

Yet this successful use of the U-boats, in defiance of the laws of humanity, at once also became a boomerang for the German Imperial Government. It recoiled upon Germany by aligning against her the one power on earth that would mean defeat for the Central Powers. When it was found that the German Imperial Government intended to persist in its unlawful undertaking, the United States broke off relations with that government, and war with the German Empire became inevitable.

The cynical conduct of the German Imperial Government was a direct challenge; and there was no course other than to hand the German Ambassador his passports—to have no more dealings with a government that had broken its pledges when it felt strong enough

---

[1] "The immediate effect of the new campaign was to double the rate of losses which had been incurred during 1916, and these losses rose rapidly to a climax in March and April."—Report of British War Cabinet, 1917.

to do so. On February 3, 1917, the President of the United States addressed both houses of Congress, and announced that diplomacy had failed, and that relations with Germany had been severed. In this address President Wilson drew the sharp distinction between the German people and the autocratic German Imperial Government—a distinction which was destined to influence the whole remaining course of the war: "We are sincere friends of the German people and earnestly desire to remain at peace with the Government which speaks for them. God grant we may not be challenged by acts of wilful injustice on the part of the Government of Germany."

These acts of injustice were not long delayed. The German Ambassador, after receiving his papers, had asked his government to suspend action until he had made a plea for peace to the Emperor. But the Imperial Government refused to change its policy, and carried forward its campaign of unrestricted U-boat warfare. On March 13 orders were given to arm American merchantmen against submarines.

On March 1, the United States Government had published an intercepted letter written by the German Foreign Secretary, Zimmermann, to the German Minister in Mexico. It was dated at Berlin, January 19, 1917:

"On the first of February we intend to begin submarine warfare unrestricted. In spite of this, it is our intention to keep neutral the United States of America. If this attempt is not successful, we propose an alliance on the following basis with Mexico: that we shall make war together and together make peace. We shall give general financial support and it is understood that

Mexico is to reconquer the lost territory in New Mexico, Texas and Arizona.

"You are instructed to inform the President of Mexico of the above in great confidence as soon as it is certain that there will be an outbreak of war with the United States and suggest that the President of Mexico, on his own initiative, should communicate with Japan suggesting adherence at once to this plan; at the same time, offer to mediate between Germany and Japan.

"Please call to the attention of the President of Mexico that the employment of ruthless submarine warfare now promises to compel England to make peace in a few months.   ZIMMERMANN."

Aside from all other matters, this outrageous letter was in itself a cause of war. It is hard to see how anything could have been written that would show more unmistakably the utter hostility of the German Imperial Government toward the United States. Another point of view, as to this letter, should be emphasized. Even after the short decade which has elapsed, it is difficult to realize that such an abnormal structure as the German Imperial Government of 1917 could have existed. It was against this German Imperial Government that the United States went to war—not against the German people. And here, in this Zimmermann letter, the German Imperial Government of 1917 has written a description of itself which could not be more damning if the whole lexicon had been exhausted.

In all sections of our country there was no longer any possibility of doubt as to the character of the German rulers and their hostile intentions in regard to the United States. Additional provocation soon followed from the ruthless conduct of the U-boat campaign, and on April 6 Congress passed the resolution of war with the German Empire.

There can be no question of the fact that the United States was thus driven into the war by the hostile acts of the German Imperial Government. The German rulers have set forth their own record too plainly to leave any doubt in the matter. These hostile acts were not only the inexcusable attacks upon the seas, but also the proved German attempts to incite Mexico and Japan to war with the United States, to disrupt the country, and take away its territory. If ever a nation was justified in entering a war, the United States was justified and in the right—and we should believe that this right prevailed.

Our nation was made strong by the self-evident fact that there was no trace of selfish aims in our participation in the World War. In all other respects our position was above question. The conditions which had brought on the war were not in any way created by us. We had not committed any hostile act. On the contrary, in our relations with the German Imperial Government, we had exhausted all the resources of peaceful diplomacy. Our President had stated our objects so plainly that they could not be mistaken, and, in spite of all accusations, even our enemies were forced to believe that the United States fought for a principle and not for gain. A striking testimony of this was rendered by Ludendorff himself, all unconsciously in a tirade: "For American soldiers the war became as it were a crusade against us."

So evident was this that the United States became a moral force in the World War, and this had a disturbing effect upon the nations allied with Germany. Especially in Austria-Hungary, it was noticeable that the entrance of the United States against the Central Powers exerted a widespread effect in arousing enmity against the German Imperial Government, which was arbitrarily dictating the policies of the Central Powers. Even in Germany, where every attempt was made to brand the United States with hypocrisy and self-seeking, the German people could not help seeing that our nation was fighting for a cause, and that our nation believed this cause to be just.

The most wise distinction made by our President between the German people and the German Imperial Government became an issue in the very heart of Germany, and it became the cause of a rift in the hitherto united nation. It was no mere coincidence that the German Emperor, in the month of our declaration of war, made tentative proposals of popular legislative government for the Germans. This simply meant that the German leaders had read the signs of the times. The attitude of the United States toward the German Imperial Government had given the vague dissatisfaction of the German people a tangible basis, and, in spite of all attempts to divert attention, the beginning of a cleavage was there. As Ludendorff bitterly expressed it, "By working on our democratic sentiments the enemy propaganda succeeded in bringing our Government into discredit in Germany." In fact, from the time of the entrance of the United States, the German Imperial Government was being scrutinized and held accountable by the German people.

This was the strong moral force exerted upon the war

by the United States, apart from all our physical force, and this was a disturbing and disintegrating influence that was always working within the Central Powers throughout the rest of the World War. It is true that this moral force would not have prevailed if it had not been backed up by physical force. If the German Imperial Government had won its war, the German people would have stood by it. But if the German Imperial Government did not win, the German people would condemn it and repudiate it. Consequently, this moral force arrayed against the German Imperial Government must be counted as a very real and potent factor, in conjunction with the unexpected fighting strength of the United States, for bringing about the disintegration and destruction of the carefully built German Imperial structure.

It cannot be stated too strongly that the physical military force exerted by the United States upon the World War was an utter surprise to the German leaders —a thing outside all their calculations. These calculations of the German leaders had been founded entirely upon their own German formulas. Their methods of creating armies involved years of training, and from their point of view it was impossible that our nation could organize an army in time to have any effect upon the World War.

The German leaders had appreciated our great resources in material and wealth, and they had been reluctant to involve the United States in the war. Twice, in 1915 and in 1916, the German Imperial Government had yielded to the United States to prevent these resources from being at the command of the Entente

Allies. But in 1917, when the German calculations seemed to assure victory in spite of these resources, the German Imperial Government made the fatal error of thinking it impossible for the United States to be a military factor in the World War.[1]

The main reason for this error on the part of the German Imperial Government was the fact that the great lessons of the American Civil War had never been suspected, much less learned, by the formal school of the German General Staff. After the defeat in the World War, Freytag-Loringhoven, the leading exponent of the Prussian military régime, ruefully admitted: "The American Civil War might have furnished us many a hint which was left disregarded." The excellence of the American armies of both the North and the South, which had been so quickly produced in the white heat of that extraordinary war, had never been understood in Europe. Consequently, the German leaders were unable to realize that an intelligent people, absolutely united in a just cause, would be capable of a great uprising for warfare.[2]

---

[1] "We had a new enemy economically the most powerful in the world. . . . It was the United States of America, and her advent was perilously near. Would she appear in time to snatch the victor's laurels from our brows? That, and that only, was the decisive question! I believed I could answer it in the negative."—Hindenburg, *Out of My Life*.

[2] "I will tell you about America. She came into the war at a time when the need for her coming was most urgent. Her coming was like an avalanche. The world has never seen anything like it. Her great army of all ranks gave service that no man would, in 1917, have believed possible."—Lloyd George.

CHAPTER II

.

BEFORE giving an account of the effort of the United States in the World War, it is necessary to state, beyond any misunderstanding, that the aim and object of that effort must be a strong military reinforcement for the Entente Allies on the Western Front. If the United States had not provided this strong reinforcement, all our effort would have ended in failure and all our resources would have been wasted. Yet, at the time we entered the war, no one on earth had any adequate conception of the vast scale of the demands that would be enforced upon the United States at the crisis of the war.

The Entente Allies themselves had no premonition of what was to come, although their leaders were greatly disheartened and at once informed the Government of the United States that the situation was very bad for the Entente Allies. Soon after our entrance, a British and French special commission arrived in this country for an international war conference. The British Commission was headed by Mr. Balfour, the French Commission by M. Viviani and Marshal Joffre. Their message to our Administration described the serious dangers for the Entente Allies, and they reflected the reaction of the leaders of the Allies, from an ill founded optimism

at the first of the year 1917, to their gloomy realization
of the actual facts of the case. The menace of the U-boat
campaign had upset their whole strategy on the seas.
Not only were they much depressed by the unexpected
losses inflicted by the German submarines and the
desperate situation[1] which had been reported to the
Navy Department by Admiral Sims, but both the British and the French military offensives on the Western
Front, from which so much had been hoped, already
bore the stamp of failure. And, even though they lacked
a full comprehension of the actual loss of Russia from
the ranks of the Entente Allies, it had become evident
that the expected "series of offensives"[2] had broken
down. Instead of there being any chance for the Entente
Allies to "inflict a decisive defeat"[3] in 1917, which at
the beginning of the year they had been confident of
accomplishing, the true facts had already forced them
to perceive that the Entente Allies themselves faced
defeat.

It was obvious that the first pressing need was naval
assistance to the Entente Allies in the struggle to overcome the menace of the U-boat campaign. This call for
naval forces at once changed the conception of our
immediate naval aims to building up the greatest possible anti-submarine forces, consisting of destroyers and
other anti-submarine craft abroad. And Admiral

[1] "'Things were dark when I took that trip to America,' Mr. Balfour said
to me afterwards. 'The submarines were constantly on my mind. I could
think of nothing but the number of ships which were sinking. At that time
it certainly looked as if we were going to lose the war.'"—Admiral Sims,
The Victory at Sea.

[2] Sir Douglas Haig's Despatches.

[3] Lloyd George.

Jellicoe has made it a matter of record that the presence of thirty-four American destroyers in British waters in July, 1917,[1] was the deciding factor to clinch the matter of the convoy system, which then hung in the balance. The importance of this American naval assistance will be evident when we realize that it was the change to the convoy system which turned the scale against the U-boat campaign.

This continued coöperation of the United States Navy in the fight against the submarines must be kept in mind as a help rendered to the Entente Allies, but it was not even a beginning of the great task of the United States in the World War. Threatening as was the menace of the U-boat campaign, it was not the crisis of the World War. That crisis came later. The defeat of the U-boat campaign did not release the Entente Allies from danger. On the contrary, while one danger was passing, a new and infinitely greater menace was arising, as the year of 1917 ran its fateful course.

The inexorable forces of the World War, which had burst all bounds of former wars, were then moulding a situation that would make a call upon the United States so urgent that all else would be cast into the shade. The actual crisis of the war was destined to come when the collapse of Russia allowed the Central Powers to concentrate all their forces on the Western Front and to establish a military superiority that would have won the World War, if it had not been for the military reinforcement provided by the United States.

---

[1] "... providing that eleven American destroyers continue to be available." Mem. of First Sea Lord, July, 1917. It will be noted that three times that number were there that same month, and continued "to be available."

It is this situation which we must appreciate in order to understand the ensuing course of the war. It was not apparent at the time. Yet, behind the war clouds that obscured all Europe, events were moving as inevitably as a Greek tragedy to that climax when the United States must be present on the European field of battle —or else German militarism would win the war. Consequently, to provide that necessary military reinforcement in Europe must be considered the great object of the United States in the World War.

But what an unprecedented national effort was implied by that phrase! It meant that the United States must raise, equip, and train a great army; that supplies must be provided for this army; that transportation overseas and naval protection must be provided for this army, and for its vast volume of supplies. All this must be done in the haste demanded by the approaching crisis—or the war would be lost. And this condition implied in itself that everything at the outset must be on the vast scale set by the unprecedented demands of the World War. There was no time for the gradual development of forces, as in the case of other nations in the war.

No nation in history ever faced such a task, and a miracle was accomplished when the peaceful United States was able to coördinate its military, naval, and industrial forces, to gain its full strategic object, in the time set by a crisis and on the enormous scale of the World War. In fact, our whole effort, in this main object of the United States, should be thus considered as one great concerted operation performed by our Army, our Navy, and our Industries. To study the great causes which brought about the successful result of this American national effort is one of the most interesting things in connection with the World War. And, in the following account of the development of our threefold forces, we must always keep in mind that the whole fate of the Entente Allies lay in the question, whether the United States would be able to provide sufficient military reinforcement in time to meet the approaching crisis of the World War. The time factor was critical and controlling.

CHAPTER III

THE PEOPLE OF THE UNITED STATES

WITH the whole outcome of the World War thus depending upon the solution of the great problem for the United States, which was then being formulated in the concealing war clouds of 1917, it is no exaggeration to state that the right solution was actually being worked out in America long before this problem itself became visible to the world. It might be said that there was some instinctive sense awakened in advance, among our people, to call into immediate action vast unmeasured American forces, to counteract the overwhelming hostile forces which were being accumulated against the Entente Allies in the World War.

This awakening was the direct result of a steady development in the American people of national characteristics, strongly inherent to insure the one basic condition, which was most important of all, that the United States was actually united in every sense of the word. Only a united nation could have given America's wonderful response to the inordinate demands of the World War. And it is simply a statement of fact to say that, in 1917, something was happening in the United States so extraordinary that it must be classed as one of the great uprisings of a people which have shown the world that human forces, welded by some powerful fusing impulse, can be stronger than artificial military conditions.

To find a comparison, with the exception of the American Civil War, it might almost be necessary to go back to the great movements of the Northern races which overran Europe. France, after the Revolution, has always been considered an outstanding example of a united uprising of humanity, finding in Napoleon the required leader. Yet, with all the enthusiasm for the Emperor, only the military and industrial forces reached full strength. Napoleon was never able to vitalize the naval arm. In the case of the United States in the World War, all three forces were coördinated into our reinforcement on the distant battlefield of Europe, and, in the words of Ludendorff, "America thus became the decisive power in the war."

This is written in no boastful spirit. In fact, there is every reason against individual American complacency. It should be stated at once that, in every military sense, we were unprepared. We must resolve never again to allow ourselves to be caught in this predicament. As a consequence, everything was retarded at the start. For a time it looked as if European prophecies of our helplessness in war would prove to be true. Then, from confusion and delays, emerged the miracle, our American military reinforcement on the Western Front, projected into its mission by our industrial and naval forces. It is true that many kinds of mistakes were made, but all details of individual errors were cast into the shade by the one dominating fact, that, behind our operation, was the thrust of strong national forces which had not been measured since the Civil War.

As has been said, the Civil War offered the only basis for comparison, and it should also be stated, with emphasis, that having the Civil War behind us was one of the component factors in our national structure. The extraordinary influence of that epoch-making war was still strong with Americans, transmitted through the men who took part in it. In fact, to these veterans of the Civil War, North and South, must be given the credit of having been the most valuable elements, throughout the communities of the United States, for inculcating the national spirit.

The full measure of the service of these men to their country can only be appreciated when we realize that the whole strength of our national structure has been derived from our local self-governing communities. The first instinct of our ancestors was to form self-governing communities, and this was passed on from colonies to states, from the fringes along the coast to our accessions over wide areas from sea to sea. Our greatest need was, in all our rapid growth, that these communities should retain the American spirit which had been their original breath of life.

In this regard, it should be reiterated that the veterans of the Civil War, in their home communities throughout our country, had made it their charge that those who lived there should be Americans in thought and deed. This good influence had been continued through the long interval of years after the Civil War, when there had been so great a stream of immigration into the United States. No one can now doubt the result of this influence, and every American owes a debt of gratitude to the men of the Civil War.

The fearful test of the World War at once proved that the American spirit was still vital within us. For, beyond any mistaking, the outstanding feature of the entrance of the United States was the instant surge of united Americans, which made it evident to all that the American people had become a united nation—that the "melting pot" had accomplished its work.

This last was utterly contrary to European beliefs. Both friends and enemies abroad had held to the mistaken European idea that a nation made up of so many elements from immigration could not be fused into a structure which would be strong enough to withstand the crucial test of war. It was forgotten that Europeans had also held the same opinion as to the North at the outbreak of the Civil War. That opinion had been conclusively shown to be erroneous in 1861, and Americans who had studied the history of the Civil War had no doubts as to the unity of our people in 1917. The faith of these American students of the Civil War was vindicated in the result. At the great summons of 1917, it was again self-evident that the American people had become an American nation, and that all who had come to us had alike become Americans with us. At the shock of war there was no disintegration. On the contrary, all differences of races and creeds and all divisions of parties were forgotten. And it is no mere figure of speech to say that the American people rose as one man to the appointed task.

This was a fearful disappointment for the German Imperial Government. The German leaders had been overconfident in their mistaken opinion that the United States was made up of different factions which could not coalesce, and, in the years of preparation before the World War, the German Imperial Government had made great use of propaganda to align with Germany racial groups among our population. The German leaders had acquired an almost childlike faith in these imaginary rifts among our people.[1] After the outbreak of the World War in 1914, the German Imperial Government had also organized an elaborate system of German agents for hostile plotting throughout our country. But, upon the declaration of war in 1917 by the United States, all this was swept away like cobwebs. At once our citizens of foreign origin showed themselves to be loyal Americans, and, throughout our local communities, there was aroused so universal a spirit of Americanism that all the efforts of the German plotters could not make headway. For, instead of finding sympathizers, these agents of the German Imperial Government found each American local community so patriotically aroused and vigilantly on the watch that they could not get a foothold. This was true of all sections of our country.

There was, of course, some sabotage. But, taken altogether, it is probable that so great pains and so great expense had never accomplished such small results. Far from having the effect, on any serious scale, of impeding the effort of the United States in the World War, the agents of the German Imperial Government only scored failure. And all the elaborate ramifications of the German spy system can be thus dismissed as negligible, in the sense of counting for any percentage of delay and damage in the accomplishment of our vast undertaking in the war. So absolute was this failure of the German

---

[1]Tirpitz's list of those to whom the Germans might appeal showed a pathetic ignorance of the make-up of the American people: ". . . the Germans, the Irish, the Quakers, the cotton interests."

agents that it will hardly be necessary to refer to them again in the ensuing narrative of the effort of the United States.

In order to get the true perspective of this narrative, the reader must always keep in mind that, from the beginning to the end, the American people was zealous and unstinting, with every energy devoted to its purpose of carrying the war to a successful conclusion, and with no dissenting faction in any part of the country. This united response of the American people was the greatest impelling force in the accomplishment of the American mission in the World War.

CHAPTER IV

THE INFLUENCE OF OUR INDUSTRIES

IN ADDITION to the assured impulse derived from this surge of a united American people, there were other new elements of strength in the national life of the United States which were most important contributing factors for our great national effort. These had come into being in the forty years preceding the World War. They were the results of far reaching changes in the make-up of our nation. And these changes were almost entirely due to the development of our industries.

In those years American industries had grown beyond localized units. The kindred activities of industrial groups had included areas that extended over many states. As a result, great industrial organizations had been created, with great producing and manufacturing establishments, of which the operations were no longer sectional but nationwide. Products and commodities were being handled on a gigantic scale never before known. It was natural, following this development of our industries, and from our new habits of mind in dealing with great figures and great dimensions, that the American people had become accustomed to thinking in terms of vast quantities and in terms of nationwide operations. All this was, in itself, a preparation for our tremendous tasks in the World War.

But, in addition, and as a direct result of this industrial development, there had been a corresponding change in our organizations of government control. Just as our industries had expanded from local to nation-wide activities, so there had been an advance from state to national control in our methods of government. This was due to the necessary special legislation, and the creation of new special departments of our government, in order to deal with the new problems which had arisen from our industrial expansion.

The first step in the creation of these new agencies for national supervision and control of our industries had been the Interstate Commerce Commission in 1887. This had been followed by the Department of Agriculture in 1889, and afterward the Departments of Commerce and Labor. But the most important of all was the creation of the Federal Reserve Board (1913). This last was given authority by act of Congress over a system of Federal Reserve Banks established throughout the United States. The country was divided into districts. To each district was assigned its own Federal Reserve Bank. And yet all these banks were coördinated into one system. They thus became a clearing house for the finances of the nation. Vexed questions of exchange were by these means eliminated, and there was also the best possible restraint against domination by any section of the country, and against any local stringency.

The benefits to our nation of this system of Federal Reserve Banks cannot be stated too strongly. Through its operation, successful from its inception, the United States had achieved a national control of finance and currency which was far superior to anything existing in other nations of the world. It gave to the nation at once an organization of its finances, which was not only stable but flexible in its stability. In times of peace it had already proved its value. But, at the summons of war in 1917, it was providential that it was already in successful operation, as it supplied the one means by which it was possible to solve the whole problem of our finances in the World War.

Through these processes of our national development, within ourselves, we had grown to a national strength that had not in the least been estimated abroad. It had all been so absolutely different from conditions in Europe, that to Europeans it was incredible. Here was the same story as their failure to appreciate the unity of the American people. To European eyes so many different elements had been hastily put together, in our vast industrial structure, that they could not believe it would be able to stand up under the pressure of a world crisis. But, on the contrary, instead of any collapse, this development of our industrial and financial systems proved to be the main cause of our ability to conceive and to perform the enormous tasks which must be the share of the United States in the World War.

These new conditions in the United States had come into being long before there was any thought of the World War, and they provided the real explanation of the readiness of the American people to rise to the emergency, and to show our ability for both thinking and acting on the vast scale set by the World War. But there had been other developments of our national industries, which were direct results of the state of war in Europe, and these had given to the United States an additional preparation for our tasks in the World War.

In the first place, there had been heavy demands upon American industries for furnishing war material to the combatants in Europe. These had almost all been orders from the Entente Allies. As the Allies had held command of the seas, they had been able to bring in supplies from over the seas. On the other hand, the Central Powers were shut off from the seas, and consequently were only able to bring in such supplies indirectly through neutral countries. As a result, the war material which Germany and her allies were able to secure from the United States did not compare with the great quantities which were obtained by the Entente Allies.

These orders of the Entente Allies for war material from the United States had grown on a large scale, and, as can easily be understood, the result had been to stimulate American industries in the very direction that would increase our ability to produce just what the United States would need, when our nation in turn was forced into the World War. Consequently, the three years of warfare before our own entrance must be counted as having made a great difference in regard to our readiness for war. They had added to the general development of our industries, which had been described, a special development for the production of war material. If the reader will keep these established conditions in mind, it will be evident that, so far as concerned our ability to produce supplies and material for a great war, the United States was not in the usual predicament of a peaceful nation suddenly hurried into war.

Besides all this, there were other conditions existing in the United States in consequence of the threatening attitude of the German Imperial Government; and these will be described in the following chapter.

CHAPTER V

THE EFFECT OF THE WORLD WAR UPON THE
AMERICAN PEOPLE

THE influence of the World War itself upon our nation was a natural matter of cause and effect. With this great devastating war going on before our eyes, its object lessons were gradually arousing the American people to the need for a national defense. And this idea grew, as the hostile attitude of the German Imperial Government made it more and more evident to the minds of our people that the United States might be forced into the war by the conduct of the German leaders.

The first event of the World War which really came home to the hearts of the whole American nation was the sinking of the *Lusitania* (May 7, 1915), with the appalling slaughter of women and children. Throughout the long negotiations which followed, before the German Imperial Government yielded to the contention of the United States, the position of the German Imperial Government had been shown unmistakably, and the American public could not fail to see the threat involved. The second crisis, which was brought about by the inexcusable torpedoing of the Channel steamer *Sussex* (March 24, 1916), was sharp and decisive, as the German Imperial Government surrendered to the

27

United States at once. But it had been made clear to all our people that we were very near war.

And here it should be emphasized that the position of the United States, at the times of these two crises in our relations with the German Imperial Government, can no longer be misunderstood and must no longer be misstated. In the *Lusitania* case, the impression that there was a long-drawn, ineffective correspondence was far from being the truth. The fact was, the protests of the United States had actually dominated the German Imperial Government to the extent of forcing the abandonment of the German U-boat campaign as originally planned. Since the World War, the open recriminations of the German leaders, following their first bitter disappointment at defeat, have drawn aside the veil from events which were going on behind the scenes to a degree that is perhaps unique in history—and these records can never be expunged. As to the *Lusitania* case, the chagrined Tirpitz called the resultant enforced order of the German Imperial Government in 1915 a "practically complete cessation of all employment of submarines."

In the case of the *Sussex*, in 1916, at the first equivocating reply of the German Imperial Government to our protest, the American Government had sent an ultimatum.[1] When actually brought face to face with this ultimatum from the United States, the German

---

[1]This ultimatum, called by Tirpitz "the well-known American bullying Note," stated: "Unless the Imperial Government should now immediately declare and effect abandonment of this present method of submarine warfare against passenger and freight carrying vessels, the United States can have no choice but to sever diplomatic relations with the German Empire altogether." (April 18, 1916.)

Imperial Government at once capitulated,[1] "and sent orders to the Naval Staff to the effect that submarine warfare was henceforth to be carried on in accordance with the Prize Law."[2]

These facts are beyond dispute. And any insinuations that the United States did not assert its rights and any reproaches as to our "late entrance" can now be dismissed absolutely. In both cases, the United States had stood out for its principles and had forced the German Imperial Government to abandon its illegal warfare. It was the act of the German Imperial Government, in violating its pledges in 1917, which caused, and set the time of, our entrance.

When our nation began to read the danger signals, which were so plainly before our eyes, it was natural that public opinion was first aroused to our naval needs. This public opinion was a matter of slow growth, but, as the German Government was breaking away from the usages of the seas, it became evident that the United States was a nation which must recognize the necessity for its defense "to be strong upon the seas." This had been the phrase which was emphasized in President Wilson's message to Congress in 1914. Consequently, the result was that our first steps in preparation for war were made in regard to the United States Navy.

This does not mean that anything was done that would in any degree correspond to the part the United States was destined to play upon the seas, but, on the

---

[1]"Yielding to Wilson . . . the *Sussex* note was a decisive turning point of the war, the beginning of our capitulation."—Admiral Tirpitz, *My Memoirs.*

[2]Admiral Scheer, *Germany's High Sea Fleet.*

other hand, definite strides were taken in 1915, which were of real value in preparing our navy. A Naval Reserve was constituted in 1915, and this was to be the germ of our future great Naval Reserve Force. There was also a most important provision in the Naval Bill of 1915, by which the office of Chief of Naval Operations had been created in our navy.

By this provision, the bill had constituted one of the most powerful offices of Chief of Staff in the world, and at one stroke had eliminated an outstanding defect in the organization of the United States Navy. For no other word should be applied to the former system of the different bureaus functioning independently under the Secretary of the Navy, with only advisory functions assigned to the Aide for Operations and the General Board. Under the new act, the Chief of Naval Operations was to be appointed by the President with the consent of the Senate, for a period of four years, and would, "under the direction of the Secretary of the Navy, be charged with the operations of the fleet, and with the preparation and readiness of plans for its use in war."

By this act, not only was there created the very thing the Navy most needed, an efficient office of Chief of Staff, but also the act came at the very time it could do the most good. For the new office was most fortunately in being when the approaching enlargement of the United States Navy and the extensions of its scope of operations were destined to bring about the greatest need in our history for a strong naval administrative organization.

In response to the President's call for a program of

national defense, the Secretary of the Navy had also made an innovation which was destined to accomplish great results. In October, 1915, Secretary Daniels had constituted the Naval Consulting Board, of civilians whose scientific and industrial affiliations made them of value, and this Board appointed an Industrial Preparedness Committee, which did useful work in gathering data from over eighteen thousand industrial plants. This may be considered one of the first moves toward our industrial mobilization.

In 1915, as has been stated, the *Lusitania* crisis had suddenly changed the whole aspect of the war in the eyes of the United States. The long interval of doubt, before the German Imperial Government yielded to the United States, had confirmed our people in their growing conviction that the United States must maintain a strong naval force against aggression. Consequently, even after the German Government had given the promise that merchantmen would not be sunk without warning, American public opinion remained aroused to such an extent that the time was propitious to propose, in the naval bill for 1916, the recommendations of the General Board of the United States Navy. These stated: "The Navy of the United States should ultimately be equal to the most powerful maintained by any other nation of the world. It should be gradually increased to this point by such a development, year by year, as may be permitted by the facilities of the country, but the limit above should be attained not later than 1925."

With the force of public opinion behind it, Congress passed this naval bill (August 29, 1916) carrying the unprecedented appropriation of $312,678,000, and authorizing the Naval Building Program of 1916, which marked an epoch in the United States Navy. In view of events after the World War, it should be noted here that this was a measure for national defense only, with no hint of imperialistic policies, and incorporated in the measure was a provision for abrogating this naval program upon any satisfactory international agreement. And, at the Washington Disarmament Conference, although the 1916 Building Program had given us the lead over any navy of the world, the United States proved its good faith by cutting down the American battle fleet to an equality with Great Britain.

In the spring of 1916, the tension with the German Imperial Government had carried our people far beyond the mere idea of a naval defense. So pressing was the danger that it had become clear that the whole nation must be arrayed for a national defense. At last public opinion in the United States was thoroughly aroused. Under this stimulus there emerged the National Defense Act (June 3, 1916) and the creation of the Council of National Defense, attached to the army appropriation bill of August 29, 1916. These two measures may truly be said to mark the beginning of the change which was destined to transform our nation, as will be shown in the ensuing narrative.

CHAPTER VI

WHEN we look backward, from the vantage point gained by the after knowledge of the mighty torrents of the last year of the World War, it becomes evident that, in 1915, when the President called for "adequate programs for national defense," no one, in America or abroad, had any conception of what was destined to be the meaning of the words "adequate programs" for the United States. This statement has been reiterated here, because the best proof of it came from the actual tests of battle in the year 1915, which conclusively showed that the World War was moving far beyond *all* ideas of even the combatants themselves.

In order to carry out the campaigns of 1915, each of the three great nations of the Entente Allies had intrusted its preparations to a military dictator—for such had General Joffre practically become in France. Lord Kitchener had been given military control in Great Britain. The Grand Duke Nicholas was paramount in Russia. Each of these was the typical soldier of his nation, and each made preparations according to the accepted ideas of 1915. These preparations were then considered adequate for victory, and the Entente Allies undertook their military operations with optimistic confidence. Herein lay the failure of the Entente Allies.

Their preparations proved to be totally inadequate to meet the greater tasks which they encountered, and, consequently, 1915 became a year of tragic defeat for the Entente Allies.

Knowing all this, it is impossible for us to believe that in 1915 there was any prescription in sight that would have met our needs. Aside from the necessity for restraint in militaristic activities, in order that the Administration might maintain the proper attitude in diplomatic negotiations, it is now clear that what was called "preparedness" in those days would not even have made a beginning of the share of the United States in the World War.

But in 1916 it was another story. The awakening of the American people had given to our nation the very qualities that were needed to accomplish our tasks. Here was an approaching crisis which had not been measured, but which our aroused instincts told us would make unprecedented demands upon the United States. It can be laid down as an axiom that the test of a nation's power to cope with unexpectedly great dangers of war must be found in the ability of the nation to improvise forces to meet such dangers. In 1916, this ability to improvise great forces had become inherent in the American nation, as a direct result of the developments which have been described in the preceding chapters.

Abroad, in 1916, the Entente Allies had learned from the bitter lessons of their military failure that the World War had outgrown all ideas of 1915. In America, our people had seen the United States on the verge of being drawn into this war which was assuming such colossal proportions. It was no wonder that "prepared-

ness" had grown to a broader meaning, and the realization of our lacks and shortcomings served to stimulate
our awakening to our needs. In this awakening, the
necessity for industrial preparedness asserted itself, as
our people began to realize what was implied in gathering our forces to meet the great danger. Throughout our
industries, their leaders began to be heard in advocating
industrial mobilization. As a result, these leaders came
into consultation with the Administration, and the
National Defense Act of 1916 (June 3, 1916) strongly
reflected these conditions.

This "Act for making further and more effectual provision for the national defense, and for other purposes"
contained many provisions for improving and expanding
the military forces of the United States. It provided for
a General Staff Corps, Officers Reserve Corps, Enlisted
Reserve Corps, Reserve Officers Training Camps, with
measures to increase the efficiency of the Regular Army,
and the National Guard, this last especially in view of
being called into the Federal service. These military
provisions will be considered in the ensuing narrative.
But an outstanding feature was the control of our
nation's industries in case of war.

The Act provided (Section 120): "The President, in
time of war or when war is imminent, is empowered,
through the head of any department of the Government,
in addition to the present authorized methods of purchase or procurement, to place an order with any individual, firm, association, company, corporation, or
organized manufacturing industry. . . . Compliance
shall be obligatory. . . . and shall take precedence over
all other orders and contracts. . . ." Moreover, in case

of refusal to carry out any such order, the President was authorized "to take immediate possession" of the offending plant. In addition, refusal was made a felony liable to three years imprisonment and fine of $50,000. These additional powers given to the President were destined to be far-reaching in their effect.

The Secretary of War was directed to make a list of munition plants in the United States, and the President was authorized to appoint a "Board on Mobilization of Industries Essential for Military Preparedness." But this last idea was more effectively carried out by the creation of the Council of National Defense, which was embodied in the Military Appropriations Act shortly afterward (August 29, 1916).

The general scheme of some such body was not new, and several proposals of the kind were before Congress, but the actual form of this Act had been made a matter of much study, as founded upon the powers of the President amplified by the National Defense Act. It provided: "That a Council of National Defense is hereby established for the coördination of industries and resources for the national security and welfare, to consist of the Secretary of War, the Secretary of the Navy, the Secretary of the Interior, the Secretary of Commerce, and the Secretary of Labor.

"That the Council of National Defense shall nominate to the President, and the President shall appoint an advisory commission, consisting of not more than seven persons, each of whom shall have special knowledge of some industry, public utility, or the development of some natural resource, or be otherwise specially

qualified, in the opinion of the Council, for the performance of duties hereinafter provided. . . ."[1]

President Wilson's own statement of the aims of this
Act should be quoted: "The Council of National Defense has been created because the Congress has realized
that the country is best prepared for war when thoroughly prepared for peace. From an economical point
of view there is now very little difference between the
machinery required for commercial efficiency and that
required for military purposes. In both cases the whole
industrial mechanism must be organized in the most
effective way. Upon this conception of the national
welfare, the Council is organized in the words of the
Act for 'the creation of relations which will render possible in time of need the immediate concentration of the
resources of the nation.'

"The creation of the Council likewise opens up a new
and direct channel of communication and coöperation
between business and scientific men in all departments
of the Government, and it is hoped that it will, in addition, become a rallying point for civic bodies working
for the national defense. The Council's chief functions
are:

"1. The coördination of all forms of transportation
and the development of means of transportation to
meet the military, industrial, and commercial needs of
the nation.

"2. The extension of the industrial mobilization work
of the Committee on Industrial Preparedness of the
Naval Consulting Board. Complete information as to

[1] Text given in full, Appendix, page 365

our present manufacturing and producing facilities adaptable to many-sided uses of modern warfare will be procured, analyzed, and made use of.

"One of the objects of the Council will be to inform American manufacturers as to the part they can and must play in national emergency. It is empowered to establish at once and maintain through subordinate bodies of specially qualified persons an auxiliary organization composed of men of the best creative and administrative capacity, capable of mobilizing to the utmost the resources of the country.

"The personnel of the Council's advisory members, appointed without regard to party, marks the entrance of the non-partisan engineer and professional man into American governmental affairs on a wider scale than ever before. It is responsive to the increased demand for and need of business organization in public matters and for the presence there of the best specialists in their respective fields. In the present instance, the time of some of the members of the Advisory Board could not be purchased. They serve the Government without remuneration, efficiency being their sole object and Americanism their only motive."

This description is well worth studying, and above all the reader will note, standing out among its academic sentences, the tense phrase "the part they can and must play," as applied to American industries. These words reflected the amplification of the powers of the President conferred by the National Defense Act.

The men appointed to the Advisory Commission were as follows, with the fields of activities for which they respectively assumed responsibility early in 1917:

Daniel Willard (president of the Baltimore & Ohio Railroad), transportation and communication.

Bernard M. Baruch (financier), raw materials, minerals, and metals.

Howard E. Coffin (vice president of the Hudson Motor Company), munitions, manufacturing, and industrial relations.

Julius Rosenwald (president of Sears, Roebuck & Company), supplies, including food, clothing, etc.

Dr. Hollis Godfrey (president of the Drexel Institute, of Philadelphia), engineering and education.

Samuel Gompers (president of the American Federation of Labor), labor, including conservation of health and welfare of workers.

Dr. Franklin Martin (secretary general of the American College of Surgeons, Chicago), medicine and surgery, including general sanitation.

In the act creating the Council, the Secretary of War was named first. It was, therefore, considered as prescribed by law that the Secretary of War should be Chairman of the Council of National Defense. This was altogether right, as the greatest and most difficult problems were those of the War Department, and more depended upon the guidance and control of the Secretary of War than upon any other factor. On March 9, 1916, Newton D. Baker had become Secretary of War. It is merely a statement of fact to say that the tasks which confronted the new Secretary were not alone greater than had ever been the lot of a Secretary of War, but were greater than had ever been presented to any war minister in history.

At a joint meeting of the Council and Commission,

held December 7, 1916, Walter S. Gifford (now President of the American Telephone & Telegraph Company) was appointed Director of the Council of National Defense. Mr. Gifford had gained experience with the Industrial Preparedness Committee of the Naval Consulting Board, and he at once showed courage and ability in developing the opportunities for national industrial organization offered by means of the Council of Defense. He remained in office throughout the war activities of the Council.[1]

A kindred measure, which was later to be an important factor, was the creation of the United States Shipping Board (under the Federal Shipping Act of September 7, 1916), "for the purpose of regulating foreign and domestic shipping and promoting the development of an American merchant marine." This was in process of organization at the first of 1917, and was to function as a war board after the declaration of war.

From the foregoing, it must be clear to the reader that great changes had taken place in the United States in 1916. It would be an exaggeration to state that much tangible work had been done toward our great undertaking in the war. Neither can it be said that, as the fateful year of 1917 began its course, the actual agencies had come into being which were to produce the American reinforcement in the World War. It would be more truthful to call these events of 1916 the basis of our preparation, as they were the first stages of the chemistry that was destined to develop the vast resources of the United States into a mobilization of the nation's

[1]Mr. Gifford did not resign as Director until October 29, 1918, when Germany was already suing for peace.

industrial forces, which must be behind the armed forces of the United States in order to accomplish our mission in the World War.

That this was all a potent chemistry will be at once apparent, if the reader will realize what it all meant. Its significance came from the development of two essential elements. The first was the establishment of the executive powers of the President as the source of authority for our improvisations of forces. Our people do not realize it, but the powers of the President of the United States are far greater than those of the executives of other nations. And these carry with them greatly increased powers in times of national emergency. In addition, what was specified and implied in the National Defense Act had amplified the President's authority. This increased power of the President was also recognized in the way the Council of National Defense was constituted, as an advisory body for the President, with all authority for carrying out its recommendations derived from the Executive only.

The second essential element lay in the fact that the Council of National Defense was in reality a call from the Administration summoning our industrial leaders for consultation and action as to a national emergency. Consequently, at this stage in 1916, the Administration had already associated with itself these leaders from our civil life. And, although the definite bodies had not then been formed which were to control our industrial mobilization, the activities of these industrial leaders were already making themselves felt throughout the country. They were not only bringing the men of our industries into touch with the Administration, but they were also stimulating the industrial centres to work in the right direction. The result was a real beginning of leadership and control from the top down, and the uprising of our people was thus given intelligent direction from the start.

These two essential elements may be summed up by stating that, in 1916, the course of events had already determined that the source of authority would be the increased powers of the President, exerted with the advice and guidance of the leaders of our industrial system.

CHAPTER VII

FINANCE AND MANPOWER

THE preceding chapter has stated the situation in the United States in the months before our nation was forced into the World War by the hostile acts of the German Imperial Government. Our declaration of war was the electric shock which galvanized into life the accumulating forces of the United States. The immediate results gave proof to Europe of how entirely the spirit of America had been misunderstood abroad —and this proof was shown in short sequence.

It is enough to state the following facts. War was declared on April 6, 1917. Before the end of May, three measures had been adopted which presaged the doom of the German Imperial Government. President Wilson had signed the seven-billion-dollar War Bond Bill. The largest Army and Navy Bill in the history of nations had reached a total of nearly four billion dollars. And the President had signed the Selective Service Act, calling upon all men between twenty-one and thirty. These quickly enacted measures meant that the United States was to make the greatest effort that had ever been made in war by a united people. Thus early was inscribed upon the wall the writing which foretold the fall of German militarism.

Two of these enactments implied the complete and

final solutions of two great problems for the United States in the World War, and an account of these should be written at the outset, in order to give the right perspective to the other difficult tasks which confronted our nation.

In the first place, this War Bond Bill marked the beginning of a financial policy for the United States, which was carried on successfully, and even triumphantly, throughout the war. There had been grave fears as to the financial side of our effort, and these fears were increased when it became evident that the sums to be raised must be of staggering magnitude. Not only was it a question of the enormous costs of our own war expenditures, which were made heavier by the urgent necessity for haste, but we must also make large loans to the Entente Allies, who were all at extremity financially. For these reasons, the financial problem of the United States was unprecedented in the vast sums required in short order.

It was the quick recourse to our self-governing communities themselves which provided the solution of the financial problem of the United States. Just as the strength of our Government was derived from these, so it was also shown that the strength of our financial resources would come direct from our American communities. War taxes were imposed, but the bulk of the enormous total required to meet this double drain upon the nation's finances was actually raised by a series of issues of United States "Liberty" bonds, taken by popular subscription in the different communities throughout our nation.

The wise policy was followed of allotting a proportionate part of the bond issues to each community in the country. Each city or town knew the amount of its share, and local pride was joined to patriotism to make sure that each did its part in carrying on the war.

In this case, popular subscription meant that the people really subscribed for the bonds. All classes participated in the patriotic service of taking these bonds in proportion to their means, and the local communities vied with one another in their zeal, and in their local campaigns to arouse enthusiasm. By these means, the success of each of the loans was notable, and, as a result of this direct appeal to our communities, the financial part of our nation's task at home and abroad was never in jeopardy. But it should be emphasized, beyond any misunderstanding, that, no matter how great the zeal of our people might be, the complicated machinery of these loans and the war finances of the United States could not have been operated by any conceivable means other than the system of Federal Reserve Banks. But, through this newly established agency, which had been created by our national development as described, our American communities were enabled to provide this first great essential for our mission in the World War.

In order to understand the vast scale of our financial problem, it is only necessary to state that the direct war expenditures of the United States amounted to about $22,000,000,000, "or nearly enough to pay the entire cost of running the United States Government from 1791 up to the outbreak of the European War."[1] To this enormous total must be added the sum of

---

[1] Colonel Leonard P. Ayres, A Statistical Summary, General Staff, U. S. A. He also has given the cost as "more than $1,000,000 an hour."

$8,500,000,000 loaned by the United States to the Entente Allies.

Before the World War it would have been held impossible that any means could be devised to make it possible to raise these huge sums of money by popular subscription. But it is all now a matter of record, and must be scored as a result of the national development of the American people which has been described.

The second of these measures, a law that solved what was thought to be even a more difficult problem, was the Selective Service Act. It had been assumed abroad that the United States would not be able to enact conscription until after a long delay, as had been the case with Great Britain where the Military Service Bill had not been introduced until January 5, 1916. At home, also, there were many misgivings, and the word "draft" seemed to presage discontent and disorder. But here again it was the same direct appeal to each American community that proved to be the foundation of success. In this case of the United States, conscription was not a last resort, but an immediate first call upon each city or town to do its share in the war.

The raw material of American manhood for the necessary enormous expansion of our armed forces was assured by this form of Selective Service—and our success was due to the fact that this was so quickly enacted. One of the fortunate elements of preparation, long before the World War, had been the establishment of an efficient General Staff of the United States Army when Elihu Root was Secretary of War in 1902. The value of this organization was soon proved in the emergency of 1917. A month before our declaration of war, the Chief of Staff, General Hugh Scott, had brought to the Secretary of War the suggestion for the Selective Service form of conscription. Secretary Baker was so converted to the idea that he laid it before President Wilson. After a short explanation, the President had said: "Baker, this is plainly right on any ground. Start to prepare the necessary legislation so that if I am obliged to go to the Congress the bills will be ready for immediate consideration."[1] The Secretary of War at once called a conference. "In that conference we laid out the main lines of the bill, which was thereafter drawn by General Crowder in more or less conference with us."[2] In this direct and businesslike way was the Selective Service Act prepared for its immediate and successful operation.[3]

One outstanding feature in the Act not only gained a great deal of time, but also had a most favorable influence upon the administration of the Act throughout the country. It will be evident that to build up a new Federal organization, in order to carry out the widespread and manifold operations of this law,[4] would have taken a long time—and the military necessity demanded haste above all things. Instead of anything of the kind, the wise decision was made to use the existing governmental organizations of the various States, and the statute authorized their use.

[1] Newton D. Baker, Secretary of War.

[2] *Ibid.*

[3] "The administration of the Act under General Crowder was as splendid a piece of executive business as I have ever seen in public or private life." —Newton D. Baker.

[4] Four thousand five hundred and fifty seven local boards were necessary to conduct the physical examination of registrants, etc.

This was unprecedented, but, in the actual working of the law, it brought success. Not only was there a great saving of time, but the effect of handing over the administration of the Selective Service to the local authorities was most beneficial, and this must be noted as marking an epoch in the conscription of the manpower of a nation. Instead of a summons from the Federal Government, backed up by military authority and enforced by soldiers, the call came to each citizen as an appeal from his own community to stand by his home institutions. For he saw the operation of the law placed in the hands of his neighbors and acquaintances, in order to secure adequate representation of his own town or city in the effort of the American nation.

The effect of this was beyond any mistaking. Instead of any idea that they were being dragged reluctantly into service, the American citizens inducted under this Act took pride in their feeling that they were rendering a first service to their communities and representing their communities. They saw the absolute fairness of the working out of the law, all in public and under the supervision of their own authorities. Consequently, there was a zealous spirit among those inducted, and their morale was very high. With this unusual basis for our American conscription, there was no trouble in the operation of Selective Service. Instead of resistance to this law, there was universal acceptance. And this fact furnished additional evidence of the futility of hostile propaganda in the United States, as the German agents had concentrated great efforts to stir up discontent against the enforcement of this measure.

The Selective Service Act was "based upon the lia-

bility to military service of all male citizens, or male
persons, not alien enemies, who have declared their
intention to become citizens, between the ages of 21 and
30 years, both inclusive." The several States, Territor-
ies, and the District of Columbia were to furnish quotas
determined in proportion to the population of each.
Plans had already been made for the operation of the
law, and the Judge Advocate General had been detailed
as Provost Marshal General to supervise the work.
The first immediate need was a registration of every
male of draft age.

To effect this, each state was constituted a separate
unit, and each governor was charged with the execution
of the law in his state. Each state was divided into districts of approximately 30,000, in each of which a registration board was appointed by the governor. Cities of
over 30,000 were treated as separate units, with their
mayors acting as intermediaries of the governors.
The sensible plan was followed of using the election
district system, so that the usual election machinery
of the precincts could be utilized, and a registrar
for each 800 was appointed by the local registration
board.

The reader will see at once what a great gain in time
was accomplished by relying upon the local authorities.
In fact, General Crowder's office was able to complete
this organization and furnish all necessary material in
the short period of sixteen days. The whole operation
was thus placed in the hands of leading citizens who
knew their localities and inspired confidence, and these
citizens gave their voluntary and energetic efforts to
this work for their own communities. The President had

proclaimed Tuesday, June 5, 1917, registration day throughout the United States.[1]

"Registration consisted in entering on a card essential facts necessary to a complete identification of the registrant and a preliminary survey of his domestic and economic circumstances."[2] So promptly and efficiently had the organizations of the States been completed that on the day set about 10,000,000 male citizens of the designated ages were registered, and by this means, in an astonishingly short time,[3] the first phase of the Selective Service had become an accomplished fact. After a drawing by lot to determine the order of liability for call to service, all matters of physical examination, elimination, and induction remained in the hands of the local boards. The case of an American citizen of age liable to military service was thus, from first to last, under the control of his own neighbors.

So general was the acceptance of this well conceived and well executed measure, and so smoothly and efficiently was it carried out through the duration of the war, that few of our people have any idea of the scope and magnitude of the problem which it solved. To fix the large numbers eventually at call for service through the operation of this law, it is sufficient to state that, after the subsequent registrations had been extended to ages from 18 to 45, of the 54,000,000 males in the United States, 26,000,000 were either registered or already in service.[4]

[1]With the exception of Alaska, Hawaii, and Porto Rico.
[2]Report of the Secretary of War, 1917.
[3]The Act was signed by the President, May 18, 1917.
[4]A Statistical Summary, General Staff, U. S. A.

CHAPTER VIII

THE CREATION OF THE GENERAL MUNITIONS BOARD

IN VIEW of what has been told in the preceding chapter, it must be clear that the main problem in the United States had become a question of material—not of manpower. This last was assured, at once and for all, by the operation of the Selective Service Act, even for the enormous American Army which was eventually to be called into being. But the problem of material for our ever growing armed forces was also ever growing in size and difficulty—with constantly increasing demands upon the industries of the nation. And the extent of these demands had never been measured, in any true sense of the word.

In the first place, even with the added knowledge of 1916, no one in America or abroad had yet advanced to the point where there was any conception of the vast size of the armed forces which would be required of the United States. On the part of the Entente Allies, there is a significant record of this. Secretary Baker has quoted General Joffre, when in America with the French Commission in May, 1917, as speaking of our "great army which may some day be as great as 500,000 men." This is notable, because it reflected the most optimistic view that a European soldier could take of our military possibilities.[1] The ensuing situation was so surprising in its overturn of all previous ideas that it went beyond all prophecies. It is a mere statement of fact to write that, from the European military point of view, a military impossibility was accomplished when the total of the United States Army in the World War reached 4,000,000, of which 2.084,000 had actually been transported to Europe.[2]

These totals give proof at a glance that the tasks of the Secretary of War were greater and more surprising than those of anyone else. And these totals of manpower also give the reason why the problems of material became so difficult. If the minds of men had not conceived the vast hosts of our armed forces, how much less had they estimated the huge volumes of material that would be demanded! Even after the achievement has become a matter of history, it is hard to grasp the meaning of such enormous figures.

In this case, material did not simply mean arms, ammunition, and equipment. These hosts of men must be housed, clothed, fed, and supplied. They must be cared for and transported. The means must be provided for taking them overseas, and for transporting overseas the great quantities of material which they would need in Europe. And, in Europe, the drain upon American material for them would increase, with the necessities for terminals, bases, services of transportation and supplies, to be built and maintained abroad. Nothing like our

[1] "How amazed he would have been could he have looked into the crystal and seen what this country transported to France in men and material during the eighteen months."—Admiral Albert Gleaves, *A History of the Transport Service*.

[2] Colonel Leonard P. Ayres, A Statistical Summary, General Staff, U. S. A.

military operation had ever occurred in history. And, consequently, it is not surprising that nothing like these matters of material had ever been formulated.

For this reason, the war problems of the United States must be considered as concentrated upon these hitherto undreamt questions of material which must be provided by means of the American industries. And the main difficulties of these war problems must also be considered as concentrated upon the Secretary of War. Consequently, it will be evident that Secretary Baker's principal task must be to coördinate our American industries in the production of war material so urgently needed by the War Department. In this great undertaking the Secretary of War was compelled to start practically at the beginning, as the General Staff of the United States Army had not progressed beyond the usual Army channels of purchase and supply. It was from the first evident that these would be hopelessly inadequate. Some other organization for procuring material must be found at once. This was the most difficult situation for an improvisation of forces that had ever been faced in the world's history.

Secretary Baker has given a vivid picture of the results of the national development which has been described: "The whole country had caught the impetus of this development, and, when we went into the war, there surged over Washington not only the unanimous approval of the people, but also the urgent desire of the great masters of business and industry to throw into the national service the experience they had acquired in private pursuits. All this great organizing and constructive talent was eager to serve the country, and our problem was limited to assimilation rapidly into the mechanism of the Government." For this very task, of making the best use of the invaluable help of the leaders of our industries, Secretary Baker was especially well equipped. He was a skilled lawyer of wide practice. He had the advantage of experience of public service, and of intimate association with leaders of great industries. These qualities made him resourceful and energetic in assimilating these industrial leaders "rapidly into the mechanism of the Government."

One of the most important questions to be considered by this group of industrial leaders was the problem of coördinating the production and purchase of war material for the Army and Navy. As has been stated, the first step in this direction had been the Naval Consulting Board, created in 1915. It was obvious that the matter of procuring war material for the Services must be included in the field of work for the Advisory Commission of the Council of National Defense, and the importance of this was soon appreciated. In 1916, Mr. Gifford, the Director of the Council of National Defense had been in consultation on this subject with Howard E. Coffin, Chairman of the Industrial Preparedness Committee of the Naval Consulting Board, whose experience was of great value, and the ideas for a controlling body were taking form.

A beginning was made by the creation of a subsidiary body of the Council of National Defense called the Munitions Standards Board, "to insure speedy and efficient quantity production of munitions, to standardize munition specifications."[1] (March 20, 1917.) It soon

---

[1]Historical Branch, War Plans Division, General Staff, U. S. A.

became evident that the scope of this new Board was not adequate for the conditions which confronted the Administration, and that it was necessary to evolve a new body under the Council of National Defense, which would have a broader field of efficiency.

The chairman of the Munitions Standards Board was Frank A. Scott, of Cleveland, who, although a comparatively young man, had been the head of a large manufacturing industry. He had also made a study of military matters, in the years preceding the World War, especially concerning the production of war material when on trips to Europe. This unusual double qualification was known to Secretary Baker, who had been well acquainted with Mr. Scott, and, consequently, the Secretary consulted him in regard to the need for a more comprehensive agency than the existing Munitions Standards Board.

After consultation also with Mr. Gifford, Mr. Coffin, and Major Palmer E. Pierce, a memorandum was drawn up of a scheme for a new subsidiary body of the Council of National Defense. This was an evolution from what had gone before. The idea was, instead of branching off in any outside experiment, to constitute a new Board of the Council of National Defense, which would consist of officers representing the different departments of the Army and Navy, and associated with them civilians who would represent our industries. The essential basis of this organization was the intent to retain and make use of the existing Army and Navy authorizations for purchase, derived from the war powers of the President and increased by the National Defense Act, as has been explained. The civilian members of this body were to act with these officers, to guide them to an increased and coördinated program for the acquisition of war material. It will at once be evident that this new Board was not only an evolution from what had gone before, but that it also preserved the same processes and authorities for purschase which formed the foundation of our whole scheme of action.

The working basis for this new body was the belief that officers of our Army and Navy would be able to respond to the broad ideas of the civilian leaders of industry associated with them, and would follow the guidance of these civilians in their own familiar fields of industry. Along these lines the General Munitions Board of the Council of National Defense was created, "and began work on April 9, 1917, under the chairmanship of Frank A. Scott."[1] The results proved that this faith was well founded, as officers and civilians worked well together. The success of this joint board of officers and civilians sitting together was largely due to Mr. Scott, to his confidence in the ability of the officers of the Services, and to his cordial relations with them. As General Crozier has expressed it, "Into this turbulent situation, to the great good fortune of the Government, there came a man of sanity."[2] General Crozier's praise was well deserved, for, above all things, the activities of this new body were sane in conception and execution.

It was, in fact, a commonsense and direct way of getting at a solution of one of the most pressing questions of the times. In this regard, it is interesting to study the situation in Great Britain when the British

[1]First Annual Report, Council of National Defense.
[2]Major General William Crozier, U. S. A., *Ordnance and the World War.*

were suddenly confronted with the problem of securing munitions on a greatly increased scale. When Lord Kitchener's régime in the British War Office had failed utterly to provide adequate war material, in 1915, the British had created an entirely new department of government, the Ministry of Munitions, with Lloyd George as the first Minister of Munitions. In America, in 1917, there were many who strongly advocated the use of the same remedy for the United States. But this would have meant that we conceded the failure of all existing machinery, and we would have been compelled to begin all over again—to build up a new organization. The delay involved would have seriously retarded our effort in the World War. For, even admitting that an enabling act might have been quickly framed that would accomplish the difficult task of creating this proposed new department of the Government, it is obvious that it would have taken a long time to build up the working machinery of any such new organization. On the other hand, the advantages of the scheme of the new General Munitions Board lay in its two fundamental ideas. It not only at once made every possible use of the already existing machinery, but also, at the same time, it added the means for greatly expanding the scope of the existing machinery. It was most fortunate that this direct plan was adopted in America.

At first the intention had been to call this new body a "Purchasing Board." But this would have been altogether an improper and misleading title, because, as has been emphasized, all actual contracts and purchases were to be made through the different departments of the Services, with authority derived from the war powers of the President strengthened by the National Defense Act of 1916. Consequently, this mistaken title was abandoned, and by resolve of the Council of National Defense, the Secretary of War appointed the General Munitions Board, Council of National Defense, "to be composed of Army and Navy Department heads, or officers appointed by them, and representatives appointed by the Advisory Commission, the purpose being to coördinate the buying of the several Departments; assist in the acquirement of raw materials and manufacturing facilities; the establishment of precedence of orders, etc., including the ordinary commercial and industrial needs and the military requirements of the nation." In the wording of this resolve the distinction was made, which has been explained, that the Board itself was not to be the purchasing agency, but that contracts and purchases should be "as at present by the departments." This distinction has already been emphasized, and must be constantly kept in mind, as it was upon the framework of this General Munitions Board that all subsequent means for our improvisation of war material for our fighting forces were drawn.

The first membership of the General Munitions Board was announced as follows:

Frank A. Scott, Chairman

From the Army: Brig. Gen. Thomas Cruse
Colonel F. G. Hodgson
Colonel H. Fisher
Lieut. Col. J. E. Hoffer
Major Palmer E. Pierce
Major Charles Wallace
Captain A. B. Barker

From the Navy: Rear Admiral H. H. Rousseau
                     Rear Admiral W. S. Capps
                     Commander R. H. Leigh
                     Commander T. A. Kearney
                     Surgeon R. C. Holcomb
                     Paymaster J. H. Hancock
                     Lieut. Col. W. B. Lemly, Marine
                        Corps
                     Mr. L. McH. Howe, representing
                        the Secretary of the Navy
                        and representatives of the follow-
                        ing committees of the

Council of National Defense:

Raw Materials	Bernard M. Baruch, Chairman
	L. L. Summers
Industrial	Howard E. Coffin, Chairman
Supplies	Julius Rosenwald, Chairman
Medicine	Dr. Franklin Martin, Chairman
	F. F. Simpson

The Secretary
of the General
Munitions Board, Chester C. Bolton

CHAPTER IX

THE NATION AT WORK

SECRETARY BAKER has frankly stated: "The early stages of our war preparations in Washington have always seemed a more or less confused episode." This is no matter for surprise, when one considers the full extent of the national emergency which confronted the American people. Here was a sudden call for the greatest improvisation of forces in history. Would the United States be able to meet this test of its power to improvise its manpower and material into a fighting force adequate to perform its part in the World War?

It is no wonder that the first impression of the situation in Washington was of bewildering confusion. How could it be otherwise? The very rush of those eager to help in Washington seemed on the surface to make things worse. We know now that it was a situation for which we cannot imagine the possibility of a ready-made remedy—and our nation had also been slow in awakening. But there were qualities in the zealous surge of our people that redeemed the shortcomings of our sluggish minds. As has been explained, real elements of leadership had already been developed. Our ablest citizens were already working with the Services. And already, underneath the surface of this confused vortex, great currents were running guided by intelligent direction.

The important results which have been described, and which were so quickly obtained, show that all was not confusion, even at this stage. But, on the other hand, we must realize that there was no clockwork of well-ordered machinery. All kinds of mistakes were made—duplications, diversions of effort into useless channels, conflicting efforts without number. But the one most necessary basis was under it all. At last our Industries and our Services were in touch. Civilians and officers were working together. As has been said, it was a chemistry—an evolution. But, with the elements in the situation which have been described, the trend was leading toward doing the right thing in the right way, and, from the vague supervision of the Council of National Defense, there were being evolved national agencies of control which were to take over industrial administration, each with its own corps of experts in its own branch.

The creation of the most important of these, the General Munitions Board, has been described. The kindred necessities, food and fuel, were kept separate from the Munitions Board, and each had its own administrative organization. There is no need to dwell on the fact that it was a colossal undertaking, to apportion these products of food and fuel among our armed forces, our people at home, and the needs of the Entente Allies abroad. In the case of food control, the basis of our policy was again at first an appeal to each American community. On May 17, 1917, President Wilson directed Herbert C. Hoover "to start a preliminary organization that would have as its principal function food conservation."[1]

This was the beginning of Hoover's work as Food Administrator, which made his name a household word throughout the United States. This preliminary work was the first nationwide "food-pledge drive" of the Woman's Committee in the State divisions (June, 1917), and it brought home to our people the necessity for economic use of food products in all homes. Drastic powers were afterward given to the Food Administration, through the President, by means of the Food and Fuel Control Act (August 10, 1917). These included a strict license system and fixing of prices. But always these powers were used to supplement the appeals for voluntary coöperation among our people.

After the passage of this Act, President Wilson, on August 23, 1917, appointed Dr. Harry A. Garfield, President of Williams College, United States Fuel Administrator. The organization of the Fuel Administration of the United States can be said to begin with this appointment. This also developed into an important system of national control.

Another offspring of the Council of National Defense was the beginning of the government control of the railroads. On April 11, 1917, the railroad organizations of the United States had promptly offered their services. On April 21, 1917, the Railroads' War Board was organized, "to direct the policies of the Special Committee of National Defense of the American Railway Association in coördinating the operations of the railroads of the United States in a continental system dur-

[1]Historical Branch, War Plans Division, General Staff, U. S. A.

ing the period of the war, merging their individual and competitive activities in an effort to produce the maximum degree of efficiency."

From the sub-committee of the Advisory Commission of the Council of National Defense there was also being developed a control of Labor, both through the Department of Labor and by means of other bodies, affiliated with the various activities which were being inaugurated.

The different states formed organizations for national defense, and to coöperate with the work of the national organizations. All over the country associations and organizations were being formed, with the object of coöperating in our great national effort. And social and philanthropic societies devoted their activities to this one object. Throughout the land there was a wonderful outburst, not only of united patriotism but of practical endeavor to be of actual assistance in the work.

Secretary Baker has given an inspiring picture of this national uprising: "Out of the body of a nation devoted to productive and peaceful pursuits and evidencing its collective spirit only upon occasions for the settlement of domestic and institutional questions, there arose the figure of a national spirit which had lain dormant until summoned to embody loyalty to our institutions, unity of purpose, and willingness to sacrifice on the part of our entire people as their underlying and dominant character. Those who believed that the obvious and daily exhibition of power which takes place in an autocracy is necessary for national strength, discovered that a finer, and freer, and greater national strength subsists in a free people, and that the silent processes of democ-

racy, with their normal accent on the freedom of individuals, nevertheless afford springs of collective action
and inspiration for self-sacrifice as wide and effective
as they are spontaneous."

In addition to the efficient personnel thus provided
for our industrial effort, the zealous offers of their services by American citizens were of the greatest value to
the Army and Navy in their immediate necessity for
expansion. In the case of the Army, it proved to be an
expansion from a 200,000 basis to a 4,000,000 basis.
This was multiplying by twenty. Aside from the organization of the fighting forces, this meant that, in
the various administrative departments of the Army,
where there had been one officer there would be need
for twenty. To meet this need for a great expansion
came these offers of the services of our citizens, among
them large numbers of specially trained men who were
well adapted for these duties.

As has been stated, before we entered the war, the
Secretary of War had already associated with the War
Department groups of voluntary assistants from civil
life. From the day of our entering the war, these men
were multiplied and given commissions and assignments
throughout the War Department. The great numbers of
skilled men who offered their services made it possible
to select a personnel, for the administrative departments of the Army, of a high standard of trained efficiency—in fact, such a personnel as had never before
been available. The influence of these men, experienced
in the great industries of our nation, was beneficial in
the War Department. In addition to their ability to
undertake their tasks, they aroused the Army officers

associated with them to broader views of the problems of the hour. It is to the credit of the United States Army that its officers were able to respond to the views of these civilians from our great industries, and to work in full coöperation with them in the broadened fields of Army administration. The same good effect was felt in the United States Navy, but of course the expansion of the Army was much greater.

The United States Shipping Board had become an active war board, by the incorporation of the United States Emergency Fleet Corporation (under the laws of the Dictrict of Columbia, April 16, 1917, with a capital stock of $50,000,000) for the "purchase, construction, equipment, lease, charter, maintenance, and operation of merchant vessels in the commerce of the United States." The powers of the Shipping Board were greatly increased by an Executive order of July 11, 1917, "wherein the President delegated to the Shipping Board all the power and authority vested in him by the emergency shipping fund provision of the urgent deficiencies act of June 15, 1917." These powers were passed on by the Shipping Board to the Emergency Fleet Corporation, which thus acquired "the power and authority of a Government agency." This was another case of the wise use of the amplified powers of the President of the United States, instead of attempting to build up some new body, which would have involved delays in organization.

In fact, behind all these nationwide activities stood the authority derived from the war powers of the President of the United States, and it must be here again emphasized that this was a more direct and practical means of putting these great forces to work than could have been found by any other method.

It was altogether an amazing scene, this sudden transformation of a broad, peaceful country into a nation aroused and intent on the work at hand. This describes the situation all over the land. It was a nation at work, and with that work already under the leaders who were to find the right guidance for the zeal of our workers.

CHAPTER X

THE BEGINNINGS OF OUR ARMED FORCES

FOR the production of the armed forces of the United States, the successful operation of the Selective Service Act has been described. And this means of securing the great numbers for the United States Army from the manpower of America must always be kept in mind, throughout this narrative, as at work and accomplishing its task by the most efficient use of conscription in history. The total added to the United States Army by means of the Selective Service reached 3,091,000.

But there were also great increases in the personnels of both the Regular Army and the National Guard. And naturally, as these were already existing forces, the enlargement of these forces became the first task of the War Department, in providing for the increase of the United States Army. Again the totals will tell the story. At our declaration of war, as has been stated, the United States Army had consisted of 200,000 officers and men. Of these, 133,000 were Regulars, 67,000 were in the National Guard. At the Armistice, the Regular Army had been increased to 527,000, the National Guard to 382,000.

Of course these totals were matters of a year and a half, and in both cases were attained not only by enlistments but by additions of recruits obtained from the Selective Service. But the immediate response in enlistments to fill the ranks to the authorized increases was another demonstration of the willingness of our people to take their part in the war. The act of May 18, 1917, had been framed "to authorize the President to increase temporarily the Military Establishment of the United States." The actual strength of the Regular Army on June 30, 1917, had grown to 250,157 officers and men. On the same date, the total of officers and men in the National Guard was 111,123.

In 1916, there had been, both for the Regular Army and the National Guard, an element of actual preparedness, which was one notable exception in that period of unformed ideas and military unreadiness. Just as Secretary Baker assumed the duties of his office, it had become necessary to send United States troops to the Mexican border. Mexican bandits, led by the outlaw Francisco Villa, had crossed the border and raided New Mexico, and this created a situation which demanded the presence of American military forces. A strong force of Regulars was organized, under the command of Major General John J. Pershing, and ordered across the border in pursuit of the raiders (March 10, 1916). It also became necessary to have additional troops to patrol the long border between the United States and Mexico. The President, therefore, used the authority vested in him to call into the Federal service the Organized Militia and National Guard. The first call (May 9, 1916) was upon Texas, Arizona, and New Mexico. Later (June 18, 1916) the President called out a large part of these forces of the other States of the Union and the District of Columbia. This summons came at the time when the Organized Militia was in process of transition into the National Guard, in accordance with the provisions of the National Defense Act.

Instructions were given, on June 23, to transfer each unit to the border as soon as it was reasonably equipped for field duty. The presence of this force on the border insured the protection of life and property for citizens of the United States in that region. This tour of duty in the Federal service gave to the various units of the National Guard the opportunity for thorough drill and for perfecting their organizations. It also gave them experience in camp life and service in the field. Most of these units of the National Guard had been returned to their homes before the United States entered the World War. But the benefits of this experience were afterward evident in the improved efficiency of the National Guard, and this Mexican border field duty must be counted as a contributing cause for the high morale which was shown by the National Guard in the World War.

General Pershing's command of Regulars was not withdrawn from Mexico until February 5, 1917. The real reason for keeping this force of United States troops so long in Mexico has never before appeared in print. The following is the explanation. At first General Pershing's command had entered Mexico in pursuit of Villa's bandits. These outlaws had scattered and concealed themselves in the mountains. It would have required a distribution of troops over a large area to keep up the pursuit. It was more important to use our troops in Mexico to check any attempts at renewing the raids across the border into the United States.

In this regard, Secretary Baker has written: "As a consequence, the capture of Villa became an entirely secondary object. The presence of General Pershing's force a hundred miles south of the border had, however, an immensely quieting and reassuring effect. It hung like a pendulum down into Mexico ready to close in behind any group of bandits which made trouble on the border. If that trouble took place west of Columbus, the pendulum would swing west and advance north to meet corresponding groups coming south and so capture the bandits between them, correspondingly if the attack was east of Columbus. As a piece of strategy, I think this plan was brilliant. And, of course, it worked with complete success, and there was no trouble on the border so long as General Pershing was in Mexico."

For these troops of the Regular Army, also, this eleven months field service was very valuable. There was another beneficial result from this service in Mexico, both for the Regular Army and the National Guard. This came from their experience in using the services of supply, under actual campaign conditions, in connection with the various supply departments of the Government. And it was found that this provided a most useful foundation upon which to build in the larger expansion of the Military Establishment for the World War. In this regard, another valuable object lesson had been given, which was a great help afterward in our war effort. The transportation of the units of the National Guard to the Mexican border had involved

the railroads of most of the States. Every possible assistance had been rendered by the American Railway Association, the Pullman Company, and the passenger
associations and officials of the different railroads.
Consequently, the Quartermaster Corps of the United
States Army had been put in especially close touch with
the railroads of the country, and this also gave a basis
for greater things to come.

The question of providing the increased number of
officers for the enlarged Army was another pressing
problem of the War Department for which progress had
been made toward solution before we entered the war.
There had been a larger number of courses for military
training in colleges and schools, but the most important
step in that direction had been the "Plattsburg experiment" by which "Major General Leonard Wood, then
Chief of Staff, put into operation a plan for camps of
instruction at which students were permitted to attend
for training without cost to the United States. The
plan was later enlarged to permit the attendance of
business men, and carried forward year by year with
increasing success and interest."[1] In 1916, "five camps
were held at Plattsburg, two at Oglethorpe, one at Fort
Wadsworth, in the Eastern Department, with a total
attendance of 12,200 men and boys. In the Western
Department camps were established at the Presidio
and American Lake. A satisfactory camp was held at
San Antonio, Texas."[2]

So satisfactory had been the result attained in these
training camps that Secretary Baker stated, as to the

[1] Report of the Secretary of War, 1916.
[2] *Ibid.*

urgent need for officers in 1917: "Accepting the Plattsburg experiment as the basis and using funds appropriated by Congress for an enlargement of the Plattsburg system of training, the department established a
series of training camps, sixteen in number, which were
opened on the 15th of May, 1917. The camps were scattered throughout the United States so as to afford the
opportunity of entrance and training with the least inconvenience and expense of travel to prepare throughout the entire country. Officers previously commissioned
in the Reserve Corps were required to attend the camps,
and, in addition, approximately 30,000 selected candidates were accepted from among the much greater
number who applied for admission. These camps were
organized and conducted under the supervision of department commanders; applicants were required to
state their qualifications, and a rough apportionment
was attempted among the candidates to the several
States. At the conclusion of the camps, 27,341 officers
were commissioned and directed to report at the places
selected for the training of the new army. By this process, we supplied not only the officers needed for the
National Army, but filled the roster of the Regular
Army, to which substantial additions were necessary
by reason of the addition of the full numbers provided
by the National Defense Act of 1916. The results of the
first series of camps were most satisfactory, and, antici-
pating the calling of further increments of the National
Army (the troops raised by means of the Selective Service Act were so designated until Regulars, National
Guard, and National Army were all placed under the
one designation of the United States Army), a second

series of camps was authorized, to begin August 27, 1917. . . ."

The further development of these means for the increase of our armed forces will be an important part of the ensuing narrative. But the foregoing statements of facts must make it evident to the reader that there was a much earlier and better beginning of the production of armed forces than has been realized by our people. However, one important point should be emphasized at this stage. Most fortunately, there were no hysterical attempts to hurry driblets of troops to Europe, which would have actually delayed the flood that was needed.

Instead of anything of the kind, the War Department followed the very practical plan of making the plants for producing the troops before trying to force the production of troops. This was taking pattern from our American industries on a large scale. The whole country was divided into districts in proportion to the men who would be forthcoming for the Army, and great camps and cantonments of standardized buildings were projected. These were, in fact, to be like manufacturing plants, as they were to receive the raw materials of manpower and convert them into military forces by processes of organization and training.

Not only did these camps and cantonments follow the patterns of our industries, but they were themselves a notable contribution given by our industries to our preparations for warfare, as will be shown when the construction of these camps and cantonments is described. Secretary Baker has stated: "The preparation of places for the training of the recruits thus brought into the service was a task of unparalleled magnitude.

On the 7th of May, 1917, the commanding generals of the several departments were directed to select sites for the construction of cantonments for the training of the mobilized National Guard and the National Army."

The accompanying map shows the locations of these camps and cantonments. As will be seen, the National Guard camps were placed in the Southern States. This was to take advantage of the open winter weather, and permitted the use of tents to a large extent. The National Guard, as was natural because it was an already existing force, would be called into camp before the National Army, which was to be raised by the Selective Service Act. As the National Guard had already received training, its term of training in the camps would be shorter. In fact, some of its units would be ready to send abroad in a very short time. Another thing made the problem of the National Guard camps easier. They would not have to receive such large units as the National Army cantonments.

The Regular Army divisions were, of course, composed of frameworks of thoroughly trained men, with only the new recruits to assimilate. These Regular Army divisions received their war preparation "in part at one or another of these 32 centres, in part as separate units at various Army posts."[1]

Thus was begun on a broad scale the production of armed forces, of which an account will be given.

---

[1] A Statistical Summary, General Staff, U. S. A.

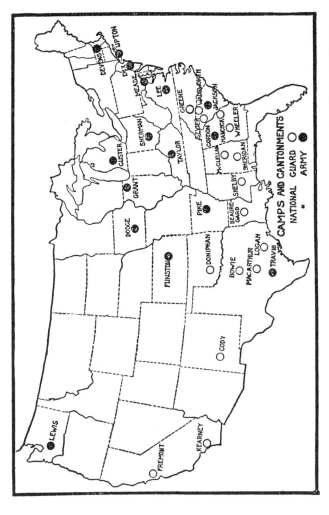

LOCATIONS OF CAMPS AND CANTONMENTS IN THE UNITED STATES

CHAPTER XI

THE DEVELOPMENT OF AMERICAN STRATEGY

IT HAD soon become obvious that an American expeditionary force must be sent overseas, although the emissaries of the Entente Allies had not at all grasped the future size of that force. Not only were the Entente Allies utterly ignorant of the military possibilities latent in the American nation, but they also had no conception of the greatness of the danger that was destined to fall upon them in 1918—and only to be averted by the utmost effort of the United States. Consequently, it can be stated positively that, upon our entering the war, the Administration did not receive any information that would set the scale of our future great joint operation.

In this situation, it was providential that two things were done by the Administration, upon our own initiative. First, as has been told, the operation of the Selective Service Act was from the beginning cast upon so comprehensive a scale that it would be effective for any military force we might be called upon to furnish. Secondly, the far seeing determination was made to select the future commander at once, and to send him overseas with his staff, in advance, to study on the ground the whole program of our military coöperation on the Western Front. We may call these two decisions of the Administration the foundations of the success of our military effort. The first provided the means of increasing the volume of our military forces to the flood that was needed at the crisis of 1918. The second provided the means of quickly obtaining military information, which would set the vast scale of our operation, far ahead of any military information possessed by the Entente Allies.

General John J. Pershing was the choice of Secretary Baker for Commander-in-Chief of the American Expeditionary Forces—and, as should be emphasized at the outset, this appointment meant that General Pershing would be Commander-in-Chief in every sense of the word. It was to be one outstanding case where there would be no interference with the commanding officer. In his preface for this book, Secretary Baker has told of his assurances to General Pershing in this respect, and this was the beginning of an unusual and cordial relationship between Secretary of War and General.

Interference and meddling in military matters on the part of war ministers can be cited as responsible for many failures in war. Secretary Baker has stated the reason which made him alive to the dangers of any such meddling, and his firm resolve that nothing of the kind should be allowed to hamper General Pershing. With our knowledge of the inspiring influence of the Civil War for Americans, it is a wonderful thing to see put on record this lesson of the Civil War, passed on by a veteran of that war to his son, and destined to bear fruit in the strength of purpose so urgently needed for this momentous decision in the World War.

In this spirit, General Pershing was allowed to select

an ample staff, and he was immediately sent overseas with his staff, long before there could be any question of an army for him to command. He had assumed the duties of his office on May 26, 1917. He sailed for Europe on May 28, was in London on June 9, and, after spending some days in consultation with the British authorities, had reached Paris on June 13. Upon arrival in France, General Pershing and his staff at once began to work out the plans and scale of the American reinforcement.

The policy of the Administration and the wisdom of the Secretary of War, in sending General Pershing and his staff so soon to France, had been quickly rewarded by practical results, which moulded American strategy into its right form. It is an undeniable fact that General Pershing and his staff foresaw more clearly than did the French and British how great a reinforcement would be demanded from America. General Pershing's vision was in this respect prophetic of his later able conduct of affairs, as his military information to Washington and his initial military plans were so much more comprehensive of the approaching crisis than were the military forecasts of the leaders of the Entente Allies, that every aspect of our effort was constantly expanding in response. These broadening views of General Pershing and his staff, as to the vast scope of our operation, were confirmed and aided by the great number of American business men from our industries, who were actually on duty with the War Department or were working with the Administration, as has been described.

In this regard, the services of these men from civil life were most valuable, because, both from their training in affairs on a large scale and from their knowledge of European conditions, they were able to foresee the possibility of our effort being required on an unprecedented scale. Consequently, their views were of much assistance to the General Staff, with which they were in contact, for casting military plans upon a basis that would permit expansion, as our program of the necessary reinforcement for the Entente Allies grew into large proportions.

General Pershing had arrived on the ground at just the right time to estimate the situation in France, after the failures of the Entente Allies in their attacks upon the German lines on the Western Front. The effect of these reverses upon the morale of the Allies had been very serious. The French had placed great hopes upon the overconfident plans of General Nivelle for defeating the Germans, and the complete failure of these plans had brought about an actual crisis in France. General Pershing in his report thus described the situation:

"The relatively low strength of the German forces on the Western Front led the Allies with much confidence to attempt a decision on this front: but the losses were very heavy and their effort signally failed. The failure caused a serious reaction, especially on French morale, both in the army and throughout the country, and attempts to carry out extensive or combined operations were indefinitely suspended. . . . Allied resources in manpower at home were low and, there was little prospect of materially increasing their armed strength, even in the face of the probability of having practically the whole military strength of the Central Powers against them in the spring of 1918.

"This was the state of affairs that existed when we entered the war. While our action gave the Allies much encouragement, yet this was temporary, and a review of conditions made it apparent that America must make a supreme material effort as soon as possible. After duly considering the tonnage possibilities, I cabled the following to Washington on July 6, 1918: 'Plans should contemplate sending over at least 1,000,000 men by next May.'

"A general organization project, covering as far as possible the personnel of all combat, staff, and administrative units, was forwarded to Washington on July 11. This was prepared by the Operations Section of my staff and adopted in joint conference with the War Department Committee then in France. It embodied my conclusions on the military organization and effort required of America after a careful study of French and British experience. In forwarding this project I stated: 'It is evident that a force of 1,000,000 men is the smallest unit which in modern war will be a complete, well balanced, and independent fighting organization. However, it must be equally clear that the adoption of this size force as a basis of study should not be construed as representing the maximum force which should be sent or which would be needed in France. It is taken as the force which may be expected to reach France in time for an offensive in 1918, and as a unit and basis of organization. Plans for the future should be based, especially in reference to the manufacture of artillery, aviation, and other material, on three times this force—i.e., at least 3,000,000 men.'"

Thus early, and far ahead of all European conceptions, was the Administration at Washington given the vast scale of the necessary American reinforcement. As a result, the American effort, industrial, military, and naval, was being cast in this greater mould for all three component parts. This followed inevitably, because, when the military reinforcement was thus defined in such great totals, it also implied a corresponding increase in the means of transportation and in the volume of material which must be provided by our industries. This meant that the tasks of the General Munitions Board, and the other agencies which have been described, were rapidly growing to more enormous totals. From week to week these demands upon our industries were increasing to undreamt proportions, and our newly awakened nation at work was facing problems that were going far beyond all prophesies.

The rapid march of these ideas was well described in other paragraphs in General Pershing's report: "While this general organization project provided certain Services of Supply troops, which were an integral part of the larger combat units, it did not include the great body of troops and services required to maintain an army overseas. To disembark 2,000,000 men, move them to the training areas, shelter them, handle and store the quantities of supplies and equipment they required, called for an extraordinary and immediate effort in construction. To provide the organization for this purpose a project for engineer services of the rear, including railways, was cabled to Washington, August 5, 1917, followed on September 18, 1917, by a complete service of the rear project, which listed item by item the troops considered necessary for the Services of Supply.

"In order that the War Department might have a clear-cut program to follow in the shipment of personnel and material to insure the gradual building up of a force at all times balanced and symmetrical, a comprehensive statement was prepared covering the order in which the troops and services enumerated in these two projects should arrive. This schedule of priority of shipments, forwarded to the War Department on October 7, divided the initial force called for by the two projects into six phases corresponding to combatant corps of six divisions each."

Here was shown a definite progress, from stage to stage, in conceptions and plans. To quote again, from General Pershing's report: "The importance of the three documents, the general organization project, the service of rear project, and the schedule of priority of shipments should be emphasized, because they formed the basic plan for providing an army in France together with its material for combat and supply." And it should also be again emphasized that these progressive conceptions gave information and warnings to the War Department which were reflected throughout our country in calls upon our industries for material.

The dependence of the whole enormous scheme of operations upon the industrial and naval factors of the program was most vividly set forth in another paragraph of General Pershing's report: "For all practical purposes the American Expeditionary Forces were based on the American Continent. Three thousand miles of ocean to cross with the growing submarine menace confronting us, the quantity of ship tonnage that would be available then unknown, and a line of communications by land 400 miles long from French ports to our probable front, presented difficulties which seemed almost insurmountable as compared with those of the Allies."

Whole volumes could not depict the necessity of the industrial and naval factors more clearly than this. The reader must understand all that was implied in the phrase "based on the American Continent," an operation such as had never been undertaken in history.

While the Administration was thus being informed of the scope of the American effort, and the War Department was responding to the increasing estimates of General Pershing, one exception was made in hurrying American troops overseas as soon as possible. This was for a very good reason. While on his mission to the United States, Marshal Joffre had made an urgent request "that an American combat division should be sent at once to Europe as a visual evidence of our purpose to participate actively in the war." This was held to be of so great importance, as a stimulus to the morale of the French, at the time of their great depression in consequence of their military failure, that the First Division was formed of Regular regiments and ordered overseas. An account of this first venture in transporting our fighting troops to France will be given in the following chapter.

CHAPTER XII

THE FIRST TRANSPORTATION OF AMERICAN TROOPS OVERSEAS

SENDING the First Division of American troops overseas was the beginning of the "great adventure," from which was evolved the decisive result of transporting across the Atlantic the reinforcement for the Entente Allies upon the Western Front. The reason for the haste of this undertaking, in response to the urgent request of Marshal Joffre, has been explained in the previous chapter. The command of this first transportation operation of the United States Navy was assigned to Rear Admiral Albert Gleaves, who had been in command of the Destroyer Force of the United States Atlantic Fleet. On May 23, 1917, Admiral Gleaves was summoned to Washington, and on May 29 received his formal orders designating him Commander of Convoy Operations in the Atlantic. In his flagship U. S. S. *Seattle*, an amored cruiser, he proceeded at once to New York to expedite the preparations for this first expedition to France.

The regular transports of the Army could not be used, as they "were not suitable and ready for trans-Atlantic convoy operations."[1] The United States Navy had only three vessels available for transport work,

---

[1] Admiral Gleaves, *A History of the Transport Service, 1917–1918.*

Hancock, Henderson, De Kalb. It was typical of the unexpected course of the World War that U. S. S. *De Kalb* should be the former *Prinz Eitel Friedrich*, the German converted auxiliary cruiser which had been through a checkered career in the German Navy. She had shared the adventures of Admiral Spee's Squadron and, having been left behind in South American waters, had to play her last part by keeping up a succession of wireless signals for the purpose of concealing from the British the fact of Admiral Spee's departure. Afterward she had made her way north to internment at Newport News—only to be seized by the new enemy of Germany and rechristened to act as a warship against Germany. In the United States Navy, as U. S. S. *De Kalb*, she was not only a useful troopship but also an able armed vessel for escort duty with the convoys.

As only these three vessels of the Navy were available, "it was necessary to commandeer such ocean-going vessels as could be found and alter them as quickly as possible for carrying troops."[1] The following table shows from what varied sources were collected the extemporized troopships at this sudden emergency:

NAME	GROSS TONNAGE	LINE
Saratoga	6,391	N. Y. & Cuba Mail S. S. Co. (Mail Steamer)
Havana	6,991	N. Y. & Cuba Mail S. S. Co. (Mail Steamer)
Tenadores	7,782	Tenadores S. S. Co. (United Fruit Co. Line)
Pastores	7,781	Pastores S. S. Corp. (United Fruit Co. Line)

[1]Admiral Gleaves.

NAME	GROSS TONNAGE	LINE
Momus	6,878	Southern Pacific Co.
Antilles	6,878	" " "
Lenape	5,179	Clyde S. S. Co.
Mallory	6,063	Mallory S. S. Co.
Finland	12,229	Int. Mercantile Marine
San Jacinto	6,069	Mallory S. S. Co.
Montanan	6,659	American S. S. Co. (Cargo Carrier)
Dakotan	6,657	American and Hawaiian S. S. Co.
E. Luckenbach	2,730	Luckenbach S. S. Co. (Cargo Carrier)
El Occidente	6,008	Southern Pacific Co. (Cargo Carrier)

It is no wonder Admiral Gleaves stated that "the somewhat motley assemblage of ships finally gathered together for the first expedition did not long survive the duty imposed upon them." And his additional comment vividly depicted the situation: "Looking back to the first expedition of June, 1917, it seems indeed that the hand of Providence must have been held over these 'arks' or the task never could have been accomplished. Who would have dreamed at that time that we were laying the foundation of the greatest transport fleet in history?"

This last has now become one of the astonishing records of the World War, for, from that motley assembly, actually grew the Cruiser and Transport Force of the United States Navy—and it was symbolical of this unprecedented growth that the designation U. S. S. *Seattle* was destined to become not only that of the ship which remained Admiral Gleaves's flagship, but also the letterhead of a tall office building in Hoboken. Throughout the "decks" of this building were to be distributed the administrative offices developed from a flagship staff, and from its "bridge" on the high roof were to be directed the movements of many transports laden with the armed manhood of the United States.

An account of this first expedition should be given here in some detail, as the narrative is in itself a true picture of conditions on the seas, and of the able and careful conduct of affairs which made possible the transportation of American troops overseas.

The original date set for the departure of the first convoy of transports was June 9, 1917. But Admiral Gleaves changed the sailing to June 14, "not without consideration of the phase of the moon as affecting night submarine attack at the expected time of arrival off the French Coast"[1] The expedition started to sail. from New York on June 14, 1917, in a thick fog. The craft were divided into four convoy groups on the commonsense basis of speed.[2] Group I proceeded at 15 knots; Group II at 14 knots; Group III at 13 knots; Group IV at 11 knots. As Admiral Gleaves very clearly explained: "The groups sailed at intervals of two hours from Ambrose Channel Lightship, except Group IV, which was held by the Department twenty-four hours for belated dispatches and stores. Group I was the fastest, Group IV the slowest, and their departure was timed to avoid congestion at the eastern terminus. It is obvious that, as the expedition advanced, the intervals between the groups opened out, thus

---

[1]Admiral Gleaves.

[2]A table of the organization of the convoy groups will be found at the end of this chapter.

increasing the difficulties of submarines lying in wait to attack."

Each of the four groups was provided with a very strong escort, in proportion to the number of transports. Group I of four troopships was led by Admiral Gleaves in the *Seattle* with the *De Kalb* and three destroyers. The converted yacht *Corsair* had also started with this group, but poor firing service had obliged her to fall back to Group II, and she was replaced by the destroyer *Fanning*. The other groups were protected in a similar way by the escort of cruisers with auxiliaries and destroyers. For the destroyers, the oil tanker *Maumee* had sailed from Boston, a few days before the expedition left New York, to a secret rendezvous on the route of the convoys, in order that the destroyers might refuel at sea.

"Oiling at sea was one of the manœuvres which had been developed in the Destroyer Force three months before the war. A division of destroyers had been oiled en route to Queenstown at the rate of 35,000 gallons per hour in a moderate sea, and with the wind blowing a half gale. Without the ability to oil at sea, the destroyers would have had to be towed and the eastward movement correspondingly delayed. Only the newest destroyers, those which could get over to the other side by one refuelling, were designated to go all the way across,[1] while the old boats, the short-legged fellows, as they were called, went only half way or as far as their oil could carry them, and then returned to New York, or

---

[1]Of the thirteen destroyers, with this first expedition the following were listed as having gone all the way across: *Wilkes, Fanning, Burrows, Allen, Shaw, Ammen, Parker.*

in case of necessity called at St. Johns or Halifax, and as a rule they had to steam against strong headwinds on the way back."[1]

Admiral Gleaves's description of the special precautions taken as to these groups of troopships should also be carefully studied, as giving the basis of the future success of the great movement of American troops overseas.

"The work of converting the requisitioned cargo ships was pressed to the utmost. They were armed with guns, fitted with lookout stations, a communication system and troop berthing accommodations. The method of commissary supply and messing was worked out and the sanitation of the ships improved as far as possible. Life belts were supplied in a quantity 10 per cent. in excess of the number of passengers carried. Special measures were taken to protect life in case of casualty, and sufficient rafts were provided so that if lifeboats on one side could not be launched, because of the listing of the ship or other reason, all hands could still be accommodated. Attention was given to the paramount necessity of landing the troops in good health and in good spirits.

"The instructions issued to all ships were, in brief, as follows, and every man had to be as familiar with them as with the Lord's Prayer:

"1. The use of maximum speed through the danger zone.

"2. Trained lookout watches made effective by an efficient system of communication between officers of the deck and fire control watch.

---

[1]Admiral Gleaves.

"3. Continuous alert gun watches in quick communication with lookouts through the fire control officer.

"4. Constant zigzagging.

"5. Minimum use of radio; reduction of smoke to a minimum; darkening of ships at night; throwing nothing overboard lest it point to a trail.

"6. A trained officer always alert and ready to use the helm to avoid torpedoes.

"7. Special prearranged day and night signals between ships on manner of manœuvring when submarines were sighted.

"8. Use of guns and depth bombs by all transport and escort vessels.

"In addition, it was directed that Abandon Ship drills be held daily, that in the danger zone at daybreak and twilight, the hours most favorable to submarine attack, troops be assembled at Abandon Ship stations fully equipped and prepared to leave the ship; that watertight doors always be kept closed; that all communication pipes and ventilators be kept closed as much as possible; that the watertight bulkheads be frequently examined—in short, that everything possible be done, first, to guard against disaster, and second, to save the ship and to save life if mined or torpedoed."

These terse sentences, from the able officer who commanded the first expedition, have in themselves painted a vivid picture of the new conditions on the seas, and this picture was destined to remain a true portrayal of the difficulties and dangers to be encountered throughout the successful operations of Admiral Gleaves's vastly enlarged command. No one can help seeing that such infinite painstaking, in thoughtful preparation in advance, must inevitably gain results of efficiency in the trying service which was to ensue. In this respect, the mere narrative of the American transport service will be sufficient testimony of the value of a good command and a good organization from the very start.

In Admiral Gleaves's secret order before leaving New York it was stated: "Reports of enemy submarine activity indicate that the area of greatest activity is East of longitude twenty West, and within a circle radius five hundred miles from Fayal, Azores." On the passage across the Atlantic the groups had moved undisturbed, until, as Admiral Gleaves has stated, "at 10:15 P. M. June 22nd, in Latitude 48° 00′ N., Longitude 25° 50′ West, the first group was attacked by enemy submarines." This was when Group I was crossing the line from North Ireland to the Azores. The lookouts on the *Seattle*, which was ahead and to starboard of the troopships, reported "sighting in the extremely phosphorescent water the wake of a submarine crossing our bow from starboard to port toward the convoy."[1] Simultaneously the *De Kalb*, ahead and to port of the troopships, sighted two torpedo wakes, one ahead and one astern, and opened fire. Admiral Gleaves has stated that two torpedoes passed close to the troopship *Havana*, and that Captain Gherardi of the *De Kalb* "handled his ship to perfection and disaster was avoided." "The ships of the right and left columns of the convoy turned to starboard and port, respectively, and ran at full speed as per instructions. There were no torpedo hits and no evidence of injury to the enemy. The convoy

---

[1] Admiral Gleaves.

re-formed at daylight and proceeded on its course."[1]
Group I was met by American destroyers from Queenstown in the afternoon of June 24, at an appointed
rendezvous.[2] The next day this group met the French
escort of two small destroyers. There was no further attack, as this group moved toward port.

Admiral Gleaves has stated that Group II was attacked as follows: "The second group encountered two
submarines, the first at 11:50 A. M., 26th of June in Latitude 47° 01′ N. and Longitude 6° 28′ W., about 100
miles off the French coast, and the second two hours
later. The group was under escort of six additional
American destroyers at that time. Both submarines
were successfully evaded, and the destroyer *Cummings*,
when sighting the second submarine, headed for it
at twenty-five knots. The submarine immediately sub-
merged and the periscope was lost to view, but the
course of the submarine was plainly disclosed by a
wake of bubbles. The *Cummings* passed about twenty-
five yards ahead of this wake and dropped a depth bomb,
the explosion of which was followed by the appearance of
several pieces of lumber, oil, bubbles and débris upon
the surface. There was no further evidence of the submarine, and if not destroyed, it is probable that it
was at least badly damaged. Commander Neil, who
made the counter attack on the submarine in the
Cummings, was decorated by the British Government
for this exploit."

---

[1]Admiral Gleaves.

[2]"We had joined up with them on time at the appointed rendezvous, which
was a good piece of navigation on both sides."—Admiral Gleaves.

Admiral Gleaves has stated that Group IV was attacked (June 28), and that the commanding officer of the *Edward Luckenbach* reported: "About 10:30 A. M., this vessel was attacked by a submarine, and one torpedo was seen to pass within about 50 yards of the *Luckenbach*. The course of the ship had just been changed by the Commanding Officer to avoid this torpedo, and the torpedo was seen to come to the surface in the wake of the *Luckenbach* at the point where the change of course took place." Admiral Gleaves has also stated that, at this time, the German U-boat was under fire from U. S. S. *Kanawha,* one of the two armed colliers with the expedition. Of the *Kanawha's* gunfire Admiral Gleaves wrote, after describing its accuracy: "It may well be that those shots so confused the aim of the submarine as to cause her torpedoes to miss." This was playing a rôle far removed from the usually accepted peaceful task of a collier.

There were no other attacks encountered on the passage. All the three slower groups had been met by additional American destroyers at appointed rendezvous, as had been the case of Group II, and all four groups arrived at the small port of St. Nazaire without any loss. The last to arrive, Group IV, came into port July 2. In France all ostensible preparations had been made with the idea of giving the impression that the convoy groups were to come into Brest, the natural point of disembarkation instead of the small and ill adapted harbor of St. Nazaire. This was undoubtedly a very wise precaution, as it is now known that the Germans at the time had laid many mines off Brest. In fact, the French cruiser *Kléber* was there sunk[1] by one of these mines, and the inconveniences of disembarking and unloading at St. Nazaire were well worth enduring, in view of the comparative safety.

By this well-conceived and well-conducted naval operation, the first step was taken on the path to the battlefield of France. There was no question of the fact that the actual appearance of American troops in Paris was a great stimulus to French morale, and the request from General Joffre that they should be hurried to France was justified by this result.[2] But it was also a stimulus for us, in our great task, to have this proof that it was feasible to span the Atlantic. In this regard, it should be emphasized that this first adventure of transporting American troops overseas was to be considered, at the time, a very hazardous undertaking. Now that the successful achievement of transporting our troops overseas has become a matter of history, it is difficult to realize how threatening was the situation, and how many people thought the operation of transportation on a great scale an impossibility. Consequently, this first expedition was a test which aroused great anxiety.

As to this, Secretary Baker has written: "I very well remember the anxiety I felt while those ships were in the danger zone. . . . My own feeling at the time was that if the submarines had managed to sink two or three ships in that first convoy, with the loss of seven or eight

---

[1]The French cruiser *Kléber*, 7,700 tons, was sunk by a mine in the Loire, June 27, 1917.

[2]"The arrival of the First Division and the parade of certain of its elements in Paris on July 4 caused great enthusiasm, and for the time being French morale was stimulated."—General Pershing, Report.

thousand men, the country would have been disposed to regard the task of transporting American troops to Europe under the circumstances as impossible. There would certainly have been enormous pressure brought to bear to limit American participation to financial, economic, and purely naval operations. When, however, Admiral Gleaves succeeded in getting the whole of the first convoy over safely, the problem of coöperating with our Army was at once seen to be soluble, and there was no more discussion of the submarine peril than of any of the other hazards of war."

At this time there had also been begun naval preparations for safeguarding the arrival of our troopships in the waters adjacent to France. On June 9, there had sailed from New York a squadron of six converted yachts,[1] which were to be the nucleus of a special American Naval force, U. S. Patrol Squadrons Operating in European Waters. This force was at first commanded by Rear Admiral William B. Fletcher, who was succeeded on November 1, 1917, by Rear Admiral Henry B. Wilson, who remained in command through the rest of the war. From this beginning grew an important element in American operations overseas. Brest was the headquarters of this force, and it remained a separate American command to the end. Admiral Sims has described it as "a force which was ultimately larger than the one we maintained at Queenstown; at the height of the troop movement it comprised about 36 destroyers, 12 yachts, 3 tenders, and several minesweepers and tugs." As will be evident in the ensuing narrative of the great movement of American

[1] *Noma, Vedette, Christobel, Kanawha, Harvard, Sultana.*

troops, this patrol of the waters about the great American bases was an essential factor in the operation.

ORGANIZATION OF THE FIRST EXPEDITION

Convoy Group I

Train Troopships	Escort
Saratoga	Armored Cruiser *Seattle* (flag)
Havana	Auxiliary Cruiser *De Kalb*
Tenadores	Converted Yacht *Corsair*
Pastores	Destroyers *Wilkes, Terry, Roe*

Convoy Group II

Train Troopships	Escort
Momus	Scout Cruiser *Birmingham*
Antilles	Converted Yacht *Aphrodite*
Lenape	Destroyers *Fanning, Burrows, Lamson*

Convoy Group III

Train Troopships	Escort
Mallory	Cruiser *Charleston*
Finland	Armed Collier *Cyclops*
San Jacinto	Destroyers *Allen, McCall, Preston*

Convoy Group IV

Train Troopships	Escort
Montanan	Cruiser *St. Louis*
Dakotan	Cruiser Transport *Hancock*
El Occidente	Armed Collier *Kanawha*
E. Luckenbach	Destroyers *Shaw, Ammen, Flusser, Parker*

CHAPTER XIII

THE AMERICAN TRANSPORTS

AFTER the success of this first expedition, it was established that our main effort on the seas must be to transport the men and material of the American military reinforcement to the Western Front. As has been stated, our conception that the reinforcement must be on a large scale had leapt far ahead of any grasp of this idea on the part of the Entente Allies. For this reason, our prompt realization of what would be the best use of American naval forces was equally far ahead of any forethought of the Allies. In the light of the knowledge of ensuing events, it was providential that this decision made the transportation of American troops overseas the principal mission of the United States Navy in the World War.

As has been explained, the United States Navy had the advantage over the Army in preparations for war. But these preparations had been for the usual mobilizations of naval fighting forces, with their auxiliaries and material. This was natural, as, up to the time we entered the war, there had been no information from the Entente Allies of any impending change. In fact, the Entente Allies had been following the usual naval policies, and there had been very little to go on, very little data upon which to base any definite plans.

The German campaign of unrestricted U-boat warfare had been a complete surprise for the naval leaders of the Entente Allies. And the sudden revelation of this threatening situation by their naval representatives in America brought an equally sudden change in our naval plans. The first pressing need for destroyers and other craft, to assist in the fight against the U-boats, must be recognized as a valuable and necessary service of the United States Navy, which was being rendered throughout the period covered by this narrative. But all this was dwarfed in importance by the new call upon our Navy, as a result of the military information received in advance by the Administration.

It can be stated positively that neither before our entering the war nor upon our entrance was there any intimation of the vast scope of this main objective of the United States—no inkling of the gigantic naval operation which was to be our Navy's component part. The giant shape of the impending danger was still hidden from the Allies themselves, and, as it was to be a military danger, it could only be revealed to our Navy through this military information obtained by the Administration. Consequently, from this time on, the service of the United States Navy must be considered as dictated by the Civil and Military authorities.

This situation can be summed up as follows. The Administration had found that there must be a mighty American Army on the Western Front. This Army could only be delivered on the Western Front by the coöperation of the United States Navy. Upon the delivery of this American reinforcement depended the fate of the war. Consequently, all other naval undertakings were of minor importance, and the safeguarded transportation of this American Army and its supplies became the main task of the Office of Naval Operations. This summed up the new developments which radically altered our naval plans.

Under the stress of these new calls upon our Navy, an expansion of personnel was going on akin to that of the Army. Of course the numbers of the increase of the Navy were not so enormous. But the total was unprecedented in naval history. At the time we entered the World War, the personnel of the United States Navy, Regular and Reserve, was in round numbers 95,000. At the Armistice, the total, Regular and Reserve, was over 530,000—a personnel far greater than that of the British Navy at its maximum in the World War.

These changes in plans, and the need to assimilate the increasing numbers which were being taken into the Navy, brought about corresponding changes in the Battle Fleet. The dreadnought battleships were conserved as a potential reinforcement for the British Grand Fleet, but many units of the Atlantic Fleet were destined to various services of anti-submarine work, convoying, and becoming training schools on a large scale. This last use of the ships of the Atlantic Fleet was of special value, in view of the greatly enlarged personnel which was pouring into the United States Navy. By these means the new recruits were being brought quickly into contact with the experienced personnel of the Navy, and were adapting themselves to their duties with astonishing quickness. A good beginning, for obtaining the great number of necessary additional officers, had been made at the "Naval Plattsburg," held on a division of the reserve battleships in the summer of 1916. Of 2,000 young men who received this naval instruction, the great majority became officers of the United States Navy after our declaration of war.

The vital question, as to the possibility of transportation overseas on a large scale, was a problem for which the United States must be the one nation to provide an answer. Before the surprising developments of the World War, it would have been assumed that, if we could raise the troops, transportation by means of Allied shipping would be a matter of course. But the need came at the very time when there had been so great losses inflicted by the U-boats that it was impossible for the Entente Allies to furnish anywhere near the amount of transportation required. As a result, transportation must be provided by the United States.

This is another matter which has been misunderstood by the public—the amount of transportation which must be supplied by the United States. It is true that eventually Allied shipping, and of course this meant for the most part British shipping, provided a greater share of the ships.[1] But we must realize that, as Admiral Gleaves has pointed out, "Until May, 1918, almost all of our troops were embarked in our own Naval transports." And it should be emphasized at once beyond misunderstanding, as an absolute factor in the situation, that, if the United States had not been able to provide this early shipping, our reinforcement would have been

---

[1] By British shipping 49 per cent., by the United States 45 per cent., by other nationalities 6 per cent.

too late. For the troops sent before May, 1918, gave the Allied armies the additional strength necessary to turn the tide, and delay would have had a fatal effect upon the war.

It seemed a desperate situation, and was in truth one of the great difficulties. That the Army Transport Service was hard put to charter ships for the first expedition was evident from the list of ships given in the preceding chapter. Yet these were the best that could be gathered from American shipping by experts who went over the registry. The Army transports, controlled by the Transport Service, had the fatal defects of being slow with small bunker capacity. They were used for other purposes, but had to be discarded for transportation of troops over the Atlantic.

Consequently, the ships in the first expedition became the nucleus of the fleet of American troopships and cargo carriers of our great undertaking. It should be stated here that, before these ships of the first groups had returned to America, one great drawback in this service had been obviated. For the first expedition, there had been much delay and confusion in getting the troops and their belongings on board ship, and there had been a hectic experience at the piers. But this was not to be repeated, as, from that time, the Army Transportation Service perfected a system for the increasing volume of transportation, which loaded ships from the piers as fast as the troops arrived at the water front.

But this first beginning of a fleet could only carry some 15,000 troops and 40,000 tons of freight, which was a small percentage of what was needed. It will give a measure of this to state the fact that in one month of 1918 over twenty times 15,000 troops were transported across the Atlantic. But, strangely enough, the element which meant the turning point from failure to success was provided by the enemy. Again, this was an example of the extraordinary overturns of the World War. The German merchant marine, so enthusiastically developed by the controlling German régime, became a decisive weight thrown into the balance which turned the scale against Germany.

On April 6, 1917, when the United States declared war against Germany, there were lying in the harbors of the United States and its colonies 104 ships of German ownership. Of these, twenty were German liners, passenger ships best adapted to be used as troopships, many of them built with the idea of eventual use as transports.

Upon our declaration of war, all these German ships were seized by the United States, following the proper precedents of international law. After inspection, it was found that the engines of these German ships had been wrecked, in the opinion of the Germans, beyond repair.

The United States Government had received ample warning, as early as the *Lusitania* crisis in 1915, that the Germans would attempt to disable these ships. But the status of these interned German steamships was all in favor of damage by their own crews. An interned ship remains in the possession of its owners and crew. Possession is not taken by the authorities of the nation in whose port the ship has been interned. It was a parallel to what occurred after the Armistice. Under the terms of this preliminary treaty of peace, the German warships were not surrendered, but were interned at Scapa to await their disposition under the terms of the final treaty. They were thus in the possession of their German crews, and, upon the news of the final disposition of the warships of the German Fleet, the German crews sank all these ships in Scapa Flow.

The damage done to the German steamships interned in America in 1917 had been a definite part of the German naval program, as stated in the memorandum of the Chief of the German Admiralty of December 22, 1916[1]. In this memorandum, Admiral Holtzendorff expressed absolute confidence that these German steamships interned in American ports could not be used for transportation during the decisive months of the war, and they were thus eliminated from the German calculations as a means of sending American troops to Germany. But here, as often in the World War, German calculations did not take into account any factor outside of their own German formulas.

All of these German steamships had cylinder engines, except the *Vaterland*, which had turbine engines. The German efforts were mainly directed toward wrecking the cylinders, as the greatest harm that could be done to a marine engine, following the idea that the one thing impossible was to run with defective cylinders. To their minds, this meant so extensive a need of replacement that it would involve a delay beyond the decisive period

[1]See *The Naval History of the World, The United States in the War, 1917– 1918*, Appendix A.

of the war. That these cylinders could be repaired in a short time, to be as good as new, was outside their calculations.

Yet this was what actually happened. At the first inspection, the Shipping Board experts had taken the pessimistic view that it was a long replacement job before the German ships could be put into operation. But the United States Navy, in the case of the two German auxiliary cruisers, had recommended that the cylinders be mended by electric welding. Upon this, the Navy Bureau of Steam Engineering was asked to examine all the German steamships, and, after examination, the recommendation was made that all should be repaired by electric welding.[1]

As a result, on July 11, 1917, the unprecedented task of repairing sixteen damaged German steamships was turned over to the United States Navy, and the Navy accomplished this task in an astonishingly short time, and with an efficiency that made the job complete once and for all. It is no wonder that at first it had been considered a hopeless case. Cylinders had been smashed, and in many cases great pieces had been knocked out of them. The German crews had done everything to the machinery that their minds could conceive. There was something almost pathetic in the amount of strenuous work put in by the Germans, and their assured

[1]The process of electric welding was first proposed by G. H. Wilson, an electrical engineer, introduced to the naval authorities by Commander A. B. Hoff (U. S. N. retired). Captain E. P. Jessop, engineer officer at the New York Yard, believed in this process, and Admiral R. S. Griffin, Chief of the Bureau of Engineering, sent his assistant, Captain O. W. Koester, for a thorough inspection. This officer was convinced that the process was practicable, and it was at once adopted.

complacency as to the result—only to find that a new element, outside of the German mind,[1] was to upset all their calculations, and the very ships they had deemed useless were destined to transport over 550,000 troops to fight against the Germans at the crisis of the World War.

The success of the new process was never in doubt. The following quotations from Admiral Gleaves's book will give the reader at a glance the picture of what can only be called one of the most remarkable feats in the history of marine engineer work.

"The biggest job, of course, was the work of repairing the main engines. This was most successfully accomplished by electro-welding large cast steel pieces or patches on the parts of the castings which remained intact. This was completed in a few months, whereas to make new cylinders would have taken over a year.

"This electric welding was an engineering feat which the Germans had not calculated on. The enemy had broken out large irregular pieces of the cylinders by means of hydraulic jacks. Where these parts had been left in the engine room, they were welded back into place, and in cases where the pieces had been thrown overboard new castings were made.

"Electric welding is a slow and difficult process and was carried on day and night, Sundays and holidays, to the full capacity of the available skilled mechanics. After each casting had been welded, the cylinders were machined in place—special cutting apparatus being

[1] "We were accustomed to attribute to these men a knowledge and ingenuity almost superhuman, and yet they failed to take into account electric welding, to say nothing of Yankee ingenuity, perseverance, and skill."— Admiral Gleaves.

rigged for the purpose. Finally, each cylinder and valve chest was thoroughly tested under hydrostatic pressure. The repairs to the cylinders were perfectly successful. In actual trial they held up perfectly under hard operating conditions, and there was not an instance of the welded portion breaking away."

This last is the true measure of this most successful exploit. It was not a temporary makeshift job of repairs, but one that made the machinery as good as new. In fact, in many cases these steamships did better with their repaired engines than with the original engines. The other damages to these ships, to machinery, piping, valves, wiring, etc., were repaired with the same ingenuity and dispatch. All were ready in six months, some in a few weeks—and in many cases the damage wrought by the Germans was repaired before the working gangs had completed the alterations necessary to change the ships into transports for troops.

Again a quotation from Admiral Gleaves will give in a short space a résumé of all this: "In addition to the long list of machinery repairs, extensive alterations were effected, including the installation of thousands of 'standees' or bunks; large increases in the bathing and sanitary plumbing arrangements; the enlargement of the galleys and increase of commissary equipment; the installation and equipment of hospitals; the provision of life rafts, boats and life belts for four or five times the normal number of passengers; the installation of guns and ammunition magazines; and scores of other smaller, but important changes necessary to permit the great increase in passenger capacity, and at the same time to keep the ships safe and sanitary."

The first idea had been that the Army would man and operate the American transports, with the Navy providing guns and gun crews. But, after it had become clear that a great American Army would be sent overseas and the vast plans for the Army began to take form, it became evident, not only that the United States Army had enough on its hands without operating troopships, but also that the operation of the American troopships at sea was logically entirely a naval operation and should be the province of the United States Navy. Consequently, the American troopships were armed by the Navy, manned by the Navy, and operated by the Navy.

Admiral Gleaves has shown how well this worked out, even before the ships were in commission, in the preparations to put into active service this great addition to the Cruiser and Transport Force under his command, and it will be evident that the presence of the naval crews hastened these preparations.

"Before these ships were commissioned, several naval officers and a skeleton naval crew were ordered on board each of them to assist and supervise. Daily reports of progress were made, and each week I held a conference on board the Flagship with my staff and the officers assigned to the different ships for the purpose of interchanging ideas and devising means to expedite the work. The damage done to auxiliary machinery piping, and fittings by deterioration from lack of care was, in general, even greater than that done wilfully. The boilers, the most sensitive part of a ship, had suffered woefully through neglect, and the ships throughout were dirty beyond description. The naval crews were gradually filled up to strength, and while machinery repairs were going on, they went ahead with scrubbing, scraping, cleaning, painting, disinfecting, and fumigating, to make the ships habitable and sanitary for the troops.''

This acquisition of the German ships was the most important factor in the solution of our great problem of transporting troops overseas. For they were available at the very time when troops were to be sent over in increased numbers, and afterward for the ensuing crisis when the maximum of numbers must be sent. The astonishing, totals of 557,788 American troops transported overseas by means of these German ships tell the whole story.[1] This acquisition put the whole matter of troopships on a different basis.

But the work was not yet done, as the demand for cargo ships was growing out of all proportion to pre-war ideas. This will be appreciated when the figures are compared. At the time of the Armistice, 500,000 dead-weight tons of American shipping were engaged in carrying troops, 2,000,000 deadweight tons of American shipping were engaged in carrying supplies for the American Expeditionary Force—that is, for every ton carrying troops, four tons were needed to carry supplies. The public has thought of this operation too much in terms of ships carrying troops. The great fleet of cargo carriers has not been taken into consideration, but, after the gain of the German ships had thus helped the troopship situation, the most difficult part of the operation was to get hold of enough cargo carriers.

As a first step toward an increase of American ship-

[1]See table on page 109.

GERMAN MERCHANT STEAMSHIPS USED AS TROOPSHIPS BY THE UNITED STATES

German Name	Rechristened	Gross Tons	Speed Knots	Date of First Departure with Troops	United States Troops carried Overseas
Vaterland	Leviathan	54,282	24.	12–15–1917	96,804
Kaiser Wilhelm I	Agamemnon	19,360	23.5	10–19– "	36,097
Koenig Wilhelm II	Madawaska	9,410	15.5	11–12– "	17,931
President Lincoln	President Lincoln	18,167	14.5	10–19– "	20,143
President Grant	President Grant	18,072	14.5	12–26– "	39,974
Barbarossa	Mercury	10,983	14.	1– 4–1918	18,542
Groser Kurfurst	Æolus	13,102	15.5	11–26–1917	24,770
Hamburg	Powhatan	10,531	15.	11–12– "	14,613
Friedrich Der Grosse	Huron	10,771	15.5	9– 8– "	20,871
Prinzess Irene	Pocahontas	10,893	16.	9– 8– "	20,503
George Washington	George Washington	25,569	18.5	12– 4– "	48,373
Martha Washington	Martha Washington	8,312	17.2	2–10–1918	22,311
Prinz Eitel Friedrich (Austrian)	De Kalb	8,797	16.5	6–14–1917	11,334
Amerika	America	22,622	17.5	10–19– "	39,768
Neckar	Antigone	9,835	14.	12–14– "	16,526
Cincinnati	Covington	16,339	15.5	10–19– "	21,628
Kronprinzessin Cecile	Mount Vernon	18,372	24.	10–19– "	33,692
Rhein	Susquehanna	10,057	14.	12–14– "	18,345
Kronprinz Wilhelm	Von Steuben	10,492	16.	10–19– "	14,347
Prinzess Alice*	Princess Matoika	10,492	16.	5–10– "	21,216
					557,788

*The *Prinzess Alice* had been interned at Cebu, Philippine Islands, all others in United States ports.

ping for this purpose, the United States Shipping Board, on August 3, 1917, requisitioned at the shipyards all steel vessels of 2,500 deadweight tons or over, which were then under construction.[1] This assertion of eminent domain, though ultimately of great effect, was not the only official act which immediately added the most tonnage to the Government's merchant fleet. On October 15, 1917, the Shipping Board commandeered all commissioned and going American steel cargo steamers of 2,500 deadweight tons or over, and also all American passenger vessels of more than 2,500 gross tons that were suitable for foreign service. "This action added instantly to the federal marine 408 merchant vessels, of more than 2,600,000 deadweight tons."[2]

Every effort was also made to acquire foreign tonnage, by seizure of enemy ships, by charter of enemy ships seized by others in the war, by purchase and charter from neutrals, by granting privileges for export in exchange for chartered tonnage, and by seizure of neutral tonnage in our ports, as will be narrated. But it should be frankly stated that things were going very badly in respect to cargo carriers in the first six months of our participation in the war, not only from the scarcity of ships, but also from the confused situation as to allocating the available tonnage among the demands of the various industrial activities and the needs of the armed forces.

---

[1] "Before the Armistice, 255 of them were in commission—nearly 1,600,000 dead-weight tons."—Crowell and Wilson, *The Road to France.*

[2] Crowell and Wilson, *The Road to France.*

CHAPTER XIV

CANTONMENT CONSTRUCTION

FROM the beginning, a most pressing problem for the War Department had been the question of constructing camps and cantonments for the new troops of the United States Army. As has been stated, these were to be the plants to manufacture the raw material of American manpower into the product necessary for our military effort in the World War. It is only by looking backward, after the test of the great totals thrown on to the battlefield, that we can appreciate how difficult was this undertaking. And it is no wonder that Secretary Baker called it a "task of unparalleled magnitude."

It was another fortunate thing that the newly created General Munitions Board of the Council of National Defense at once perceived that the vast amount of construction involved would be one of the most exacting demands upon our American industries. There would also be the need for the supplementary construction of great additions to the Government arsenals and outside plants for the manufacture of war material and supplies. In the very month of our entering the war, this whole question was made a matter for action by the General Munitions Board—and, again, in this regard, it should be stated that only by looking back at the events of the World War can we appreciate the importance of this prompt action.

For it brought about a quick start, where every day of time was afterward proved to be of value. As early as April 29, 1917, the Committee on Emergency Construction was organized by the General Munitions Board, with the following personnel:

C. W. Lundoff, Cleveland, Ohio, Chairman; W. A. Starrett, New York, N. Y.; Major Wm. Kelly, United States Engineers; Frederick L. Olmstead, Boston, Mass.; M. C. Tuttle, Boston, Mass.

Shortly after the formation of this committee, Mr. Lundoff resigned as chairman, and W. A. Starrett (Major, U. S. R.) was appointed in his stead.

The resolution of the General Munitions Board defining the duties of this committee was in part as follows:

"To suggest forms of day-work contracts, applicable to the construction of cantonments and similar enterprises where rapidity in construction is essential; to formulate plans and methods of expediting the construction of housing facilities in connection with engineering and construction work and activities essential thereto."

The War Department had also been prompt in action. On May 7, 1917, the commanding generals of the several departments were directed "to select sites for these camps and cantonments for training the mobilized National Guard and the National Army." And on May 17, the Cantonment Division, Quartermaster Corps, U. S. A., was created to "take charge of the work of construction of cantonments and camps." This organization of the United States Army worked in close coöperation with the Committee on Emergency Construction, and here again was shown the benefit of that coöperation between the Services and civilian experts, which was the basis of the scheme of the General Munitions Board. The recognition accorded by the Army to the guidance of the civilian experts of this Committee was proved by the significant fact of "the selection of the contractors being left in the hands of this Committee."[1]

The commonsense of this decision will be at once apparent, when the reader understands that these enormous projects of construction went far outside the scope of all normal Army activities. The usual Army methods of advertising for bids and awarding contracts to the lowest bidders were out of the question in the emergency, not only because there must be no delay in getting the work started, but also because no completed plans and specifications would be available. For not even the sites of these cantonments had been determined, and the only way to get the quick results which the crisis demanded was for construction and design to go on together. "Since no form of Government contract would fit the situation a new form had to be developed."[2]

It was obvious to the industrial experts of the General Munitions Board that some form of percentage and day-work contract must be devised to meet this emergency. Accordingly, the Committee on Emergency Construction worked on these lines. Such a form of

[1]Historical Branch, War Plans Division, General Staff, U. S. A.
[2]First Annual Report, Council of National Defense.

contract must imply mutual knowledge and confidence between the contracting parties. In order to collect the information necessary for drawing up a workable form of contract, the Committee called into consultation large numbers of the leading engineers and contractors of the country, and discussed with them the desirable features of these contracts and especially the matter of compensation.

"The result of this study was embodied in a report, dated May 9, which outlined the principle which seemed to the Committee desirable to embody in such a contract. This report was brought before the General Munitions Board, was discussed, certain changes were suggested and embodied, and the matter again brought before the General Munitions Board and the report approved. After which the Committee, in coöperation with the legal committee, drew the cantonment form of contract which was approved by the General Munitions Board and has since been used on a large amount of the Government construction."[1]

These contracts were on a day-work basis, with compensation adjusted on cost and a percentage allowed for profit, running from 10 per cent. on cost of under $100,000 in a graduated, decreasing scale on larger amounts to 6 per cent. on $3,500,000 and a maximum fee to any contractor of $250,000.

After arriving at this decision as to the form of these contracts, the Committee on Emergency Construction continued to do important work. When the Cantonment Division of the Army was constituted (May 17, 1917), Colonel I. W. Littell, U. S. A., was assigned by

[1]First Annual Report, Council of National Defense.

the Secretary of War to take charge of this new Army organization, and the Committee immediately assisted him in building up his novel command. With the advantage derived from a wide knowledge of industrial conditions, the Committee suggested the names of men who were especially fitted to head the different departments of the work. These suggestions were largely accepted by Colonel Littell and approved by the Secretary of War.

As the sites were selected, it became necessary to have them studied by experts. Consequently, a sub-committee was formed for this purpose, consisting of Leonard Metcalf, of Boston; George W. Fuller, of New York; Asa E. Phililps, of Washington, D. C. This sub-committee appealed to local experts for aid in investigating the conditions at each cantonment. The work of the members of this sub-committee was of the greatest value. If they had not conducted these investigations, weeks would have been lost in the construction of the camps and cantonments. "They studied particularly transportation facilities, topography, water supply, and sewage disposal, and after the submission of their report the sub-committee coöperated actively with Colonel Littell's engineering organization in solving the problems that their reports brought out."[1]

But the most difficult work of the Committee on Emergency Construction was the perplexing task of investigating and listing those who could be relied upon as contractors for this widespread scheme of construction. This implied a nationwide investigation of standings and capabilities, in order to find men who could be

[1]First Annual Report, Council of National Defense.

depended upon as qualified to undertake construction under rush conditions. Not only were references and data checked up in the usual way, but, as it was so important not to leave any chance for failure or delay, all other methods of inquiry were used, and special information was obtained from architects and engineers throughout the country. It was an extraordinary undertaking, and could only have been carried out by men who were in touch with our industries. It is inconceivable that all this could have been accomplished by the Army itself.

But this work was done so efficiently that the Report of the Council of National Defense was merely making a statement of fact in saying, as to the result, that the Committee had "in hand probably the most complete survey of the contracting field ever made." The value of this work was shown at once, as it provided an immediate and practical basis for making contracts. As soon as a cantonment site was selected, the Committee, at the request of the Cantonment Division of the Quartermaster Corps, would use these lists to make recommendations of the most suitable contractors. Then, upon approval by the General Munitions Board, the contracts would be thus awarded, and these contracts would be signed by the Army authorities.

From the above, it will be evident to the reader that, in this great and novel undertaking, the problem was solved by using the same source of authority which has been described—the amplified war powers of the Executive, transmitted through the regular departments of the Army, but guided and controlled in the wide and untried fields of industry by the special knowledge of the civilian leaders of American industry.

As a result, this whole vast scheme was being carried into effect in astonishingly short order. In June, all the sites had been selected, and all the contracts had been awarded. In the same month, work had been begun on all but two of the cantonments—and these were started early in July. The original idea had been to have all thirty-two camps and cantonments of the same special building construction, but, as has been explained, the sixteen National Guard camps in the Southern areas were simplified by using tents.

Each National Army cantonment was practically a city for 40,000 men, with water supply, sewers, lighting, heating, some 25 miles of roads, and all the adjuncts of a self-maintaining city. Each was laid out on a typical plan, which varied only in the demands of the site, with streets of standardized wooden barrack buildings, offices, storehouses, sheds, depots, hospitals, and buildings for all kinds of service and administration. These comprised some 1,200 buildings, covering 2,000 acres of ground, with another 2,000 acres devoted to parade grounds, rifle ranges, and fields for practice manœuvre. Secretary Baker has given the estimated average cost as approximately $8,000,000. The cost of the National Guard camps was much less, as tents were used, and they did not receive such great numbers of men. But, of course, they also required the installations of water, sewers, light, heat, etc., and there were also many buildings necessary for administration, services of supplies, etc. The average cost of these National Guard camps was about $1,900,000. Clearing the land on the various sites of cantonments and camps was also a difficult work.

But so thorough had been the preparations, even though they had been made in so short a time, that the great work went on most efficiently. How many of us realize that in a few months in 1917, shelter was constructed for 1,800,000 men? Yet such was the fact.

A most helpful factor in securing this extraordinary result over so wide a field and with different conditions as to labor was the creation of the Cantonment Adjustment Commission (June 19, 1917). This was brought into being through an agreement between Secretary Baker and Samuel Gompers "for the purpose of adjusting and controlling wages, hours, and conditions of labor in the construction of cantonments." The Commission was composed of three persons appointed by the Secertary of War, to represent the Army, the public, and labor, respectively. The original members of the Commission were General E. A. Garlington (the Army), Walter Lippmann (the public), John R. Alpine (labor). It was agreed that work should not be stopped while any question was being adjusted by this Commission, and that the arbitration of the Commission should be binding on the parties. This wise measure for averting trouble between workers and their employers was of great benefit. And the good effects of the adjustments of the Commission were so marked that it was also agreed between Secretary Baker and Mr. Gompers that the authority of the Commission should be extended to cover other construction work which might be undertaken by the War Department during the war.

CHAPTER XV

WHILE these great plants for the production of troops were thus being built and put into operation, and the transport service was also being organized, which was to deliver overseas the product of these American camps and cantonments, the other corollary necessary to insure success was being provided in France. This necessary factor was the creation of facilities for receiving and handling American troops and their supplies at their destination overseas. These were the three component parts of our vast operation. There must be the quick production of troops at home. There must be the means of safeguarded transportation overseas. There must be the great terminals and administrative machinery in France.

This last was another phase of our American effort which has not been appreciated by our public. But, the fact was, it was only by building up in France the equipment to receive, handle, and deliver troops and supplies that the American Expeditionary Forces were able to render their timely aid at the crisis of the war. And it was only through the foresight shown in making these essential preparations far in advance that this necessary equipment was ready at need. This foresight was of a piece with the sagacity of General Pershing and his Staff in casting the size of our army on so much greater scale than any ideas of the Entente Allies. For, included in General Pershing's early recommendations were the projects of this vast service of the rear, as has been stated.

It was also akin to the failure of the Entente Allies to estimate the strength of the American Army that European opinion actually supposed, at the time, that these most necessary projects in France were wasted effort. A note from Ambassador Page reflected this Allied opinion: "It is becoming apparent that the bulk of tonnage assigned to transport the Army is being used to bring over material to create the facilities for handling and supplying a projected army so large that it can probably never be landed in France—at least not in time to get into the game." Most fortunately, these ideas found no echo in the War Department, and the work went forward as projected by General Pershing.

At the beginning, in addition to the First Division of American troops sent overseas to encourage the French, General Pershing's immediate plans also comprised a call for "nine newly organized regiments of Engineers."[1] This was the first step in his service of the rear project, and this was the beginning of the all-important system of terminals, warehouses, and railroads which were to be built and organized by American engineers. All this was also to be another strenuous demand upon our American industries, as will be evident from the following description.

In the first place, it will be obvious that, before developing plans for the American line of communications,

[1]General Pershing, Report.

THE AMERICAN EXPEDITIONARY FORCES "1
CONTINENT"

(This map is diagrammat
Showing the American systems of bases and ports
the American Expeditionary Forces. General Headqu:
Supply, Tours. By means of these systems of bases ar
explained in the text, the great volumes of men, mat(
distributed for their allotted objects. Here was the foct
Atlantic, by means of which the American Reinforcem
field.

it would be necessary to decide upon the sector of American coöperation on the Western Front. This area of future American operations was determined in advance, and General Pershing's statement of the case was most clear and convincing.

"Our mission was offensive and it was essential to make plans for striking the enemy where a definite military decision could be gained. While the Allied Armies had endeavored to maintain the offensive, the British, in order to guard the Channel ports, were committed to operations in Flanders and the French to the portion of the front protecting Paris. Both lacked troops to operate elsewhere on a larger scale.

"To the east the great fortified district east of Verdun and around Metz menaced France, protected the most exposed portion of the German line of communications, that between Metz and Sedan, and covered the Briey iron regions, from which the enemy obtained the greater part of the iron required for munitions and material. The coalfields east of Metz also were covered by these same defences. A deep advance east of Metz, or the capture of the Briey region, by threatening the invasion of rich German territory in the Moselle Valley and the Saar Basin, thus curtailing the supply of coal or iron, would have a decisive effect in forcing a withdrawal of German troops from northern France. The military and economic situation of the enemy, therefore, indicated Lorraine as the field promising the most fruitful results for the employment of our armies."[1]

In view of the enormously increased tonnage of supplies required by modern warfare, the main problem

[1]General Pershing, Report.

was to find a way to forward the vast volumes of food, munitions, and material to this chosen American sector. It must be done by means of railroads, and the French railroads of northern France were already overtaxed by the demands of the Allied armies fighting in France. Not only were the British already crowding the Channel ports, but any attempt for the Americans to use these ports on a large scale would have meant that our supplies sent by railroads to the east, would have been obliged to cross the British and French zones of operations. This condition ruled out a line of communications based on ports and railroads in that region. As General Pershing expressed it, "If the American Army was to have an independent and flexible system it could not use the lines behind the British-Belgian front nor those in the rear of the French front covering Paris. The lines selected, therefore, were those leading from the comparatively unused South Atlantic ports of France to the northeast where it was believed the American armies could be employed to the best advantage."

"The ports of St. Nazaire, La Pallice, and Bassens were designated for permanent use, while Nantes, Bordeaux, and Pauillac were for emergency use. Several smaller ports, such as St. Malo, Sables-d'Olonne, and Bayonne, were chiefly for the transportation of coal from England. From time to time, certain trans-Atlantic ships were sent to Le Havre and Cherbourg."[1] Brest was most heavily used for landing American troops in France, as will be seen from the diagram on page 258. Later, at the time of the German offensive of 1918, arrangements were made "to utilize the ports of Mar-

[1]General Pershing, Report.

seilles and Toulon as well as other smaller ports on the Mediterranean."[1]

"In the location of our main depots of supply, while it was important that they should be easily accessible, yet they must also be at a safe distance, as we were to meet an aggressive enemy capable of taking the offensive in any of several directions. The area embracing Tours, Orleans, Montargis, Nevers, and Chateauroux was chosen, as it was centrally located with regard to all points on the arc of the Western Front."[2]

These preparations, for receiving and handling the troops and supplies of the future great American Expeditionary Forces, implied a program of engineering construction on a vast scale, which has not been generally understood. It comprised constructing port facilities at the different ports of unloading, which did not begin to possess adequate accommodations. At these ports construction included docks, railroads, warehouses, hospitals, barracks, and stables. Throughout the southern French railroad systems, which were to be used by the Americans, it was necessary to lay 1,002 miles of standard-gauge track, consisting largely of double-tracking, cut-offs, and tracks in the yards at ports and depots. 1,761 consolidation locomotives were shipped to France. Of these over a third were lifted bodily into the holds of the ships, packed in with bales of hay, and on their arrival in France required only to be lifted out on to French rails and their fires lighted to enable them to move off under their own steam. 26,994 standard-gauge freight cars were also sent to

[1]General Pershing, Report.
[2]*Ibid.*

France. Rails and fittings shipped to France, for improving the French railroads and for our own construction, aggregated 430,000 tons.

General Pershing has stated that "we assisted the French by repairing with our own personnel 57,385 French cars, and 1,947 French locomotives." He has also given the following summary of another phase of this great work: "The French railroads, both in management and material, had dangerously deteriorated during the war. As our system was superimposed upon that of the French, it was necessary to provide them with additional personnel and much material. Experienced American railroad men brought into our organization, in various practical capacities, the best talent of the country, who, in addition to the management of our transportation, materially aided the French. The relation of our Transportation Corps to the French railroads and to our own supply departments presented many difficulties, but these were eventually overcome and a high state of efficiency established."

The amount of construction of buildings was enormous. From the French we secured 2,000,000 square feet of covered storage. It was necessary to construct some 20,000,000 square feet in addition. As an example of the great scale of other construction, the hospital at Mars of 700 buildings covered 33 acres. This was practically a city, with the roads, water, sewerage, and lighting plants of a municipality. The refrigerating plant at Gieves had a capacity of 6,500 tons of meat and 500 tons of ice per day. "If the buildings constructed were consolidated, with the width of a standard barrack, they would reach from St. Nazaire across France to the Elbe River, a distance of 730 miles. In connection with construction work, the Engineer Corps engaged in extensive forestry operations, producing 200,000,000 feet of lumber, 4,000,000 railroad ties, 300,000 cords of fuel wood, 35,000 pieces of piling, and large quantities of miscellaneous products."[1]

All this work was going on overseas to create the facilities for handling the great output which was being produced in the United States. The reader must keep before his eyes this factor of the threefold destiny of our American forces, which must be "based upon the American continent." In all three components of our great operation, production of troops in America, transportation overseas, service in France, the military and naval elements are obvious. But, behind all three, there must be industrial forces which had never been sufficiently taken into account.

[1]General Pershing, Report.

CHAPTER XVI

THE FIRST MONTHS OF THE MOBILIZATION OF INDUSTRIES

FROM the preceding chapters, the reader will understand by what great leaps our conceptions of the scale of the American effort were growing into vast dimensions. And, with this growth of the ideas of what our military effort must be, with the constantly increasing projects of construction, supplies, and transportation, the mobilization of American industries was becoming a correspondingly greater problem. For all these vast undertakings, as they grew into larger proportions, implied constantly increased demands upon our industries, which must provide the material, both in America and overseas.

In order to show how these demands upon our industries grew far beyond all former ideas, it would be well here to give the totals of wartime construction in the United States alone. This construction was carried out, as has been described, by the Cantonment Division, afterward consolidated with the Construction and Repair Division and known as the Construction Division of the Army, in conjunction with the Emergency Construction Committee of the Council of National Defense.

Colonel Ayres has given these astonishing totals of costs of construction projects in the United States:[1]

[1] A Statistical Summary, General Staff, U. S. A.

National Army cantonments	$199,000,000.
Ordnance Department projects	163,000,000.
Miscellaneous camps and cantonments	139,000,000.
Quartermaster Corps projects	137,000,000.
National Guard camps	74,000,000.
Hospitals	23,000,000.
Regular Army posts	22,000,000.
Coast Artillery posts	13,000,000.
Aviation and Signal Corps projects	8,000,000.
Other construction	39,000,000.
	$817,000,000.

These totals are typical of the enormous figures which would have been thought impossible before we entered the World War. And all this was accomplished by the methods which have been described, the coöperation of the trained men of our industries guiding and controlling the great expansion of the operations of Army departments. As Colonel Ayres has stated, "The operations of the Construction Division constituted what was probably the largest contracting business ever handled in one office." These projects of construction amounted to the labour of 200,000 workmen, in the United States, continuously employed for the period of the war. They expanded from the first cantonment construction, which has been described, to the construction of enormous powder, high-explosive, and loading plants (Ordnance Department projects), warehouses, repair shops, power plants, cement piers, and many other types of construction—and they comprised building in every state of the Union.

These details will give the reader an idea of what was going on in the other fields of our industries. In all it was the same story, of increased demands which went

CONSTRUCTION PROJECTS IN THE UNITED STATES

CONSTRUCTION PROJECTS 541
AVERAGE COST $1,500,000

far beyond all former ideas, and of subordinate bodies of the Advisory Commission of the Council of National Defense guiding the expansion of the departments of the Services. The period of the first four months was most critical, as much depended on the right direction being given to the mobilization of our industries.

In the ever shifting and expanding problems of the production of war material, one of the outstanding necessities was for the coördination of purchases by the Army and Navy, to do away with competitive bidding, and to establish precedence of orders in just proportion to the requirements of the departments of the Services. Herein was also included the question of priority between the needs of the Services and the needs of our people. This was one of the earliest and most difficult tasks, especially of the General Munitions Board and of the Committee on Raw Materials, Minerals, and Metals. Similarly, the questions of supplies, such as cotton, woollen goods, and shoes, were referred to the Committee on Supplies.

As it was an emergency situation, and the greatest result in the shortest time was necessary, the sensible policy was followed of going directly to the various industries and organizing committees formed from leading representatives of these industries. This was the quickest way of using the brains and experience of these leaders, in coöperation with the committees of the Advisory Commission of the Council of National Defense and the departments of the Services. By this means, there would be the best basis for the study of sources of supply, production, and its increase, possible substitutes, and distribution between the needs of the Services, the public, and the Entente Allies.

For this purpose, coöperative committees were appointed from leading representatives of the following industries: Alcohol, Aluminum, Anthracite and Bituminous Coal, Asbestos, Magnesia, Roofing, Brass, Cement, Chemicals, Copper, Lead, Lumber, Mica, Nickel, Oil, Rubber, Steel and Steel Products, Zinc. "As subordinate to these general committees, there were appointed also advisory committees to cover special constituent fields, as, for instance, in respect of the following steel products: Pig Iron, Iron Ore, Lake Transportation, Tin Plate, Sheet Steel, Steel Distribution, Wire Rope, Malleable Castings, Ferro Alloys, Tubular Products, Cold-rolled and Cold-drawn Steel, Pig Tin, Wire Products, Scrap Iron and Steel."[1] It will be at once apparent that steel was to be one of the most important factors in production of war material, and this list of advisory committees will show how fully the field was covered.

As a result of this close relationship between our industries and the Services, it can be stated that a real system of priority had been established in the first critical four months. Moreover, there had been established a workable system of price fixing. This last was most necessary, as, before our entering the war, demand had already gone beyond supply, and, after our entrance, there was great danger of prices soaring out of all reason. The question of fixing prices was not one of compulsion by any recognized authority. On the contrary, through these committees, at the instigation of

---

[1]First Annual Report, Council of National Defense.

the Committee on Raw Materials and the General Munitions Board, the situation in each industry was made a matter of study to keep prices within consistent limitations, and this was also made a matter of personal appeals to good feeling and patriotism. By one of the earliest arrangements, the Navy was enabled to buy 45,000,000 pounds of copper at $16\frac{3}{4}$ cents at a time when the market price was about 35 cents. "This was followed by similar arrangements for the procuring of some 500,000 tons of steel for the Navy program at about one third to 50 per cent. below the market price. Large purchases of zinc and lead were also arranged for at from $33\frac{1}{3}$ to 50 per cent. below market price. This also served to break the continuity of thought toward higher prices, and to show that the business men of the country were willing to and would voluntarily reduce their prices to the Government in time of war."[1]

The work of the coöperative Committee on Lumber was also typical. As will readily be understood, this was a very important field, in view of the great construction projects which have been described, and also the ship building program, which was being inaugurated. The following from the report of this committee should be read: "The price policy recommended by the committee has been simple. It has been to eliminate middlemen, except where extreme emergency requires taking lumber from local stocks, and to induce the mills to furnish at a price well below the market in return for being afforded certainty as to what is expected of them and for being given prompt car service. This policy 'pegged' prices at a very reasonable point, whereas, if

[1]First Annual Report, Council of National Defense.

the purchasing had been unsystematized, the demands of dealers expecting to get Government business would have skyrocketed prices beyond reason. Nor would it have been possible to get a dependable supply when and where needed. Government timber requirements are continually changing with the changes of building plans, but probably a billion feet at least has been or will be bought under present plans. Probably $10,000,000 has been saved by the committee's mobilization of the producers as described in the preceding pages."

Another important field was that of the Committee on Supplies, as will be evident from the list of its co-operative committees of these industries: Cotton Goods, Woollen Manufactures, Shoe and Leather Industries, Knit Goods, Leather Equipments, Mattresses and Pillows, Canned Goods. The same methods were followed of "pegging" the prices of various commodities, making large allotments throughout the industries, eliminating the middlemen, and doing away with competition between Government departments.

As a result of these methods of industrial mobilization, the General Munitions Board was able to report, at the end of the first four months, that, in addition to the cantonment building which has been described, there had been an establishment of priorities and price fixing, that contracts had been made to provide arms, ammunition, equipments, clothing, shoes, blankets, and food, for the increased Army which was being gathered, and contracts for the emergency needs of the Navy.

In regard to the two most important items in the matter of arms, the unusual situations should be explained. As to rifles, Colonel Ayres has clearly explained the conditions existing at the time we entered the World War: "During the years immediately preceding our entrance into the war there was much discussion within the War Department, as well as in the country at large, of the need for increased military preparedness. Reference to the Department reports for 1914, 1915, and 1916 shows that what was then considered as the best military and civilian opinion was agreed that the army that would have to be called into the field in any large emergency was one of 500,000 men. In these reports attention was called to the fact that while our available resources in trained men, in airplanes, and in machine guns were entirely inadequate, our reserve stocks of rifles and small-arms ammunition were sufficient for even a larger army than the half million suggested. On the outbreak of hostilities there were on hand nearly 600,000 Springfield rifles of model of 1903. This arm is probably the best infantry rifle in use in any army, and the number on hand was sufficient for the initial equipment of an army of about 1,000,000 men. What no one foresaw was that we should be called upon to equip an army of nearly 4,000,000 men in addition to furnishing rifles for the use of the Navy."

This was a very serious situation, as the production of rifles requires special machinery, and this special machinery cannot be created in a hurry. The Government plants which had been manufacturing the Springfield rifles, did not have the equipment to increase their output to anything approaching the demands of the greatly enlarged army—and providing the necessary gauges, jigs, and tools for the large increase would have meant prohibitive delays. This was a perplexing problem for the General Munitions Board.

Most fortunately, there were in the United States several plants which were just completing large orders for Enfield rifles for the British Government, and were, consequently, equipped with the special machinery for turning out these rifles in large quantities. Our emergency was met by taking over these plants, and producing a new type of rifle for American troops. This rifle of 1917 was bored and chambered for the same ammunition as our Springfield, but it retained the general characteristics of the British Enfield to such an extent that the existing special machinery could be used. Consequently, it was only the question of a short time to convert these plants to the manufacture of American Enfield rifles in great quantities. These rifles proved to be fine weapons, with the advantage of using our American ammunition.

This was a striking instance of the benefit derived from the preparation of our industries in the years before our entering the war. The totals of rifles used by our Army in the World War showed how great was this help in our emergency. At the end of the war, the number of Springfields had increased to 900,000. But the total of American Enfields had reached nearly 2,300,000. The first divisions sent overseas were equipped with the Springfields which were on hand. The American Enfields were being produced in quantities as early as August, 1917—and, as a result, there was no shortage of supply in rifles for our troops. Colonel Ayres has also stated: "The test of battle use has upheld the high reputation of the Springfield, and has demonstrated that the American Enfield is also a weapon of superior quality. The American troops were armed with rifles that were superior in accuracy and rapidity of fire to those used by either their enemies or the Allies."

In regard to this matter of rifles for the United States Army, Secretary Baker has made a statement which should be studied by all. Not only was this one of the most important decisions, in its effects upon our military reinforcement, but the circumstances of this decision gave striking testimony of the coördination which had been established in the War Department.

"Almost immediately after we entered the war, General Pershing, having been selected as our overseas commander, was directed to report to me in Washington. On his arrival he was informed of his selection and given an office in the War Department, and he immediately began to study the situation, selecting his staff, and in conference with General Scott, Chief of Staff, and the other higher officers of the General Staff, to foresee and try to solve the problems he would face. One of these problems was, of course, the armament of his troops, and the basis of this armament was, of course, the rifle. That the Springfield was the best rifle known was the settled judgment of the Army. The Springfield rifle was the Army's pride. It could be made, however, only at the Springfield Arsenal and at Rock Island, and the machine tools necessary for its production could not be multiplied rapidly enough to assure a supply adequate to the forces likely to be used. This suggestion General Pershing, General Scott, and General Crozier considered together. The matter was finally brought to my attention, and I directed that the whole subject be discussed before me and set aside an evening for that purpose in my office at the War Department. In the meantime, I acquainted myself with the general situation through prolonged conferences with Frank A. Scott and with others in the General Munitions Board, chiefly relying, however, upon Mr. Scott, whose knowledge as a manufacturer was directly in point. At the conference there were present General Scott, General Bliss, General Pershing, General Crozier, and one or two junior officers. The matter was discussed for several hours, and all possibilities and views were canvassed. The first question discussed was as to whether we were to fight with the British or the French, on the theory that, if our army was to coöperate directly with one or the other of these forces, it would be better to adopt the rifle used by that force so as to secure complete interchangeability of ammunition. It, of course, immediately developed that the American Army would for the most part be an independent military force, some elements of it from time to time coöperating with the French and others with the British. Interchangeability of ammunition was, therefore, impossible. Next we discussed the possibility of multiplying Springfields. That took too much time. Next we discussed the use of the Enfield as the British had it, but General Crozier suggested that a change of its caliber and of its cartridge was simple, and that it could be made without loss of time to use our regular service ammunition, and that the supply of Enfields so modified could easily be made adequate to any army we might send. All of the general officers present ex-

pressed their views freely, and at the end of the conference I decided on the modified Enfield, and directed
immediate steps to work out its modification so that
complete interchangeability of parts could be secured
among the rifles manufactured in different plants and
quantity production started at the earliest day possible
after I had made my decision. I asked each of the officers
present if he had anything to say against the wisdom of
the decision. General Pershing spoke first and entirely
approved the decision. General Crozier followed with a
similar approval.

"An interesting consequence of this decision was that
we immediately took over the plants which had been
constructed to supply Enfields to the British, and with
the plants we took over their organizations and employees. It took about two weeks to design the modifications in the rifle, and during that two weeks the
employees in the plants played cards and loafed with
nothing to do, but at the expense of the Government,
since it would have entailed an enormous loss of time
to allow the organizations to be scattered and reas-
sembled when we were ready for production. Some little
scandal was attempted to be created at the wasteful-
ness of the War Department in maintaining these large
number of employees to sit around an idle factory
smoking and entertaining themselves, but I was perfectly aware of the fact that the two weeks lost were
trifling as compared with the disorganization which
would follow any other course, and in this judgment
I was comforted by Mr. Scott and his associates, whose
experience as manufacturers was, of course, incompar-

ably more reliable than the casual opinion of observers, who saw the men drawing their pay for that brief space without work."

In the other important essential, artillery, we were in the same predicament, with a supply on hand to equip an army of 500,000 men, and no possibility of increasing this supply of our types of artillery in time to meet our needs. The manufacturing plants in our country had not been prepared to produce great quantities of guns, as had been the case in the matter of rifles. The policy of the Entente Allies had been to make their own guns at home, but American industries had provided them with large quantities of the material for gun manufacture. The French were especially dependent upon these importations of material. In our first consultations with the Allies, two things had become evident. In the first place, if we tried to produce our own artillery for our troops overseas, it would involve long delays. Secondly, our attempting to do this would interfere with the supply of American gun material for the Allies.

To meet this situation, an agreement was made with the Entente Allies, as early as June, 1917, "to allot our own guns to training purposes and to equip our forces in France with artillery conforming to the French and British standard calibers. The arrangement was that we should purchase from the French and British the artillery needed for our first divisions and ship to them in return equivalent amounts of steel, copper, and other raw materials, so that they could either manufacture guns for us in their own factories or give us guns out of their stocks and proceed to replace them by new ones made from our materials."[1] In this arrangement[2] there was also the advantage that these guns would be of uniform calibers with the guns already in use in the Allied armies. But the great gain was to do away with delays that would have been a set-back for our whole operation. The Allies, especially the French, had ample facilities for gun manufacture, and, with the stream of gun material from America in payment, "it may be said that these plans were carried through successfully along the lines originally laid down."[3]

By these means, provision was made for the two principal needs of our American troops, so far as arms were concerned. Other questions as to arming the forces of the United States will be treated in the following narrative.

On July 18, 1917, the General Munitions Board was superseded by the War Industries Board. This was a smaller and more compact board, but its powers and

---

[1] A Statistical Summary, General Staff, U. S. A.

[2] "The arrangement for supplying artillery to the American troops from British and French sources was made by General Bliss in London and cabled to the War Department. The reasons for it were exactly those recited in the text. The French did not believe it possible for us to learn to make their '75's,' and particularly did not think it possible for us to make it by machine substitution for some of the hand processes upon which they thought the efficiency of the arm depended. We did make the gun, however, at Rock Island Arsenal, and the French sent to us an expert who knew the secrets of that gun, so that before the end of the war we were turning out '75's' with as high performance as the French gun, and had developed a machine process very much more rapid and equally effective. The principal difficulty was the mathematical exactness with which the bore of the recoil chamber had to be finished. This, as I recall it, the French did by hand. We did it by mechanical lapidation. I saw the process in operation at Rock Island, and the French officer there told me it was quite impossible, but that it was actually being done."—Newton D. Baker, Secretary of War.

[3] A Statistical Summary, General Staff, U. S. A.

purposes remained the same, as it was a subsidiary body of the Council of National Defense, and its functions were on the same basis of civilian representatives of industries sitting with representatives of the Army and Navy, to guide and control the production and distribution of war material for the Government. The authority for purchase remained also unchanged, as it was all done through the representatives of the departments of the Services, and thus derived from the war powers of the President of the United States. In fact, it was in all respects an evolution of the General Munitions Board.

The personnel of the new Board was as follows: Frank A. Scott, Chairman; Bernard M. Baruch, Commissioner of Raw Materials; Robert S. Brookings, Commissioner of Finished Products; Robert S. Lovett, Priority Commissioner; Hugh A. Frayne, Labor Commissioner; Colonel Palmer E. Pierce, U. S. A., representing the Army; Rear Admiral F. F. Fletcher, U. S. N., representing the Navy.

The description of the functions of the War Industries Board, as officially defined, presents not only a summary of the early scheme of mobilization of war industries, but also, in reality, a review of what had been done in the first four months—and this description should be quoted here in full:

"The Board will act as a clearing-house for the war-industry needs of the Government, determine the most effective ways of meeting them, and the best means and methods of increasing production, including the creation or extension of industries demanded by the emergency, the sequence and relative urgency of the needs of the different Government services, and consider price factors and, in the first instance, the industrial and labor aspects of problems involved and the general questions affecting the purchase of commodities.

"On this Board Mr. Baruch will give his attention particularly to raw materials, Mr. Brookings to finished products, and Mr. Lovett to matters of priority. These three members, in association with Mr. Hoover so far as foodstuffs are involved, will constitute a commission to arrange purchases in accordance with the general policies formulated and approved.

"The Council of National Defense and the Advisory Commission will continue unchanged and will discharge the duties imposed upon them by law. The committees heretofore created immediately subordinate to the Council of National Defense, namely, Labor, Transportation and Communication, Shipping, Medicine and Surgery, Women's Defense Work, Coöperation with State Councils, Research and Inventions, Engineering and Education, Commercial Economy, Administration and Statistics, and Inland Transportation, will continue their activities under the direction and control of the Council. Those whose work is related to the duties of the War Industries Board will coöperate with it. The sub-committees advising on particular industries and materials, both raw and finished, hitherto created, will also continue in existence and be available to furnish assistance to the War Industries Board.

"The purpose of this action is to expedite the work of the Government, to furnish needed assistance to the departments engaged in making war purchases, to devolve clearly and definitely the important tasks indicated upon direct representatives of the Government not interested in commercial and industrial activities with which they will be called upon to deal, and to make clear that there is a total disassociation of the industrial committees from the actual arrangement of purchases on behalf of the Government. It will lodge responsibility for effective action as definitely as possible under existing law. It does not minimize or dispense with the splendid service which representatives of industry and labor have so unselfishly placed at the disposal of the Government."

CHAPTER XVII

TRAINING THE AMERICAN SOLDIERS

THE summer of 1917 saw in active operation the great plants which had been constructed for turning the abundant manpower of our nation into soldiers. As has been explained, the supply of recruits had been at once assured—and our problem was to prepare them for service. The camps and cantonments had been constructed in short order, as has been described, and in these American training areas there was accomplished a work which can only be described as revolutionizing the production of armies.

Few of us have realized the extraordinary results which were afterward summed up in the following short paragraph: "Of the 42 American divisions which reached France, 36 were organized in the summer and early autumn of 1917. The other 6 were organized in divisions by January, 1918, but had been in training as separate units months before that time. . . . The average division had been organized eight months before sailing for France. . . ."[1]

This meant that these men had spent an average of eight months at camps or cantonments. The diagram at the end of this chapter shows the different periods of the services of all divisions that went over-

---

[1] A Statistical Summary, General Staff, U. S. A.

seas. The white spaces show the periods of training in the United States. It will be noted that the First Division and the Second Division did not have this preliminary training before they were sent to France. The troops of which they were composed were Regular Army units, made up of frameworks of trained men and recruits who had the benefit of contact with trained men. In the Second Division were included two regiments of the United States Marine Corps. The next three divisions which went overseas (26, 42, 41) were composed of selected units of the National Guard, most of whom had seen service on the Mexican border. For this reason, their terms of training could be shortened.

The reader should remember that a division of the United States Army, which was our typical combat unit organized for the World War, consisted of about 1,000 officers and 27,000 men. This was, roughly speaking, over twice the strength of a division in any of the European armies. Therefore, in reading accounts of forces in operations in the World War, which are usually given in terms of divisions by military writers, we must remember that one American division was equivalent to two European divisions. In order to identify the American divisions, it is also necessary to bear in mind that the Regulars were numbered 1—20, National Guard 26—42, National Army 76—93. These were all "organized and trained before the signing of the Armistice."[1]

This represents an achievement that was held impossible according to all European formulas. The German General Staff must have known that we were at-

[1] A Statistical Summary General Staff, U.S.A.

tempting to train a large number of men for military service, yet the German leaders never considered them a serious factor—"soldiers of a child's game mostly made of paper cuttings." But the miracle was being accomplished, and the German leaders were soon to find out the meaning of the "child's game."

Our training camps did not spring into being full armed. At first it was a hard task to get hold of the rifles to equip the large numbers of men called out in the fall of 1917. The supply of rifles for the troops who were to go overseas must first be assured. Consequently, at the beginning, it was necessary to resort to temporary expedients for drilling the troops. There were on hand 200,000 Krag-Jörgensen rifles, which had been stored for an emergency. These and other obsolete weapons were used, and supplies of Ross rifles were bought in Canada. But this time of makeshifts was soon over, and what was accomplished was sufficient testimony to prove that our young men made progress, even at this disadvantage. This confirmed the good judgment of General Leonard Wood, who definitely advised not to delay calling the men out until a full supply of American Enfields or Springfields could be assured, saying that even broomsticks could be used to occupy men's hands in the preliminary setting up exercises.

The quick results obtained at the American training camps could only spring from the mutual understanding which existed between teachers and pupils. From the first, there was no doubt about this. One reason was the absence of class distinctions among our people, and this brought about a prompt coördination throughout all ranks. All spoke the same language and thought in the same terms. Here again was the experience of the Civil War over again. The striking attribute of the Civil War soldier, the game-playing ability to handle himself and his utensil, was again present. And there was the same adaptability of Americans to receive instruction from contact with trained men.

In this regard, our most valuable asset was our Regular Army, which was a highly organized force of picked men. The officers of the Regular Army were well schooled in their profession, and soon made their influence felt throughout the new levies among which they were scattered. As Grant stated in the Civil War, concerning the value of the Regular officers who had gone home to their State troops, "the whole loaf was leavened." This was one of the wisest sentences Grant ever wrote—and it was destined to prove as true in the World War as it had been in the Civil War. With the benefits of this contact, officers and men alike were soon working together at their tasks with a zeal and a unity of purpose which transfromed them into soldiers in an incredibly short time.

There was one invaluable help in preparing our troops for the approaching crisis on the Western Front—and this has not been appreciated by our public. The doctrines of the United States Army were all in favor of teaching the very tactics which were destined to be used in the fighting of 1918. For this reason, our untaught troops were actually receiving instruction in America that was ahead of the times in Europe. As General Pershing expressed it, "The development of a self-reliant infantry by thorough drill in the use of the rifle and in the tactics of open warfare was always uppermost." At that time, "the training of the Allies was still limited to trench warfare,"[1] and the poor results gained in the Allied offensives had given the leaders of the Allied armies the habit of thinking of trench warfare as "stabilized."

Most fortunately, this idea had not gained control in the United States Army. The whole system of "hasty intrenchments," which had dominated the tactics of the World War, was the product of the Civil War. Consequently, field intrenchments were not looked upon in America as any new and abnormal factor, and trench warfare was regarded as an adjunct to open warfare, not as having put open warfare out of existence. The account of the events of 1918 will show how providential it was that this trend of thought still prevailed in the United States Army, as it gave the right basis for military training in America.

Both France and Great Britain sent many picked officers to the United States to assist in training the American troops. These officers zealously gave their services to the War Department, and they were sent throughout the country. Their experience was of great value in our training, and this benefit should be acknowledged gratefully. They showed the utmost good feeling, and won the high regard of all with whom they came in contact. But, for the reasons given above, the training of the American soldiers could not be entirely under their direction. Our own doctrines were best for our future American Army, and the fruits of their experience, and their valuable instructions, were used in combination with our own methods.

---

[1] Gen. Pershing, Report.

The wisdom of this has now been universally acknowledged, as these American ideas for the training given on so great a scale comprised the very essentials best adapted to the future demands of the war. Although nothing of the kind had ever been attempted in proportions of such magnitude, not only was it soon shown that the United States Army would have a new personnel unusually adapted for military service, but, with every trade and occupation represented in the various cantonments, new methods of administration grew up from the experience of handling the new machinery. As a result, the great training centres became well organized and well administered communities, and, aside from the efficient military training which was going on, there was also an extraordinary development of community life which made it certain that the American soldier would receive his intensive military training under the best of conditions for his health and welfare.

In the first place, as to health, how many of us realize that of the 200,000 American officers in the World War, 42,000 were physicians? These figures in themselves convey some idea of the amount of care devoted to the health of our troops. The work of these physicians, who gave up practice for the service of the country, was beyond all praise,[1] and there can be no dissent from this verdict. Their services were not alone performed in the hospitals, which were established in each

---

[1] "Probably no working force has ever been organized which contained more distinguished men of a single profession than are to-day enrolled in the Medical Department of the United States Army."—Report of the Secretary of War, 1918.

camp or cantonment, and as medical officers for the units in training, but their duties included all the problems of sanitation of cities—for each of these military training camps was a city of 30,000 to 45,000 inhabitants. Each locality had its own questions of sanitation, and all were solved under the direction of expert physicians.

The vital importance of good teeth was early recognized, and over 4,400 American dentists were in actual service in the World War. More effective work was done in social hygiene than had ever before been accomplished in an army. In this important work, the Medical Corps was greatly assisted by the Commission on Training Camp Activities, which had been "created in April, 1917, by the Secretary of War to advise him on all matters relating to the morale of the troops."[1] This prompt recognition of the value of morale led to most beneficial results.

"It became the task of the Commission to foster in the camps a new social world,"[2] and this marked a new epoch in the training of soldiers. The nation thus recognized a new need, aside from the question of military training. "Cut off from home, family, friends, clubs, churches, the hundreds of thousands of men who poured into the country's camps required something besides the routine of military training if they were to be kept healthy mentally and spiritually."[3] Our soldiers thus became the wards of the nation, and our people responded whole-heartedly for their well-being.

---

[1]Report of the Secretary of War, 1918.
[2]*Ibid.*
[3]*Ibid.*

Secretary Baker has stated: "I have always felt that the work done by that Commission under the guidance of Raymond B. Fosdick was the most original and salutary contribution made by America to the war. The merit is largely Mr. Fosdick's. My own sympathy with the program grew out of the fact that as the mayor of a large city and as the result of a lifetime of work with social agencies of one sort and another, I had an educated mind on the subject of youth. From the very beginning we discarded the idea that soldiers are necessarily brutal or irregular in their habits, and accepted as the fundamental concept of our task the fact which every social worker knows to be true, that young men spontaneously prefer to be decent, and that opportunities for wholesome recreation are the best possible cure for the irregularities of conduct which arise from idleness and the baser temptations of modern life. Dr. Salmon, Chief Psychiatrist of the Expeditionary Forces, told me in Washington after his return from France that the American Army of two million men was the sanest, soberest, and least criminal body of people of the same number that had ever assembled anywhere at any time in the world, and that this was not merely a casual judgment, but was a scientific analysis of the record of the men compared with the record of other such bodies civilian and military. I am sure that a very substantial part of this fineness of spirit was due to the work of the Commission on Training Camp Activities. I am equally sure that the efficiency of these men as an army was enormously increased by the soundness of their health and the soundness of their morals."

Much of the success of this work was due to the efforts of great organizations throughout the country, which made the welfare of our soldiers their chief task during the World War. This war work was not only performed in the United States, but was carried on overseas, as our troops were sent to France. "These organizations, the Young Men's Christian Association, the Young Women's Christian Association, the National Catholic War Council (Knights of Columbus), the War Camp Community Service, the American Library Association, the Jewish Welfare Board, and the Salvation Army, have been enormously effective in maintaining the morale of our troops at home and overseas and the value of their services is gratefully acknowledged."[1] With their assistance, a really inspiring community life was given to our soldiers in training. They had their clubs, organized athletics, recreations, theatres, music, library, and educational facilities, and opportunities for religious service. This system was extended into towns and cities surrounding the camps, with a wholesome regulation of hospitalities to soldiers, and rigid regulations against intemperance and vice. With our families throughout the country represented by young men in the training camps, this work made a universal appeal to our people, and the good results were nationwide.

None of us who saw these great training centres in operation could fail to see that here was something far reaching in effect upon American young men, and which went beyond all former ideas of military training. This was perhaps best expressed in their music. Their magnificent mass singing was most impressive to all who

[1] Report of the Secretary of War, 1918.

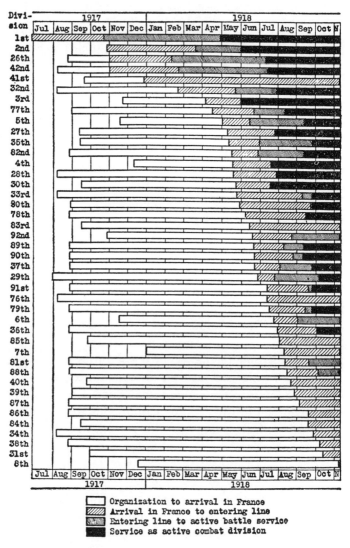

AMERICAN DIVISIONS SENT TO FRANCE

PLACE OF ORGANIZATION OF DIVISIONS AND SOURCES BY STATES

Division	Camp	States from which drawn
Regulars:		
1st	France	Regulars.
2nd	France	Regulars.
3rd	Greene, N. C.	Regulars.
4th	Greene, N. C.	Regulars.
5th	Logan, Tex.	Regulars.
6th	McClellan, Ala.	Regulars.
7th	MacArthur, Tex.	Regulars.
8th	Fremont, Calif.	Regulars.
9th	Sheridan, Ala.	Regulars.
10th	Funston, Kans.	Regulars.
11th	Meade, Md.	Regulars.
12th	Devens, Mass.	Regulars.
13th	Lewis, Wash.	Regulars.
14th	Custer, Mich.	Regulars.
15th	Logan, Tex.	Regulars.
16th	Kearny, Calif.	Regulars.
17th	Beauregard, La.	Regulars.
18th	Travis, Tex.	Regulars.
19th	Dodge, Iowa.	Regulars.
20th	Sevier, S. C.	Regulars.
National Guard:		
26th	Devens, Mass.	New England.
27th	Wadsworth, S. C.	New York.
28th	Hancock, Ga.	Pennsylvania.
29th	McClellan, Ala.	New Jersey, Delaware, Virginia, Maryland, District of Columbia.
30th	Sevier, S. C.	Tennessee, North Carolina, South Carolina, District of Columbia.
31st	Wheeler, Ga.	Georgia, Alabama, Florida.
32nd	MacArthur, Tex.	Michigan, Wisconsin.
33rd	Logan, Tex.	Illinois.
34th	Cody, N. Mex.	Nebraska, Iowa, South Dakota, Minnesota.
35th	Doniphan, Okla.	Missouri, Kansas.
36th	Bowie, Tex.	Texas, Oklahoma.
37th	Sheridan, Ohio.	Ohio.
38th	Shelby, Miss.	Indiana, Kentucky, West Virginia.
39th	Beauregard, La.	Alabama, Mississippi, Louisiana.
40th	Kearny, Calif.	California, Colorado, Utah, Arizona, New Mexico.
41st	Fremont, Calif.	Washington, Oregon, Montana, Idaho Wyoming.
42nd	Mills, N. Y.	Various States.
National Army:		
76th	Devens, Mass.	New England, New York.
77th	Upton, N. Y.	New York City.
78th	Dix, N. J.	Western New York, New Jersey, Delaware.
79th	Meade, Md.	Northeastern Pennsylvania, Maryland, District of Columbia.
80th	Lee, Va.	Virginia, West Virginia, Western Pennsylvania.
81st	Jackson, S. C.	North Carolina, South Carolina, Florida, Porto Rico.
82nd	Gordon, Ga.	Georgia, Alabama, Tennessee.
83rd	Sherman, Ohio.	Ohio, Western Pennsylvania.
84th	Zachary Taylor, Ky.	Kentucky, Indiana, Southern Illinois.
85th	Custer, Mich.	Michigan, Eastern Wisconsin.
86th	Grant, Il.	Chicago, Northern Illinois.
87th	Pike, Ark.	Arkansas, Louisiana, Mississippi, Southern Alabama.
88th	Dodge, Iowa	North Dakota, Minnesota, Iowa, Western Illinois.
89th	Funston, Kans.	Kansas, Missouri, South Dakota, Nebraska.
90th	Travis, Tex.	Texas, Oklahoma.
91st	Lewis, Wash.	Alaska, Wahsington, Oregon, California, Idaho, Nebraska, Montana, Wyoming, Utah.
92nd	Funston, Kans.	Colored, various States.
93rd	Stuart, Va.	Colored, various States.

heard it, and it gave a true prophesy of the morale which was to carry them through dangers to triumph, the spirit of the men of the Civil War which was born anew within them. We can hold to the faith that these young men acquired traits which will endure throughout their lives as a factor of strength in the American nation.

CHAPTER XVIII

THE TRANSPORTS AND THE CONVOY SYSTEM

WHILE these vast preparations for our military forces were being perfected throughout our country, the corresponding preparations were being carried forward for the great naval operation of safeguarded transportation, which would be the only possible means of putting these American forces on the European battlefield. The corresponding increase of the personnel of the United States Navy has been described, and the reader must keep in mind that this personnel was to be larger than the total of any other navy in the world. Not only was there to be a greater number of men than had ever been handled before, but the United States Navy was to be called upon to perform tasks which had never been attempted before.

Moreover, not only were the performances of the new tasks difficult in themselves, but these new tasks must be performed with the constant accompanying call for additional preparation and organization to carry them forward to a constantly increasing scale. The Army's task was hard enough—to train the vast volume of untried recruits. But what can be said of these strenuous months of training and preparation for the United States Navy? More and more ships to be operated—more and more men to be trained! The ships must be schools as well as efficient on their jobs. The trained personnel must not only perform all kinds of new duties, but must also act as teachers for the new, untried personnel that was coming into our Navy in such great numbers. Few of our people have any conception of this phase of our Navy's work. But it should be reiterated that, at the very time the personnel of the United States must perform tasks greater and more varied than had ever been undertaken by any navy, the Navy's personnel must also be occupied in training a new personnel greater than had ever been in any navy.

Success was attained through the existing condition that our young men were showing the same adaptability on the sea that they were showing on land. In fact, seafaring is an attribute of Americans. We are all descended from those who came over the seas, and a great proportion of Americans have been in touch with life on water. It is true that our ocean-going ships have disappeared to a great extent, but our coastwise and inland water commerce has maintained an American merchant marine far greater than in the old days. This merchant marine was the main source of the new increase of our Navy, and the men from the Great Lakes and inland waters showed themselves able to take their places beside their salt water brethren. Large numbers of Americans had also gained practice in yachting, fishing, sailing, and boating, which helped them in the Service. In this respect, it was also the experience of the Civil War over again. And these novices of the World War learned their lessons with the same uncanny quickness from contact with experienced naval seamen. In an astonishingly short time the men of the new personnel of the United States Navy were ready, in all grades, to take up their new responsibilities and duties.

Of all these varied and exacting naval undertakings the work of operating the convoy system of the Cruiser and Transport Force of the United States Navy stands out as of unprecedented difficulty. On the one hand, the safeguarding naval forces must be at high efficiency; on the other hand, the troopships themselves must be at high efficiency—and this efficiency must be established by intensive training.

As has been explained, the convoy system was, at this stage in 1917, winning its way against the U-boats by its reduction of losses to a margin of safety for Allied and chartered shipping. Losses were still enormous, compared with any pre-war ideas, but, in this respect, the convoys were rendering a double service. Not only were they reducing the totals of actual losses, but they were also increasing the totals of available shipping, as the confidence induced by this additional security led the neutral nations to send out shipping previously kept in port from fear of the U-boats.

The United States had at once acquiesced in the obviously sound doctrine that, in general, it was best that the convoys should be under British control. There were obvious reasons for this being the best course. The fact that the greater part of the convoyed shipping must move to and from the central area, that of the British and French ports, made this focus naturally the best seat of administration. And the worldwide maritime connections of Great Britain were all in favor of British administration of this system. But there was one exception made on the part of the United States from the first. While the American cargo ships were to be operated under this British direction of the convoy system, it was decided that the convoys of American troopships were to be under American control and were to be operated by the United States Navy. Later on, when British troopships were also carrying overseas American soldiers, these British troopships were, for the most part, under the British control of the convoy system. But it was a matter of commonsense that the American troopships should remain under our own control, as the United States Army and United States Navy had early developed a system of transportation which was in every sense a perfected joint operation. By this means, better results were being obtained than could have been accomplished by any change.

At the beginning, it had become apparent that the actual operation of the American troopships should be in the hands of the United States Navy. Of course, the troops remained organized units in command of their own officers. But the whole control of these troopships, their operation, and the rules and regulations for their conduct, became the charge of the United States Navy. To the United States Navy was also assigned the task of safeguarding these American troopships.

Consequently, so far as regards the United States Army and the United States Navy, the apportionment must be considered as follows. The United States Army was to produce the trained military personnel for overseas, to transport it to the American sea terminals, and to deliver it at the docks for shipment abroad, exactly like goods delivered for export in commerce. The United States Navy was to receive these troops and their equipment on board ship, and, from that time, was to take full charge of them, transporting and safeguarding them overseas, and finally delivering them to the United States Army at the prepared base ports overseas. Again this was like the process of commerce for delivering goods to the consignees at foreign ports. At these ports overseas, the United States Army was to receive the troops and again to take full charge. The Army was then to deliver the troops at the fighting front by means of the American facilities in France, which had been prepared in advance as described. If the reader will think of the great American joint operation in these terms, the picture will stand out in its true perspective, and the meaning will be evident of General Pershing's phrase "based on the American continent."

It will be at once clear that this sensible agreement arrived at between the Army and Navy, for handling the ever growing volume of transportation on American troopships, gave a businesslike basis for operation that was better without recourse to the machinery of the British convoy control. With the great task apportioned as above, the movement overseas of American troops became a convoy system in itself, a thing apart from the other convoy operations, although the arrivals in the war zone of the American troopship convoys had to dovetail very closely into the general convoy system. The wisdom of this course, on the part of the War Department and Navy Department of the United States, received an astonishing proof of success. Of over 900,000 troops, transported overseas to France in American troopships and safeguarded by the United

States Navy, not a single man was lost through an act of the enemy. There is no need to add anything to this matter of record, except to state that it was the result of the infinite care and pains in the organization and operation of the Cruiser and Transport Force, shown in the first venture and continued throughout the war.

The successful conduct of this joint military and naval operation was also a proof of how quickly the minds of the Army and Navy leapt forward to a grasp of affairs which were suddenly cast on so vast a scale, and with complicated tasks that had never been undertaken before. Both Services demonstrated that their high training had fitted them to perform duties which were outside of all former ideas. A notable feature was the excellent teamwork between the two Services, and this was a most necessary element, in view of the constantly shifting needs for control and apportionment of the details of the ever growing operation and the huge volume of supplies. With the demands of the situation constantly swelling to new totals and new requirements, anything like a hard-and-fast program was out of the question.

The Army had instituted an Embarkation Service, with General Frank T. Hines as Chief of Embarkation, and his relations with Admiral W. S. Benson, the Naval Chief of Operations, were so cordial that they were able to adjust points at issue without cut and dried classifications, which would have inevitably caused delay, as the flood of troops poured in for transportation. It will be apparent that all this was far afield from the usual demands of the Services, and there was no time for tabulating the details of control. Matters had to be adjusted man to man. The same coöperation existed between General David C. Shanks, in charge of the great embarkation base of New York, and Admiral Gleaves, and also between General Grote Hutcheson, at Newport News, and Admiral Hilary P. Jones, who had charge of the Newport News Division of the Cruiser and Transport Force. So well did these officers of the Army and Navy work together, that, after the first confusion had been remedied by the Embarkation Service, the vast undertaking was carried out from first to last in an efficient and businesslike way, and its success was never in doubt.

Secretary Baker has written an appreciation of this cordial coöperation between the Army and the Navy, and this reveals the course pursued more clearly than could be explained in a long dissertation: "When we went into the war, Secretary Daniels and I agreed that there would be all sorts of questions between the two Services, and we appointed our respective chiefs of staff to work these questions out, bringing to us only such controversies as they could not themselves compose. For the Navy, Benson, and, for the Army, in succession, Bliss, Biddle, and March, worked together so admirably that it was only necessary for them to refer one question to Secretary Daniels and myself. That was to do with priority of access to steel, and, when that question was propounded to us, I undertook to solve it by saying that I thought the Navy was entitled to priority and preference for every project it had which could be completed in a year from the date of our entry into the war, but, at the end of the provision for things which could be completed in a year, I thought the Navy

should stand aside for the Army. Secretary Daniels
accepted this as the solution, and there were no further
controversies."

In order to complete the picture of the preparations
for transporting and maintaining the American Expeditionary Forces, "based on the American continent."
it should be stated that the American cargo carriers
were on a different basis, and their relation to the convoy system should be here defined. The operation of
this enormous fleet of cargo steamers, necessary to transport the vast volumes of supplies and material for our
troops overseas, became, it is true, more and more a
task of the United States Navy, and eventually, as will
be narrated, there was to be the Naval Overseas Transportation Service. But it will be obvious that this was
a service altogether unlike that of the American troopships.

The heterogeneous collection of cargo ships, partly
owned by the United States, partly chartered and operated by the United States, partly chartered by the
United States and yet operated by the owners, was not
favorable for a closely organized special convoy system, like that of the American troopships. Consequently, our cargo carriers were made part and parcel
of the general convoy system under British control.
This distinction should be kept in mind throughout the
narrative of ensuing events.

CHAPTER XIX

THE SPREAD OF WAR ACTIVITIES IN 1917

THE preceding account has shown how whole-heartedly the American nation was committed to its task. The month of May, 1917, might well have been called the month of awakening—and it was the waking of a giant, as was proved by the activities of the ensuing months. It is impressive to sum up the new life which had sprung into being in that fateful month of May, 1917, and which was keeping pace with an entirely new war. For such had the World War become. No one knew it at the time, but it is a fact that all former means and methods of fighting the World War were suddenly out of date. We must put it out of our minds that we entered a war which was to go on as it had before, or that we became part of the situation which had existed before. On the contrary, the Entente Allies were to face a new situation—and we must do the same. As has been stated, our awakening was an instinctive appreciation that the danger would be on a scale that was not foreseen abroad.

To sum this up: In May, 1917, the prompt passage of the Selective Service Act had insured us a strong American Army, and the great scheme of cantonments had insured its training in adequate numbers. In the same month, the commission to General Pershing, and his mission overseas in advance of his army, had insured the military information which would cast our American reinforcement in the necessary great dimensions, and the commission to Admiral Gleaves had also insured the prompt organization of the Cruiser and Transport Force. It is most inspiring, in the face of petty faultfinding, to realize these great launchings of forces which were the realities of the situation.

It is equally inspiring to realize the uprising of our citizens. In fact, so universal was the participation of Americans, throughout our country, in the activities of the ensuing months of 1917, that it would be a true statement to write that the Selective Service Act of May, 1917, not only called into the war our young American manhood, but it also enlisted all Americans in the service of our country. The quick, sympathetic response to the appeals of the training camps has been described. But it went far beyond this. The realization that all our American communities, and our American families, were represented in the Army and Navy of the United States was a direct appeal to neighbors and relatives to render service in the same cause—and the response was immediate everywhere.

The women were even more zealous than the men, and the service of American women must be acknowledged as one of the great factors in the success of the effort of the United States in the World War. The importance of this was foreseen by the Council of National Defence, and the Woman's Committee of the Council of National Defense was appointed, which had its first meeting May 2, 1917. Dr. Anna Howard Shaw was chairman. "The principal objects before this committee were to provide a new and direct channel of communication between American women and their Government; to enlist the coöperation of all women, whether organized or not; and to ascertain and report upon the patriotic work being done by them; to endeavour, through coördination and centralization, to obtain greater efficiency in women's defense work, and to impress upon women the importance of all methods of economic warfare as a vital aid to winning the war."[1]

The Woman's Committee organized divisions (woman's committees) in all States, and in Alaska, Hawaii, and Porto Rico, which in turn organized county and local units. The State divisions also coöperated with the State councils of defense. The Woman's Committee also worked in coöperation with many national organizations. "Eighty women's organizations, national in extent, were affiliated with the committee."[2] Under its control there was an efficient registration of women for service, taken on cards approved by the Council of National Defense and by the United States Census Bureau.

The work of the Woman's Committee of the Council of National Defense soon became very useful to the Government in special drives for women workers, at the request of Government departments and of the Civil Service Commission. The value of this work of the Woman's Committee will be at once evident, when the reader considers the great expansion of all the departments caused by the demands of the war, and the hosts of new employees required by the Government. This resource was also a much needed means for ob-

---

[1]First Annual Report, Council of National Defense.
[2]Historical Branch, General Staff.

taining the large numbers of intelligent women required as student nurses. In addition to these functions of Organization and Registration, the Woman's Committee carried on its work through the following departments: Food Production, Food Administration, Women in Industry, Child Welfare, Maintenance of Existing Social Service Agencies, Health and Recreation, Education, Liberty Loan, Home and Foreign Relief News. The mere list of these departments will convey an impression of the wide fields of war work for American women.

The Council of National Defense had at once recognized the value of the National Research Council, "organized in 1916 by the National Academy of Science, at the request of the President, to coördinate and stimulate scientific research."[1] By a resolution of February 28, 1917, this body was asked to coöperate with the Council of National Defense, and in our months of preparation served as the Department of Science and Research of the Council of National Defense.

In the same spirit, the Council of National Defense appointed committees to coöperate in the widely divergent fields of Shipping, Fuel, and Food. But in these three cases there were independent sources of control. The Shipping Committee of the Council of National Defense was absorbed in the United States Shipping Board, and in the later Shipping Control Committee, of which accounts will be given. The Food Administration and the Fuel Administration remained the controlling bodies in their respective fields. The work of the Food Administration was nationwide, and the

[1]Historical Branch, General Staff.

problems of Food Administrator Hoover were threefold: Conservation; Control of commodities; Coördination of purchases, exports, imports, and transportation. Each of these departments received the help of
the national and state committees of the Council of
National Defense. The appeal for conservation brought
home to the whole American people the need for saving.
This campaign was carried on by means of pledge cards,
and 11,000,000 homes were pledged to this form of conservation. The control of commodities was extended
from voluntary agreements to a strict licensing system,
which became so effective that at the end of 1918
over 260,000 firms, individuals, and corporations were
under license. Of the Division of Coördination of Purchases, it is enough to state that its activities covered
the tremendous problems of purchase and distribution
of foodstuffs, not only for the unprecedented demands
of the Army and Navy, but also for a proper allotment
to the Entente Allies, with due regard for the needs of
our own people. There was also the problem of supplying the great need of the Red Cross, as well as other organizations of war relief. Altogether, there were vast
scopes of activities which would have been considered
incredible before the World War swept aside all former
ideas.

In a similar way, the Fuel Administration was obliged
to face problems on a scale that had never been estimated. As can be readily imagined, all these nationwide activities had created demands for coal and oil
fuel beyond all calculations, and this condition was
complicated by the fact that, at the very time when
the work of the Fuel Administration had become most

difficult, the fall and winter of 1917–1918 brought blizzard weather of exceptional severity.

The severe weather had also an adverse effect upon the administration of the American railroads. This had been promptly inaugurated by the action of the American Railway Association, as has been described, in response to the Committee on Transportation and Communication of the Advisory Commission, Council of National Defense, of which Daniel Willard was Chairman and active organizing head. "The agreement contained in the resolution was signed by the executives of nearly 700 railroads,"[1] and the Railroads War Board was thus assured of the coöperation of the railroad men of the nation. At the very time when the Board was struggling with the rapidly increasing volume of traffic due to the demands of the war, which grew to enormous totals at the end of 1917, there came blizzard weather conditions. As a result, "serious traffic congestion prevailed and situations developed which rendered imperative complete unity of administration, impossible under private control."[2] Consequently, by proclamation dated December 26, 1917, "the President assumed possession and control of systems of transportation located wholly or in part within the United States, including railroads and all systems of transportation owned or controlled by the railroads, together with all equipments and properties pertaining thereto."[3]

This was a recourse to the same fountainhead of authority which has been emphasized in this work, the

---

[1]Historical Branch, General Staff.
[2]*Ibid.*
[3]*Ibid.*

power vested in the President of the United States and amplified by act of Congress. William G. McAdoo was named Director General, and at once began the organization of a system of control which became the United States Railroad Administration. But, as in other cases, it must be kept in mind that this was an evolution from the methods put into operation by the acts of the Advisory Commission of the Council of National Defense.

In fact, throughout the whole effort of the American people, the influence of the Council of National Defense was unmistakable. It had called into the service of the United States all elements among our citizens, ∟eginning with the right leadership of men experienced in their accustomed fields, and reaching out to include all local conditions. The very fact that its organizations went through a formative period was helpful. Looking backward, we can see now that any attempts to create the definite administrative bodies at the start would have been premature and founded upon inadequate knowledge—for no one could have foreseen the vast scale of our activities. But the agencies in the process of evolution were more flexible and capable of indefinite expansion. The result was, the definite bodies which were evolved not only sprang from being given the right impulse at the beginning, but they were also the product of the new conditions which were encountered. For this reason the effects of the summons of the Council of National Defense were not only felt in our preparations for fighting and in our mobilization of industries, but also in the wider mobilization of the American people, to enlist each man or woman for a share in the great work.

In this united surge of the American nation, another
notable proof of unity was the utter forgetfulness of
politics during the months when our citizens were carried beyond themselves in devotion to their country.
One of the leaders in the work of the Council of National
Defense, Grosvenor B. Clarkson, has made a striking
record of this: "The writer, who happens to be a Re-
publican, wishes to make the following statement
with regard to Secretary of War Baker and his five
Democratic Cabinet associates forming the Council of
National Defense. Looking back on the three years in
which he served the Council, he is unable to recall a
single instance in which Mr. Baker or the Council requested him to make an appointment or take an administrative action on a personal or political basis. . . .
The question was not raised at all. It was a clean business throughout in this respect, and a demonstration
of non-partisanship in a crisis that the writer would
not have believed possible before going to Washington."[1]

---

[1] *Industrial America in the World War.* Note to Chapter II.

CHAPTER XX

THE year of 1917 was thus running its course, with the great component elements of the American effort, industrial, military, and naval, growing into a strength that was not at all appreciated by the world at large. On the contrary, as the year drew to the dreary end of its succession of military failures for the Entente Allies, there was a general feeling of discouragement among the Allies in regard to the possibilities of any decisive military assistance from the United States.

The leaders of the Entente Allies were deeply disappointed at the results of the American effort so far. To them it seemed that failure was inevitable, judging from the small numbers of American troops in France. General Pershing, has stated in his Report: "On December 31, 1917, there were 176,665 American troops in France and but one division had appeared on the front. Disappointment at the delay of the American effort soon began to develop." The defeats of the Allied armies had effaced the first exultation caused by the entrance of the United States, and the Entente Allies were measuring the whole strength of America by the first thin trickles of the stream, with no conception that it would suddenly burst into a mighty torrent.

Not only did the leaders of the Entente Allies utterly fail to estimate the results of the uprising in the United States, but, even at the stage of the last months of 1917, the Entente Allies still failed to make any adequate estimate of the vast scale of the military reinforcement which must be provided by the United States to avert defeat at the crisis of 1918. A striking proof of this last, in regard to the Entente Allies, was made a matter of official record in the latter part of 1917."

This was on the occasion of the Paris Conference, begun on November 29, 1917,[1] from which eventually sprang the Allied Maritime Transport Council, a long step toward bringing about coöperation in the matter of Allied shipping. At this Conference delegates were present from practically all of the Entente Allies, and with these was associated a representative of the United States. In fact, one main object of the Conference was to urge upon the United States greater coöperation with the Entente Allies in the matter of shipping. And it was a most significant sign of the times that, even thus late in 1917, the following was adopted: "That if she [United States] take these steps, however, there is a prospect of her being able to transport and maintain an American Army of 500,000 by the early summer [1918] and of 1,000,000 later in the year."

This estimate by the Conference, set as a goal for our effort, was only half of the military forces actually provided by the United States, and it was most fortunate, as has been stated, that the military information sent

[1]"The Paris Conference, which began on November 29, 1917, was probably the most impressive expression in the war of both the range and unity of Allied effort."—*Allied Shipping Control.*

by General Pershing to the United States was far in advance of the times and our structure was already being built up to the greater scale demanded by the World War. This narrative has described the foresight of General Pershing in so quickly impressing it upon our nation that our military problem must be worked out in large figures. In this same month of November, 1917, another example of prophetic forecast on the part of General Pershing was also made a matter of official record.

In General Pershing's confidential estimate of the situation for the Secretary of War (dated November 15, 1917) he sounded these notes of warning: "The utmost energy should be put into developing America's fighting forces for active service during the coming summer. Winning the war is vital to our future, and if humanly possible it ought to be done in 1918. There is no telling what might happen if we defer our utmost exertion until 1919. . . . Finally, every possible ton of shipping should be secured by purchase, construction, or otherwise, in the Orient or elsewhere, with the least delay for use in carrying our armies to France. It should be no longer a question of how much tonnage can be spared for military purposes, but only the most imperative necessity should permit its use for any other purpose. To secure this result the whole of our shipping ought to be under War Department control, and as much more as possible from neutral or Allied sources."

This urgent call was reiterated in General Pershing's cable of December 2, 1917, to the War Department, with even more emphasis:

"The Allies are very weak and we must come to their

relief this year, 1918. The year after may be too late. It is very doubtful if they can hold out until 1919 unless we give them a lot of support this year. It is therefore strongly recommended that a complete readjustment of transportation be made and that the needs of the War Department as set forth above be regarded as immediate. Further details of these requirements will be sent later."

It was upon this question of transportation overseas that the success of the American effort depended, and the situation at the end of 1917 was far from satisfactory. As stated by General Pershing, "a complete readjustment of transportation must be made," or the American effort would fail. This question, as has been stated, resolved itself into two problems: transportation of troops overseas; transportation of cargoes to sustain the constantly growing needs of our troops abroad.

Transportation of troops was the less difficult problem. As will be seen from the table on page 109, the great fleet of German steamships taken over by the Navy was in full operation at the first of 1918. These seized enemy ships made the best possible transports for troops, and they were the backbone of the Cruiser and Transport Force. Added to these were American steamships and acquired foreign steamships, and transportation of troops already stood on a better basis than transportation of cargoes. As a result, this last became the more difficult problem. As the Entente Allies, at this stage, neither believed in the possibility of a large military reinforcement from America, nor foresaw the urgent need of such an American reinforcement, the leaders of the Entente Allies were not yet much inclined to

allot shipping to the needs of the American Expeditionary Forces.

At this time, all minds in Europe were occupied with
the great struggle between the U-boats and shipping.
The convoy system had already won this fight, as has
been described, but this was not yet apparent to the
Entente Allies, and at this Conference of November
29, 1917, a gloomy view was taken of the situation on
the seas. This was not a matter for wonder, as it was
there stated that Great Britain in the war had lost
10,000,000 d. w. tons, which meant a net loss of 4,000,000
d. w. tons over replacements and captured ships, and
the world losses of shipping had been 17,000,000 d. w.
tons, which meant a net loss of 9,000,000 d. w. tons.

Yet, at this stage, the convoy system had in fact
grown into a real system in every sense of the word,
and its operation had developed as if many regular
steamship lines were running from the outlying ports
to the central station, which was, of course, Home Waters and the ports of Great Britain and France. The
group sailings of these convoys had become scheduled
and regulated in every detail, as to departures, voyages,
and arrivals. The ships were not only protected by
warships, but they were also trained in the tactics of
self-preservation and consequently prepared in advance
to cope with the attacks of the U-boats.

This was the picture of the situation on the seas at
this stage of the World War, with these well regulated
groups of convoys arriving in due order in the infested
zones of Home Waters, where they were picked up one
by one by their assigned forces of anti-submarine protection, which made any attacks upon these convoys a

matter of operating the U-boats in an area made dangerous for them by the assured presence of enemy naval forces prepared to take the offensive against them. It was altogether a different situation from what had gone before, when scattered ships were taking their own means of protection, and arriving in patrolled areas with no assurance of striking the company of protecting warships.

This revolution in the methods of protecting shipping, by reverting to the ideas of the old convoying days, had produced an astonishing result in relation to losses from the U-boats. It is true that losses of ships in the near-by coastwise traffic, and of ships outside the convoys, still remained large, but the convoy system had reduced the losses of overseas shipping in the convoys to a point that assured the defeat of the U-boat campaign. This is best shown by the simple statement of fact, that, whereas there had been losses of ten unconvoyed ships before the introduction of the convoy system, there was only the loss of one convoyed ship after the convoy system had been put into full operation.

This balance had been swung in the direction of safety only just in time, as the demands of the war upon shipping were growing out of all proportion to former experience. The scale of operations in France was constantly increasing, with greater expenditures of munitions and supplies. Troops were still being drawn from Canada, Australia, New Zealand, and South Africa. The distant expeditions must also be maintained, and this implied services of supply to Salonica, Mesopotamia, Palestine, and East Africa.

Of course, the transportation of the troops and sup-

plies of the American Expeditionary Forces was destined to be the most important use for the shipping at
the command of the Entente Allies. But the crisis had
not yet made this evident. Consequently, all the greater
exertions were necessary on the part of the United
States. But we had the one important advantage of
General Pershing's warnings from overseas which were
spurring our nation on to these greater exertions.

CHAPTER XXI

THE FOUNDATIONS LAID IN FRANCE

THE warnings from overseas, due to the information gathered by General Pershing in France and his estimates of the approaching crisis, had thus emphasized the two outstanding factors of our participation in the World War. Not only must we provide an American Army much greater than had ever been imagined by the Entente Allies, but also that greater American Army must be on the battlefield of the European Western Front in 1918. Otherwise it would be too late. These two elementary needs became the impelling springs of the whole war policy of the Administration, and there was no deviation from this war policy.

All our military forces were being developed to provide this reinforcement in the allotted time. This military object was dictating our naval strategy, and the forces of the United States Navy were being prepared to forward it. All our industrial forces were being mobilized and set to work for the same purpose. These last must be active in every phase of our operation, military and naval—in the United States, on the seas, in Europe.

An account has been given of the preparations in France for receiving our great army when it should be ready, and of the construction projects which were being undertaken before there was any army in evidence. In the same spirit of foresight, the administrative organization for the American Expeditionary Forces was being created in France in advance—and this was an important reason for the success of our operation.

General Pershing had at once realized that there was a specially urgent need for an efficient Staff organization, as the American Expeditionary Forces were to operate so far from their base, "the American Continent." His own description of the necessities of the case was explicit:[1]

"The organization of the General Staff and supply services was one of the first matters to engage my attention. Our situation in this regard was totally unlike that of our Allies. The French Army was at home and in close touch with its civil government and war department agencies. While the British were organized on an overseas basis, they were within easy reach of their base of supplies in England. Their problems of supply and replacement were simple compared with ours. Their training could be carried out at home with the experience of the front at hand, while our troops must be sent as ships were provided and their training resumed in France where discontinued in the United States. Our available tonnage was inadequate to meet all the initial demands, so that priority of material for combat and construction, as well as for supplies that could not be purchased in Europe, must be established by those whose perspective included all the services and who were familiar with the general plans. For the

---

[1]General Pershing, Report.

proper direction and coördination of the details of administration, operations, supply, and training, a General Staff was an indispensable part of the Army."

Another paragraph of General Pershing's Report gave a graphic picture of the wide fields of activity of the Staff work of the American Expeditionary Forces.

"The functions of the General Staff at my headquarters were finally allotted to the five sections, each under an Assistant Chief of Staff, as follows: To the First, or Administrative Section—ocean tonnage, priority of overseas shipments, replacement of men and animals, organization and types of equipment for troops, billeting, prisoners of war, military police, leaves and leave areas, welfare work and amusements; to the Second, or Intelligence Section—information regarding the enemy, including espionage and counter-espionage, maps, and censorship; to the Third, or Operations Section—strategic studies and plans and employment of combat troops; to the Fourth Section—coördination of supply services, including Construction, Transportation, and Medical Departments, and control of regulating stations for supply; to the Fifth, or Training Section—tactical training, schools, preparations of tactical manuals, and athletics. The same system was applied to the lower echelons of the command down to include divisions, except that in corps and divisions the Fourth Section was merged with the First and the Fifth Section with the Third."

The mere list of these different duties gives an idea of the many problems confronting the American Expeditionary Forces, and no argument is needed to show how necessary it was that a staff organization should be provided in advance for the great army which was to be poured into France. The reader will readily understand how these problems mounted in difficulties, when the American troops increased so rapidly in numbers. The following expressed the growth of the gigantic Service of Supply, which became a great army in itself: "As the American Expeditionary Forces grew, it was considered advisable that, in matters of procurement, transportation, and supply, the chiefs of the several supply services, who had hitherto been under the General Staff at my headquarters, should be placed directly under the supervision of the commanding general, Services of Supply."[1] As can be easily imagined, the growing needs for staff officers ran beyond the numbers of those who had the training for these duties. To meet these demands, a General Staff College was organized at Langres in November, 1917, to give an intensive course for staff officers. "Officers were carefully chosen for their suitability and, considering the short time available, graduates from this school returned well equipped for staff duties and with a loyal spirit of common service much accentuated."[2]

It is impossible to conceive that our American military operation would have succeeded if it had not been for these preparations in advance. That it did succeed must be attributed to the fact that, before there was any great American Army in sight, construction projects had insured facilities for receiving and handling it, and a General Staff organization had insured its administration.

---

[1]General Pershing, Report.
[2]*Ibid.*

Yet, as has been stated,[1] the general opinion among the Entente Allies was that all these preparations were wasted efforts—that the United States was making the mistake of diverting material and shipping for the benefit of a phantom army which would never exist. This impression grew stronger in the fall of 1917, when the Entente Allies found so few American soldiers arriving in Europe. "Disappointment at the delay of the American effort soon began to develop. French and British authorities suggested the more rapid entry of our troops into the line and urged the amalgamation of our troops with their own, even insisting upon the curtailment of their training to conform to the strict minimum of trench requirements they considered necessary."[2] It was natural that this idea of scattering the American troops among the units of the Allied armies should appeal to the Entente Allies as the quickest means of gaining a military reinforcement.

This scheme was strongly urged by the leaders of the Entente Allies. It took most definite form in the project submitted in November, 1917, by General Robertson, the British Chief of Staff, to send overseas 150 individual battalions of American troops to serve in British divisions. This proposition was sent to the Administration in Washington with strong endorsements from abroad which made an impression in its favor. But the Secretary of War adhered to his determined course of not allowing any interference with General Pershing, and President Wilson was of the same mind. Consequently, General Robertson's project was referred

[1]See page 120
[2]General Pershing, Report.

back to General Pershing, giving the American Commander-in-Chief "entire freedom"[1] to make his own
disposition of his forces.

This question became a matter of discussion for a long
time between General Pershing and the British and
French military leaders. But the American Commander-
in-Chief could not be convinced of the wisdom of amalgamating our troops with those of the Entente Allies,
and his opposition turned the scale against this scheme.
The final rejection of any such disposition of American
soldiers was clearly expressed in a letter from General
Pershing to the Secretary of War (February 24, 1918):
"Since my last letter to you on the subject of training
and service of our units with the French and British
armies, there has been much discussion, with the final
result as cabled you. I think both the British and the
French now fully understand that we must look forward to the upbuilding of a distinctly American force
instead of feeding our units into their organizations.
Your decision on that point settled all thought of our
doing anything else."

This was a fine example of the relation maintained
between the Secretary of War and General Pershing,
and the result vindicated the policy of not allowing outside interference with the American Commander-in-
Chief. The subsequent course of the World War showed
that the scheme of the Entente Allies for the use of

---

[1]Cablegram from Secretary of War to General Pershing, December 18,
1917: "This suggestion is not, however, pressed beyond whatever merit it
has in your judgment, the President's sole purpose being to acquaint you
with the representations made here and to authorize you to act with entire
freedom in making the best disposition and use of your forces to accomplish
the main purposes in view."

American troops would have been a mere drop in the bucket. It would never have accomplished anything on a large scale. Of course, it was conceived in the European lack of faith in an American army on a large scale. But the American belief in that great army was destined to find its realization on the field of battle, and there is no longer any question of the wisdom of the decision to stake our hopes of success upon that cast.

There was another serious objection to the amalgamation of American troops with those of the Entente Allies. This lay in our different ideas of training, as our soldiers, if incorporated in units of the Allies, would have been restricted to a system of training which was inadequate according to American doctrines. The Allies, especially the French, did not have any belief in our tactics for open warfare. General Pershing wrote as follows to the Secretary of War: "Another point of difference was as to tactical value of open warfare. We have held that our young officers lacked experience in handling their units in the open, and that a knowledge of the methods of trench warfare was not enough to prepare them for the important duties of commanding units where there was a possibility of open warfare. I have spent much time myself explaining that our company officers must have training in handling units in open attack and defence, and that they must be thoroughly schooled in the principles of what we call 'minor tactics.' The French take the opposite view and have held that our officers do not need that training now." It was another most fortunate thing, as was shown by the sequence of events, that General Pershing continued to insist upon this training in open warfare tactics for American troops.

In his report, the American Commander-in-Chief has summed up this case most effectively: "While the Germans were practising for open warfare and concentrating their most aggressive personnel in shock divisions, the training of the Allies was still limited to trench warfare. As our troops were being trained for open warfare, there was every reason why we could not allow them to be scattered among our Allies, even by divisions, much less as replacements, except by pressure of sheer necessity."

The correspondence between Secretary Baker and General Pershing reveals a cordial coöperation from the beginning to the end of their relations. The Secretary of War pursued an admirable course in regard to the designation of officers who were to serve under General Pershing. The Commander-in-Chief was given a free hand, not only in the matter of his staff organization but also in regard to the field officers who were to serve under him. The Secretary wrote (September 10, 1917): "In the matter of selecting corps and division commanders, I constantly feel that I ought to have your advice and judgment. . . . From all you have said, supplemented by all I have learned elsewhere, the need for young and physically strong men is apparent, and I am perfectly willing to go any limit in meeting this requirement." In this letter Secretary Baker outlined the sensible policy of "planning to send practically all of the general officers to France for a visit to the front, so that they will come back to their training camps with the actual knowledge of the conditions of present methods of warfare. After they have been to France, they are to call on me individually to report, and I hope in that way to have opportunity to make personal estimate of their vigour and alertness both of mind and body. In the meantime, you of course will see them all while they are in France, and I would be grateful if you would let me have an estimate of the impressions they make on you while they are actually at the scene of war and studying the conditions at the front." In response General Pershing gave these warnings: "A division commander must get down into the trenches with his men, and is at all times subject to severe hardships. . . . I strongly recommend that no general officers who are in any way physically inactive or unsound be sent here to command units. I deem it my duty to you and to the President to give you my very best judgment in such matters, regardless of individuals."

There is no question of the fact that this last became the basis of selection, and both the American Commander-in-Chief and the Secretary of War worked together to secure officers who would be able to stand the severe strain of the approaching military operations, "regardless of individuals." It was a hard test, and many able officers were reported physically unfit for these arduous duties. These officers were used in other fields of service, and in many cases there were disappointments for officers who were eager for service in the field. But it is evident that General Pershing was always supported by Secretary Baker, and both were so united, in their desire for the greatest efficiency of our American Expeditionary Forces, that they were carried above all ideas of individual favoritism.

After reviewing the correspondence between the Secretary of War and General Pershing, it is clear beyond doubt that this was one case in the conduct of an army in the field where the general was not subject to the dictation of the war minister, and neither appointments nor removals were made through personal or political influence.

Naturally, there were officers who thought they had cause for complaint, but it is only just to recognize that the American Commander-in-Chief had set an exactingly high standard in his zeal for obtaining the best possible American Army, and in his foresight of the arduous service which must be the task of that army. That standard was made the test for service on the battlefield—and it was only through physical failure to meet its requirements that details for active service were denied. When Marshal Joffre and General Bridges were in this country, both had sounded the same note of warning to Secretary Baker, that the hardships of trench warfare were beyond the strength of men past middle life or having physical disabilities. Many general officers, indeed most of the list of major generals of the Regular Army, as that list stood at the outbreak of the war, were obviously not qualified to meet this exacting standard of fitness for active service as commanders of divisions on the battle front. It was nothing derogatory to their ability and usefulness that they should not be fit to go through the special hardships of field duty in the difficult terrain of France. In order to prevent cases of breakdown, it was a wise policy to set this rigorous physical standard for this service, and to allow the command of divisions on the Western Front to be won by younger men who demonstrated their aptitude for that kind of warfare and their physical endurance in the field.

The older general officers rendered invaluable service in other spheres, as for instance, the fine and effective organization of chemical offensive and defensive warfare by General Sibert after his return from Europe. For the most part, these older officers rendered their service in the training camps where all their experience was available and their large administrative talents were specially needed. The case of General Leonard Wood was typical, and it should be mentioned in order to correct any wrong impression left by the agitation consequent upon his not being sent to France with the division he trained. For many years General Wood suffered from a physical disability which was the result of a serious accident in Cuba. He had been twice operated on for a tumor on his brain, but the effects of the injury remained and ultimately caused his death in 1927. General Wood's energy and courage were such that he never yielded to the disability, and he was in fact given a test overseas in a tour of actual operations of the war in progress. However, the report in France as to his physical condition showed that he would not be able to stand the hardships of division command on the Western Front, and this had precluded his being assigned to field service.

"In this regard, of course, he shared the fate of General J. Franklin Bell and General Thomas H. Barry, both men of brilliant records in field and camp. All three were, of course, very eager for assignment to field service. No one of the three, however, had such assured robustness of health as to justify a detail under the rules laid down. All three of these older generals rendered fine service in the training camps and in the important task of cementing the country around its young soldiers in the difficult days of their initiation into army life."[1] General Wood's energetic conduct and notable services, from the start of the training camp activities, will always deserve the gratitude of his countrymen.

By following out these far seeing policies, the preparations were being made in France for the future great American Army, for its bases, its transportation, its depots of supply, its training in open warfare, its staff organization, and its rigidly selected officers for commands in the field. All this was being carried forward with high faith in that great military force, a faith untouched by the scepticism of all Europe, and not to be swerved from its purpose by the constant efforts to divert our energies into other courses. This faith was destined to emerge triumphant in the achievement of the American military reinforcement at the crisis of the World War, and by no other means could the success of our effort have been attained. Consequently, these preparations, which were being made in France long before the world thought there was any prospect of an American Army, must be considered as foundations of our military structure overseas.

---

[1]Newton D. Baker.

CHAPTER XXII

IN WASHINGTON, there had been a corresponding response to the warnings and constantly increasing estimates from overseas, which were dictating the great proportions of our future American Army in France. It was an essential of the foundations which were being prepared in France, that, in the United States, the whole War Department was being reorganized to cope with the problems of this future great army. The administrative staff organizations which must be provided were beyond all former ideas. It was not only the multiplication of all numbers by twenty, which, in itself, meant multiplied difficulties, but it was also a question of the many new problems which sprang from the unprecedented condition that the operations of this American Army were to be three thousand miles away, and on the other side of the broad Atlantic Ocean.

"Based on the American Continent" implied difficulties such as had never beset a general staff. But this task had been set for us by the American information from France, and all energies were concentrated upon this one great object. There was the fixed goal for the United States, and, at home as well as abroad, nothing was allowed to interfere with our struggle to attain that end. The good effect of this early committal of all our energies to that one aim cannot be exaggerated. In this respect it ended all divided counsels, and it would be hard to find another case in history where the war ministry and the military command were so unitedly committed to one plan of war, and so united against any outside attempts to change that plan of war. All the influence that was exerted abroad was powerless to impair this concentration, and nothing in this country was allowed to divert our efforts into any other channels. Of course, in a sense, this plan was dictated by the trend of the World War. But, on the other hand, our American military information had rightly interpreted that trend, and we had adhered to this interpretation—in spite of many attempts to make us change.

As was proved by the event, there was a real merit in this unchanging purpose, which guided us, abroad and at home, and this should be counted as a strong factor in providing our military reinforcement for the Entente Allies. If there had been any yielding, in changes of plan, we could not have achieved our end.

It was characteristic of this united purpose that the Secretary of War should consult the American Commander-in-Chief, in France, as to the selection of the Chief of Staff, who was to serve in the War Department in Washington. General Scott, who had rendered valuable service as Chief of Staff, was to retire in the fall of 1917, and General Bliss was to succeed him for the short time which would remain before General Bliss himself reached the age of retirement. This situation meant that there must be a new Chief of Staff in charge at the time the American Expeditionary Forces would grow into the form of an army. Secretary Baker had written to

General Pershing (September 10, 1917) in this regard: "It seems to me that coöperation in Washington is of an importance impossible to overestimate, and that we can assure it best by having a young, aggressive man, who will realize from actual observation and participation your difficulties, and be able to understand from the least hint just what it is necessary for us to do to be of the maximum support to you."

The choice was made of Major General Peyton C. March, who had been given a turn of duty in France which made him "familiar with the whole situation abroad, and whose experience in the War Department had been such that there would be no loss of time on his part in understanding the intricacies of bureau operation here."[1] The wisdom of this choice was proved by the energetic and efficient administration of General March, as Chief of Staff throughout the exacting period of the building up of the American Expeditionary Forces and their successful operations at the crisis of the war.

The increase of the various departments of staff organizations demanded by the situation leapt beyond all estimates. One set of figures will illustrate this, and will show how the United States Army was changed beyond recognition. In October, 1918, the Quartermaster Corps had grown to 11,256 commissioned officers, 200,354 enlisted men, and 84,435 civilian employees—a much greater total than had been in the whole United States Army in June, 1917. This was typical also of the expansion of its tasks. Some idea of these last can be gained from the list of the divisions of the Quartermaster Corps in contrast with the decentralized procurements in the

---

[1]Letter of Secretary Baker to General Pershing, September 10, 1917.

small depots of the old Army: Clothing and Equipage Division, Fuel and Forage Division, Hardware and Metals Division, Remount Division, Subsistence Division, Vehicles and Harness Division, Motor Divisions (later the Motor Transport Corps.)

It was the same story in the Ordnance Department, Signal Corps, Engineer Corps, Surgeon General's Office, and in the great Division of Purchase, Storage, and Traffic. All were building up the organizations and securing the increased personnel to handle the enormous work which was being thrust upon them. As Secretary Baker expressed it, "Office forces doubled and trebled in weeks and days. The work was done because of the energy and skill of the Army officers on duty and because of the fine quality of the men who offered their services for carrying forward the task. Technical, professional, and business men came to Washington by the hundreds, ready to make any sacrifice of salary or prestige, that the end might be achieved."[1]

The intelligence and adaptability of these Americans from civilian life, who were attached to the different departments of the Army, not only helped in the administrative tasks in this country, but their knowledge of European conditions stimulated the response to the demands from overseas. With such men added to the Army, and with the civilians of the bodies of the Council of National Defense actually associated with the representatives of the departments of the Army and Navy, the expansion of these departments of the Services went on with the right auspices. The Regular officers of the two Services rose to the occasion. As Secretary Baker

[1]Report of the Secretary of War, 1918.

wrote, "There the representatives of the Army, Navy, and other departments met with representatives of the manufacturers and settled the knotty questions as they rose."

The first great problems of supplies which confronted the War Department had arisen from the sudden need of providing for the new great army in the United States, as it was sent into training camps all over the country. This situation was met by the adoption of a zone system. The whole country was divided into zones, each with a great central depot for the supply of the camps within its boundary. Every effort was made to secure the supplies for each zone within its own boundaries. This materially reduced the need of transporting supplies. Whenever an increase of stocks was necessary in any zone, beyond the possibilities of procurement in that zone, immediate transfers from other depots were made, or direct shipments were made by contractors to that zone. By this system it was made possible to equip the new troops promptly, as they came into service, and to maintain them in the camps and cantonments. In this task the zealous coöperation of the Food and Fuel Administrations was a great and indispensable assistance to the War Department.

As soon as the American troops began to move from the training camps, to go overseas, these problems of supply becamse vastly more complicated.

In addition to equipping and maintaining the troops in the training camps, there were new demands as follows:

1. To maintain reserves at depots in the United States sufficient to provide a steady flow of supplies to points of embarkation to meet overseas requirements.

2. To build up at ports of embarkation reserves sufficient to insure prompt shipment of articles requisitioned by General Pershing.

3. To maintain at these ports stocks of equipment and clothing, in order to insure new equipment for embarking soldiers, to prevent waste of cargo space by sending troops with the articles of equipment and clothing which would soon demand replacement.

4. To maintain overseas supplies at ports of debarktion, at bases and intermediate depots, and at advanced stations, in order to provision and equip the operating troops and troops behind the lines.

Extensive preparations were also made in advance by the Army Embarkation Service (a separate section of the General Staff created August 4, 1917) for handling the shipments of troops and supplies to be sent overseas. Two principal ports of embarkation were established, one at New York with headquarters at Hoboken, N. J., and the other at Newport News, Va. In this case, again, the preparations were made on a scale adequate for the great needs of the future.

At New York, the Hoboken piers of the North German Lloyd and Hamburg-American Lines were taken over at once, and, later on, other piers at Hoboken and on the North River front, as will be narrated. In order to take care of the expected troop movement through New York, two camps of embarkation were established in the fall of 1917, Camp Merritt, at Tenafly, N. J., and Camp Upton, on Long Island. Each of these camps had a capacity of 40,000. Space for 20,000 more was later provided at Camp Upton. For Newport News, terminal and storage facilities were acquired at Lambert's Point, near Norfolk, at Pig Point, Va., and at Morrison, Va. In addition there were established, later, an animal embarkation depot, Camp Stuart (a rest camp), and Camp Hill, for organizing labor units for overseas.

All of these preparations were going on in our country at the time when there was no belief abroad in the possibility of a large American Army on the battlefield of Europe. And these preparations in the United States, which were to insure the presence of that army, were not understood in Europe.

CHAPTER XXIII

THE SITUATION AT THE BEGINNING OF 1918

AT THE beginning of the fateful year, 1918, the German Imperial Government was confident of winning the war. It was true that the campaign of unrestricted U-boat warfare had not accomplished the decisive results expected by the German leaders. But the military events of 1917 had brought the Central Powers into a new military situation, so favorable that the Germans were preparing the most formidable assault of the World War, in full belief in its power to sweep through the Western Front to a victory that must end the war. The elimination of Russia as a military factor had allowed Germany to concentrate all her forces against France, with the assurance that the Central Powers were not in danger elsewhere.

A survey of this military situation will show at once the domination of Germany over all military factors in Europe at the beginning of 1918. This situation had been wrought by the inexorable grinding processes of the World War, which had consumed the resources of nations as never before in history. In all former wars results had been measured by victories and gains of territory. In the World War all such results had been dwarfed by the toll of lives and the consumption of material resources. The course of the war had made this fearful drain more severe for the Entente Allies. After the first defeat in 1914 of the German General Staff's long premeditated "dry-land" plan to win the war by one military coup, the Entente Allies had the advantage. But the unsuccessful strategy of the Entente Allies had thrown away this advantage, mainly because they had failed to dominate the Baltic and Dardanelles, and had thus allowed the Central Powers to concentrate against an isolated Russia. France and Great Britain had been unable to make any military assaults strong enough to divert this pressure from Russia, as the fighting on the Western Front had only consumed men and material as fast as France and Great Britain poured their resources into the trenches, without dislodging the Germans. As a result, the losses of Russia in men and resources had been beyond anything the nation could endure, and the whole national structure had collapsed.

At the beginning of 1918 all was ended for Russia, so far as concerned any participation in the World War. The ruling Bolsheviki had agreed to an armistice in December, 1917, and this was to develop into separate peace treaties enforced upon the Ukraine and Russia early in 1918. Thus the mighty power of Russia had been shorn away from the Entente Allies. Of course, this was the greatest victory for the Central Powers in the World War. But even this was not the total of the unfavorable situation for the Entente Allies. The serious Italian reverses of the fall of 1917 had at one blow changed Italy from an allied force pressing upon Austria-Hungary to the position of an ally in distress. Instead of being a power in the war, on the offensive against the Central Powers, Italy herself needed help from the Entente Allies, and, in consequence, it had become established as a definite condition in the military situation that the Entente Allies could not have any hope of an Italian offensive in the early months of 1918.

Over all the far flung fields of battle, outside of the Western Front, it was the same story. The Central Powers had nothing to fear that would interfere with their great offensive. In the southeast, Rumania, without the support of Russia, was doomed to downfall.[1] The Allied Army at Salonica was held in check. The Turks had accomplished all the service the Central Powers required from them by holding the Dardanelles and keeping Russia shut off from the other Entente Allies. After the downfall of Russia, the work of the Turks was done, so far as concerned the German Imperial Government, and, to all intents and purposes, they were outside the German sphere of operations. Left to themselves they had become demoralized, and General Allenby's British expedition had little difficulty in capturing Jerusalem (December 7, 1917). But nothing in these outlying regions threatened to interfere in the least with the success of the projected German assault on the Western Front. The reader must realize that the ensuing decisive campaign of the World War must be fought out on the actual battlefield of the Western Front. All else had faded into insignificance.[2]

---

[1] "As a result, the Treaty of Bucharest was signed on May 7th. The terms of the treaty were of extreme severity."—British War Cabinet Report, 1918.

[2] "But it never must be forgotten that it was on the Western Front, and in the magnificent resistance there offered to the last violent onset, that victory was secured. Successes on other Fronts would not have availed, save after long years of protracted and costly sacrifice, if the Western line had been broken."—British War Cabinet Report, 1918.

Of this general military situation there can no longer be the slightest question, and the main interest in the study of the ensuing history of the World War must be concentrated upon the factors which made up the strengths of the two opposing forces in the last desperate fight to a finish.

In the first place, it should be stated that by their ability to move troops from the Eastern Front to France, the Germans had established an actual superiority in forces. In respect to numbers they were at a greater advantage than even in their great assault of 1914. Ludendorff has emphasized this fact by stating: "Numerically we had never been so strong in comparison with our enemies."

But there were also other especial reasons for the military superiority of the Germans in their impending attacks on their chosen battlefield of 1918. One outstanding reason was the weakness of the Allied armies on the Western Front, in consequence of the drain of losses in preceding years. The year 1917 had been notably costly in losses. This can be baldly stated as follows. The unsuccessful French offensive had consumed the remnant of the French power to undertake any offensive operation on a large scale. From this time on it was an arduous task to keep the French ranks anywhere near fighting strength. For the British it was the same situation, as 1917 had been a year of heavy British losses, and, when the Battle of Flanders dwindled to its ineffective end in the mud of the late fall, the casualties had reached a total which forbade any hope of increased British armies for the new year. Not only this, but Great Britain was also facing a difficult problem to keep her armies even on a fighting basis for 1918. Consequently, there was no chance of a French or British offensive early in 1918, and the Germans possessed the great advantage of being able to make their plan against Allied armies which must act on the defensive. This advantage meant that the German leaders would be able to choose their points of attack without being in danger of counter attacks.

In addition, the Germans possessed "an element of tactical surprise which had been, generally speaking, lacking in the case of previous offensives on the Western Front."[1] This was a carefully rehearsed system of disposing German divisions at graduated distances, so that they would converge upon the objective in successive instalments. It was a practical method of returning to the first principle of a concentration of superior numbers against the point of attack, and it was especially dangerous against the French and British, who looked for nothing beyond the tactics which they themselves had been using in what they had grown to regard as "stabilized" trench warfare. As the event proved, this preconceived idea of the limitations of trench warfare left the Allied armies on the Western Front unprepared for defense against the new German system of attack.[2] The military leaders of the Entente Allies were taking it for granted that military attacks would follow the fashions established by themselves on the Western Front, and that the established sys-

---

[1] British War Cabinet Report, 1918.

[2] "By this means the enemy was, during the course of the Spring and early Summer, able to attain a far greater degree of success than had been previously achieved by any army on the Western Front since the commencement of trench warfare."—British War Cabinet Report, 1918.

tems of defense would be adequate. This was a costly error.

These conditions had unquestionably established a great military advantage for the Germans at the time, and this was beyond the power of the existing Allied forces to remedy.[1] Any true analysis of the situation leads to the unavoidable conclusion that a strong reinforcement of fighting troops was necessary, and would be the only factor that could turn the balance on the Western Front. But the Entente Allies themselves were too depleted in manpower to provide this reinforcement. Only the United States could furnish the additional element of military force necessary to overcome this established German superiority. Thus the great objective of the United States in the World War, which has been emphasized, was to take definite shape in 1918.

With the battlefield of Europe only in mind, and with European factors the only elements that the German leaders would admit in their calculations, the German Imperial Government did not imagine the possibility of defeat. The Hindenburg-Ludendorff régime had won complete control of the affairs of the Central Powers. But Ludendorff had gone over Hindenburg's head and become the military dictator of Germany. Ludendorff's was the guiding will[2] that determined the strategy of 1918, and the German people

---

[1] "When on March 21, 1918, the German army on the Western Front began its series of offensives, it was by far the most formidable force the world has ever seen."—General Pershing, Report.

[2] "The last war period Germany was controlled by one will only and that was Ludendorff's. His thoughts were centred on fighting, his soul on victory."—Czernin, In the World War.

were again confident of the outcome of his plans.[1] Their leaders were positive in their conviction that the preparations of the United States could not possibly result in the actual presence of an American Army on the battlefield.[2] In this respect, the statement of Hindenburg has left no question as to German opinion of the United States: "Would she appear in time to snatch the victor's laurels from our brows. That, and that only was the decisive question! I believed I could answer it in the negative."[3] It was thus frankly a "race," as it has often been called, but one in which the German leaders did not think there was a chance for America to win.

[1] "But the Germans were persuaded that after leaving the Eastern Front they would throw themselves on to the Western Front and that the war would end before the Americans had time to come in. Their reckoning was at fault, as we all know to-day."—Czernin, *In the World War*.

[2] "Why this unexpected defeat following performances so grand? Because a military commander, intoxicated with isolated success, flushed with the omnipotence of Cæsar, twice failed to conceive a proper estimate of America as a factor."—Maximilian Harden.

[3] *Out of My Life*.

CHAPTER XXIV

THE PROBLEM OF TRANSPORTATION

AT THE beginning of 1918, the matter of transportation overseas, for troops and material, had become the main difficulty in our "race" with the German Imperial Government. In fact, with the whole question of the success of the American effort depending upon transportation, General Pershing's request for "a complete readjustment of transportation" summed up the most urgent need in the situation. For this situation was so far from satisfactory that it must be corrected. Otherwise we would fail to provide the American reinforcement.

At that time transportation for troops stood on a better basis than transportation for material. The great fleet of seized German passenger ships had come into full operation. Added to these were American troopships and acquired foreign steamships. The Entente Allies had not yet waked to the fact that transportation of American troops would be the best possible use for Allied shipping. That was to come later. But there had already been a beginning of the additional service of British troopships, which was destined to become so important a part of the great movement of American troops in 1918.

The beginning of this additional service of British

troopships came in November, 1917, when the Chief of
the Army Embarkation Service asked the British Ministry of Shipping to assign to us the White Star liner
Olympic, 46,359 tons gross. This fine steamship, at the
time, was laid up in a British port. Under an agreement
that the American Government would assume all risks,
and that the *Olympic* was to be operated by her owners
on this condition, the British Admiralty assigned this
ship for transportation of American troops. The *Olympic*
made her first trip with American troops in December,
1917. In January, 1918, the *Aquitania*, 45,647 tons gross
and *Mauretania*, 30,704 tons gross, both of which had
also been laid up in port, were added as transports for
American troops on the same conditions. These three
British ships at once added a monthly carrying capacity
of 15,000 troops, and this was the start of British transportation of American troops on a large scale to meet
the emergency of 1918. And here the distinction was
established, between the British steamships transporting American troops overseas and the American transports, which continued throughout the war. As has been
explained, the American transports were operated by
the United States Navy. But the British troopships
were operated by their owners, and their relation to the
Army Embarkation Service was that of chartered ships
employed to transport overseas what was consigned to
them. On the seas they were, for the most part, under
the British convoy system, and the bulk of the American
troops they transported overseas were landed in Great
Britain, whereas the American troopships of the Cruiser
and Transport Force landed troops at the base ports in
France.

The great training camps in the United States were turning out their products of American soldiers in greater numbers, and, in the first months of 1918, monthly transportation of American troops overseas increased to the following totals: January, 47,853; February, 49,110; March, 84,882. These figures will show that, before the crisis had been revealed, there had been great strides in our preparations. It should also be stated that, at this time, a direct assurance of the future great numbers of American troops had been put on record at a conference with British representatives. On February 4, 1918, General Pershing still had been obliged to report: "As to the question of obtaining extra shipping from the British, it does not look favorable from this end of the line, but I hope we may increase our tonnage by every possible means." It was in that same month that the Army Embarkation Service gave assurances that American troops were ready beyond all European expectations. At this conference in February, 1918, the British representatives had not been prepared to believe in the great numbers of American troops that would be ready to go overseas. General Hines had reassured them by the promise: "We will load every ship you put in our ports." To fulfil this promise, General Hines and General Shanks at once made plans to increase the port facilities of New York. By the enlargement of accommodations at Camp Upton and Camp Mills, the Army Embarkation Service provided additional space, and this enabled the Port of New York to reach its high records in the rush of troops overseas at the emergency of 1918.

By these means the problem of transportation of

American troops was well on its way to solution before the crisis. But the question of cargo carriers was a much more difficult and complicated problem, and so remained throughout the war. With every exertion that was made, we were barely able to stagger through to the end. Transportation of troops was a matter that loomed large in the public eye, but transportation of supplies, which meant the life and being of these troops, did not make the same appeal. But, as Admiral Gleaves has stated, "In making our Army in France effective, special mention should be made of the Naval Overseas Transportation Service. Little could have been accomplished without these unromantic, rusty, slow plodding tramps, transporting food, munitions and supplies."[1]

It would be hard to exaggerate any description of the difficulties experienced in collecting enough cargo carriers for the needs of the United States. These difficulties were encountered abroad and at home, and they lasted throughout the war. After the crisis of the first onslaught, in the Spring of 1918, the Entente Allies could see that everything must be done to expedite the transportation of American troops to France. But, even then, the needs of America for cargo ships did not stand out in the same proportion, in comparison with the other calls upon Allied shipping. Yet cargo shipping was equally important, as the supplies of the American Army in France must come over the seas. The necessities of the case were shown by the totals of shipments of cargoes eventually needed to support the American Expeditionary Forces in France. In the summer of 1917

---

[1] *A History of the Transport Service.*

these were 16,000 tons in a month. In the fall of 1918 they were 700,000 tons in a month.

But there were also many difficulties at home in securing cargo carriers for the material and supplies for the American Expeditionary Forces. In the United States the demands of the Embarkation Service for cargo carriers leapt so rapidly beyond all early ideas that they soon came into conflict with the other requirements of the country. That there should be conflicting demands was natural, with the many Government agencies hard at work to develop all the resources of the nation. These activities necessarily implied a great drain upon shipping, and there was a congested situation as to cargo carriers, in consequence of the confusion among so many claimants.

In 1917, the United States Shipping Board was the controlling body, which allotted shipping among these various claimants. The ships at the disposal of the Shipping Board were not only the American cargo carriers, but also all cargo carriers acquired from foreign owners. It will be readily apparent that there must be heavy demands upon all this shipping from the War Industries Board, the Food Administration, the Fuel Administration, and from the different essential industries of the country. The result was that, in 1917, the practical effect of this system had been to permit each of these activities to acquire a definite fleet of cargo carriers for its own particular use. And this method, of dividing the cargo carriers into separate groups, had not produced the best results for getting the maximum use out of the whole total of shipping.

A great deal of the confusion and delay in 1917 had

come from this cause, and, with the increased demands of the beginning of 1918, the situation was going from bad to worse. The remedy found for this state of affairs was an evolution from one of the typical Government activities which have been described—without any definite powers at first, but suddenly developing into a practical central control. At the call of the Government, there had been regular meetings in Washington to discuss the shipping situation.[1] At these meetings the Administration officials conferred with eminent American shipping men, who acted as voluntary advisers to the Government. One of these advisers, P. A. S. Franklin, president of the International Mercantile Marine, was consulted by the Secertary of War as to the bad situation in regard to shipping. Mr. Franklin submitted a plan to put the whole ocean marine in one pool under the control of one management.

This plan was at once adopted by the Secretary of War (February 7, 1918), and by resolution of the United States Shipping Board, February 11, 1918, the Shipping Control Committee was constituted. The membership of this new body was: P. A. S. Franklin, Chairman; Sir Connop Guthrie, representative of the British Ministry of Shipping; H. H. Raymond. The representation of the British Ministry of Shipping was important, because the main purpose of the Shipping Control Committee was not local, but "to centralize control of shipping, to unify the shipping resources of the Allied nations and of the United States, and to make existing shipping as liquid as possible."[2]

[1]Shipping Committee, Council of National Defense.
[2]Historical Branch, General Staff, U. S. A.

Mr. Franklin, its head, at once built up its organization, and in the same month of February, 1918, it was at work in quarters in New York, which were in the former office building of the Hamburg-American Line—another instance of the irony of events in the World War. By this means a central control of shipping was effectively established. There were no longer different fleets for the different interests. All ships were allotted to their different tasks, as if the whole mass of shipping were one great ocean line. Each allotment was made a matter of tonnage of freight, with local supervision of loading and turnarounds of the ships. In this way the maximum use of the available shipping was obtained, and the results in efficiency were equivalent to a large increase in tonnage of cargo carriers. "Through the centralized control of shipping, the employment of the 'marine skip-stop system,' which involved direct routing, unification of cargoes, full loading, and reduction of time in port, and the use of progress charts and tabulations of vessel movements, the committee was able to double the efficiency of the available shipping."[1]

This was the turning of the lane. It must not be supposed that any magic cure was found for our difficulties. On the contrary, the quest for cargo carriers for the ever expanding volume of supplies and material to maintain the American Expeditionary Forces in France was a never ending problem. But this fortunate change to a central control of all shipping came just in time to improve the situation, at the very stage when the greatest demands were to be made upon the United States.

In the spring of 1918, the Dutch shipping lying in

[1] Historical Branch, General Staff, U. S. A.

United States ports was acquired by exercising the right of angaria—seizure justified in the act by extreme necessity. Of the 500,000 tons thus taken over the Army gained 300,000 tons, allotted by the Shipping Control Committee. "The chartering of Scandinavian and Japanese tonnage during 1918, which relieved the whole tonnage position of our country, also was reflected in the growth of the Army fleet. The most ample credit must, however, be given the War Trade Board, which by drastic restriction of non-essential imports made possible the release of large amounts of shipping from the import trades."[1] This body had been created by Executive order, pursuant to the act of October 6, 1917, to prevent trading with the enemy.[2] In addition to this function, the War Trade Board thus did valuable work in conserving shipping, especially for the constantly growing needs of the War Department.

Another step forward was taken, as to the cargo carriers, early in 1918. As has been stated, it had become evident that manning and operating these ships lay in the province of the United States Navy. Through the last months of 1917 more and more cargo carriers were thus manned and operated by the Navy. At the end of the year, these had increased to such great numbers that on January 7, 1918, a special Branch of the Office of Naval Operations, U.S.N., was created, called the Naval Overseas Transportation Service, with the sole duty of operating the Government cargo carriers. This was

---

[1]Report of the Secretary of War, 1918.

[2]Chairman Vance C. McCormick, with members representing the Departments of State, Treasury, Agriculture, Commerce, the Shipping Board, and the Food Administration.

usually known as the N.O.T.S., and it grew into the largest merchantman fleet ever assembled under one management. Commander Charles Belknap, U.S.N., was Director of the N.O.T.S. in the Office of Naval Operations.

The wisdom of having this service of cargo carriers operated by our Navy, and the special advantage possessed by the United States Navy in its ability to secure crews by the appeal to patriotism for enlistment in the Navy, will be easily understood, for the difficulty experienced in obtaining civilian crews had been very great. The Navy was also best able to gather intelligent men for officers in the Naval Reserve Force, to train them quickly for their duties, and to give them special practice with experienced officers in the novel requirements of service with convoys. These Government cargo carriers were destined to be operated under the convoy system, as a matter of course. And for this arduous service, so different from anything else on the seas, the Navy, by intensive training for this particular purpose, produced with uncanny quickness a personnel of uncanny skill in convoy seamanship. The test of their efficiency was shown by the small losses in that dangerous service, which must perforce make use of the slow ships, as the ships of speed were taken for troopships. "Of 450 vessels in the N.O.T.S. fleet, only eighteen were lost—four per cent. of the total; and of the eighteen, only eight fell victims to German mines and submarines. Four went down after collisions at sea, and the rest were accounted for by fire or by stranding."[1]

For these cargo convoys, Hampton Roads was made

[1]Crowell and Wilson, *The Road to France.*

the main port of departure from the United States. It
had many natural advantages in position. It was near
the coal fields. The oil tankers from the south (Tampico)
put in there, and great reservoirs of oil were established
there. It was also nearer the cotton supply, and it had
access to the great resources of the Middle West. This
choice of Hampton Roads not only avoided train and
shipping congestion, but it also diminished the risk of
"too many eggs in one basket."

For these ships of the great fleet of cargo carriers there
were dangers that the public has not estimated, and for
their crews there were risks that had never been encountered on the seas in former wars. It was natural that the
public should not appreciate these dangers, because
there actually was almost no fighting on the seas, in the
old-fashioned sense of the word—no engagements between regular naval forces that would attract attention.
In this new warfare, there were all kinds of fights and
adventures, in the course of the U-boat campaign, for
the ships that were sought as prey, for the U-boats
themselves, and for the anti-submarine forces. But of
set actions between naval forces there was almost no
trace left in the war. Occasionally there would be a clash
of light craft, but the rival battle fleets were never near
a general action in 1917.

The reason for this lay in the changed naval strategy
of the Germans. The British Grand Fleet was retained
for its same mission of defending the North Sea area,
and was prepared to fight the German Battle Fleet, "if
it came out." But, from the time of the German decision
for unrestricted U-boat warfare, the German Battle
Fleet remained devoted to its changed mission of for-

warding the attacks of the German U-boats. Its task continued to be that of clearing the passages beyond the German naval bases for the U-boats. In this task the German Battle Fleet was, in general, successful, but this mission restricted its area of operations to these waters around the German naval bases. Consequently, with the German High Sea Fleet operating on one side of the North Sea, and with the British Grand Fleet defending the other side, there was not much chance of an action of fleets.

Aside from operations in the Baltic, the German Battle Fleet only made in 1917 what Admiral Scheer called "test-trips," to feel out the British obstructions beyond the German bases, and these were a valuable part of the new mission of the German Battle Fleet for forwarding the U-boat campaign. "Every test-trip group comprised minelayers and sweepers with their tackle for finding mines; behind them went torpedo-boats with U-boat 'kites' with which to locate nets; these were followed by barrier-breakers, and light cruisers with seaplanes for scouting. Heavy warships protected the test-trip groups on routes that were known to be free of mines."[1]

The British were making great efforts to strew mines in the egresses from the German bases, and British minelayers were constantly kept at work in these areas. But these obstructions could not be expected to prove as effective as if they had been protected by armed naval forces. In February, 1918, preparations had been begun for the great Northern Barrage of mines, extending from Norwegian waters to the Orkney Islands, which had

[1]Admiral Scheer, *Germany's High Sea Fleet.*

been devised in the United States, but this would not be effective before the fall of 1918.

The bases and areas of patrol of the British Battle Fleet lay to the north, and this British main naval force was not a coördinated part of the U-boat struggle, as was the German Battle Fleet. Admiral Jellicoe, the First Sea Lord of the British Admiralty, had asked that a division of battleships of the United States Navy should be sent to reinforce the British Grand Fleet, and also that these should be coal-burning owing to the great scarcity of oil in Great Britain. Accordingly, under the command of Rear Admiral Hugh Rodman, the following American battleships joined the Grand Fleet in December, 1917: *New York* (flagship), *Texas, Wyoming,* *Arkansas.* Later were sent *Florida* and *Delaware.* These American battleships became a division of the Grand Fleet under the command of Admiral Beatty, and from that time took part in its routine of duty.

But, as will be evident from the foregoing, 1917 was a drab year for the main naval forces. It was the reverse of this for the other elements of naval forces and shipping which were on the seas. Although the World War had not produced the naval actions of old, it had brought back the old conditions when all on the seas were obliged to scheme and fight for their ships and their lives. The great currents of the war had swept all seafaring shipping into the struggle, and naval warfare was no longer a question of regular naval forces. Never, in all the history of pirates and predatory nations, had captains and crews been compelled to cope with such great dangers—and the vast multiplication of shipping used for war purposes had brought down to the sea great numbers of men to whom seafaring was a new adventure.

This was especially true of the United States, for the greatest expansion of forces must come from our nation, and this constant increase of our fleets for transportation meant that our personnel in the United States Navy was growing to over 500,000 men. In addition to the demands of the American Expeditionary Forces, there was the increasing share of the United States in the antisubmarine warfare. Our Queenstown anti-submarine forces remained under the British Naval Command, as did the other American naval units with the British Battle Fleet. But in July, 1917, the decision was made to establish an American naval base at Gibraltar, and in August began a gathering of American light forces which performed valuable service at this important centre of convoys. The establishment of an American naval base at the Azores soon followed.

As has been stated, the American naval forces in the Brest area remained an independent American command. This was natural because this area had been given over to the bases for American troops, supplies, and material. For this reason, it was apparent that here was one case where putting American naval units under a foreign command would not have produced the best coördination, as their services were to be devoted mainly to safeguarding the arrival of the American Expeditionary Forces, their supplies, and material. This could best be accomplished under the control of the United States Navy, and Admiral Wilson's command became a necessary element in this great joint operation of the United States Army and United States Navy.

An important factor in the future success of the American Expeditionary Forces was another independent American fleet, of which little has been known.It was the American Cross-Channel Fleet, which was being created at this time for carrying cargoes and men from Great Britain to France. This was a very necessary part of our transportation system, and it grew to over 300,000 dead weight tons by the end of the war. All sorts of small steamships were utilized, and it is notable that, with chartered Swedish and Norwegian shipping, were used numbers of American steamships from the Great Lakes. These were known as Lake boats, for their names were *Lake Arthur*, etc. The association of these craft, from our great inland waters, with craft from Denmark and Norway in the waters of the English Channel, was an instance of the unexpected bunkmates brought together by the demands of the World War. The most notable service of the Cross-Channel Fleet, a service which was indeed indispensable, was bringing Welsh coal to the American bases. The ships of this fleet were subject to constant U-boat attack, and their hazardous service deserves great praise.

The foregoing gives a picture of the strenuous situation on the seas. It had seemed to the world that the extremes of effort and activity were being called forth at the end of the year 1917. But, in fact, the new year of 1918 was destined to bring the summons for still greater exertions, to cope with the new situation which would change the whole aspect of the World War.

CHAPTER XXV

THE DEVELOPMENT OF AMERICAN INDUSTRIAL FORCES

THESE great military preparations in the United States and in France, which were destined to bear fruit in the unexpected strength of the American Expeditionary Forces on the Western Front, and these great naval preparations, which made possible the presence of the American troops on the battlefield, implied in themselves correspondingly great developments of American industrial forces. Our effort must be threefold, military, naval, and industrial. If any one of the three factors had been found wanting, the whole American effort must have failed. This should be reiterated until it stands clear—the underlying condition of the whole problem.

The ships of the United States Navy, which transported and safeguarded American troops and supplies overseas, were as much in action with the enemy as if they had been present on the firing line. The same thing can be said, even more forcibly, of those who were working in the American industries—for they were producing the power which impelled both the military and naval forces. In fact, the vast armies of American industrial workers were actually to make their presence felt upon the battlefield of Europe.

The beginning of 1918 saw a mobilization of American industries which was strong enough to carry through our task. This had come from developments of the two cardinal principles which were adopted by the Administration in the tentative organizations just before our entering the war. The first of these fundamental elements was the call upon our industrial leaders to take a direct part, and the prompt association of these experts with the Administration. The second element was the instinctive choice of the amplified war powers of the President as the source for authority.

At the time of the crisis, in the spring of 1918, our industries were under various controlling bodies which had more drastic powers than had ever before been delegated in such cases. And yet all had been evolved from the early organizations founded upon these two principles. There had not been new creations. Instead of anything of the kind, the first great chemistry had proved to be right. Its evolution had produced agents of central control founded upon the right basis, as they had sprung from the right elements. There had been no breaking off—no constituting new bodies with the delays involved in organization. Instead of a Ministry of Munitions, there was the War Industries Board. Instead of a Ministry of Shipping, there was the Shipping Control Committee. And, aside from the gain in time by not creating new machinery, these American bodies had the advantages of greater powers and of memberships composed of men whose efficiency had been proved in the organizations from which these bodies had been evolved.

The War Industries Board was a case in point, and was typical of the evolution of control from the different organizations of the Council of National Defense to the final form of drastic authority. The origin and development of this body have been described, and the value of its work, in promptly bringing together the Services and our industries to coördinate production and purchase, cannot be stated too strongly. F. A. Scott, the first Chairman, had been obliged to resign in the fall of 1917, because his health had given way. Daniel Willard, Chairman of the Advisory Committee of the Council of National Defense, acted as Chairman until January 11, 1918. "The board was reorganized March 4, 1918, by the President in a letter which asked Bernard M. Baruch to accept the chairmanship of the board, and at the same time outlined its functions, constitution, and action. . . . According to the President's letter, the functions of the board were to be: (1) creation of facilities and opening of sources of supply; (2) conservation of existing facilities, where necessary, to new uses; (3) conservation of resources and facilities; (4) advice to Government purchasing agencies as to prices; (5) determination of priorities of production and delivery, and of proportions when supplies were insufficient; (6) purchases for allies."[1]

The following paragraph in the President's letter greatly increased the power of the Chairman: "The Board should be constituted as at present and should retain, so far as necessary, and so far as is consistent with the character and purposes of the reorganization, its present advisory agencies; but the ultimate decision of all questions, except the determination of prices, should rest always with the Chairman, the other members acting in a coöperative and advisory capacity."

[1] Historical Branch, General Staff, U. S. A.

The War Industries Board was made a separate Executive Agency on May 28, 1918.

In the same way the United States Railroad Administration was an evolution from the earlier Railroads' War Board of the Council of National Defense. William G. McAdoo remained Director General of this organization throughout the war. "In handling the enormous traffic involved in the movement of troops and supplies, the Railroad Administration accomplished results which would have been impossible under private control. . . . Owing to the elimination of competition and the introduction of more effective operating methods, the congestion which prevailed when the roads were taken over was cleared up and by May 1, 1918, the railroads were functioning normally again."[1] But this wonderful result under Government control would not have been possible, if there had not been the early voluntary organization of the railroad men themselves, and the good work of the Railroads' War Board built up the structure.

The Food Administration and the Fuel Administration were other examples of the drastic authority, derived from the amplified war powers of the President, exercised over wide fields of production. But, as has been explained, these governing powers were efficient because they had been evolutions in the same way.

Under such strong control, our industries were accomplishing wonders at the fateful stage of the spring of 1918. But it is impossible to conceive this state of things, if the right direction had not been given to our energies in the early months of confusion. The Council of National Defense, with its manifold means of reach-

---

[1] Historical Branch, General Staff, U. S. A.

ing the industrial leaders of America, was certainly a providential element in our preparations for war. It was only through its agencies that the Services were enabled to get into touch with our industries. The great plants that were turning out our troops for overseas were the product of those first months, and in those months the trails were blazed that were to lead to the efficiency of 1918.

The Shipping Board had developed important branches of our industries. The Board had been reorganized on July 27, 1917 (Edward M. Hurley, Chairman; Raymond B. Stevens, Vice Chairman; John A. Donald, Bainbridge Colby, Charles P. Page, Commissioners). All continued in office through the war period. Its shipbuilding program was carried out by its offspring, the Emergency Fleet Corporation. Of this Admiral Benson has written: "This corporation engaged in probably the greatest construction task ever attempted by a single organization."[1] In August, 1917, when, by use of the authority of the Executive, all steel ships of over 2,500 tons under construction in American shipyards had been commandeered, this meant that 431 uncompleted hulls of ships had been taken over for construction—and it also meant that the shipyards had been taken over to be operated by the Emergency Fleet Corporation. It is enough to state that "by the close of 1918 nearly 90 per cent. of the construction work on this tonnage had been carried on under the Corporation direction."[2]

Rear Admiral Washington L. Capps had been General

---

[1] *The Merchant Marine.*

[2] Edward N. Hurley, *The Bridge to France.*

Manager, and Rear Admiral F. T. Bowles had been assigned to organize the construction division. Admiral Capps had resigned on December 5, 1917. On December 15, 1917, Charles Piez became General Manager.

The Shipping Board's own building program, of ships for the emergency needs of the war, was of standardized designs so far as this was practicable. "This made possible more speed in construction, and the success of the plan is shown by the fact that 1,308 contract steel vessels, with a total deadweight tonnage of 8,918,295, were delivered. The 384 requisitioned steel vessels made a total of 1,692 steel ships, with a deadweight tonnage of 11,605,561. The keel of the first contract steel vessel was laid on July 29, 1917. The first launching occurred on November 24, 1917, and the first delivery was made on January 5, 1918."[1] There were also contracts for wooden ships. The first launching was December 1, 1917; the first delivery on May 24, 1918. This program comprised 589 ships. In addition, there were 18 composite ships built. But construction of this type proved costly and unsatisfactory, and no more were built. The actual deliveries of contract and requisitioned ships in the months before the crisis were: March, 162,200 tons; April, 162,805 tons; May, 258,941 tons; June, 286,422 tons—a total of 870,368 tons. From this time on, it was a desperate struggle to attempt to catch up with the constantly increasing demands of the Army for transportation of men and supplies.

On April 16, 1918, Charles M. Schwab had been made Director General of the Emergency Fleet Corporation, and the benefit of his experience and ability was notable.

---

[1] Admiral W. S. Benson, *The Merchant Marine.*

There were four great fabricating yards, financed by means of the Executive authority delegated to the Emergency Fleet Corporation. Of these by far the largest was at Hog Island. "These four yards had a total of ninety-four ways, and when in full operation could build more tonnage in a year than ever was produced in any country before 1918."[1] The great shipbuilding projects of the Emergency Fleet Corporation required an army of over 350,000 workers, and recruiting these workers was a notable achievement in coöperation with the administration of the Selective Service Act. General Crowder had appreciated the importance of the shipbuilding program, and his administration showed much ability in apportioning the manpower of the nation to the demands of the services and to the needs of the essential industries.

The Shipping Control Committee had arbitrary powers in allotting this shipping, as well as the other acquired shipping. The ships assigned to the Government were turned over to the Navy Department on a bare-boat charter basis to be operated by the United States Navy. Those operated under the Shipping Board retained their character of merchantmen, and carried civilian crews.

The purely naval construction for the United States Navy was also a call upon the industrial forces of the nation. At the outbreak of war, the construction of the capital ships and large cruisers of the Naval Building Program of 1916 was suspended in order to concentrate the efforts of the steel shipbuilding yards upon destroyers, and of the wood shipbuilding yards upon anti-submarine craft. A program for building 250 des-

[1]Edward N. Hurley, *The Bridge to France.*

troyers had been adopted in May, 1917. This was
made operative in June, and the construction of these
destroyers was pushed to completion as rapidly as possible. This was a wise policy, especially in regard to the
building of destroyers. The use of standard parts in
their construction also increased the speed of production, and before the end of the war the United States
Navy was stronger in destroyers than any other navy.
This was the best possible addition to our Navy, as the
destroyer was the most deadly enemy of the submarine,
and to have a large number of this type in the United
States Navy provided the most effective means for safeguarding the transportation of troops and supplies overseas.

With our industrial forces thus mobilized under the
control of experts to whom had been delegated the plenary powers of the Executive, the United States was approaching the crisis under conditions that would assure
the ability to respond to the great demands that were
to be made of the nation. Throughout all this development of our industries, by means of the authority of
the President delegated to the various agencies which
have been described, Congress had shown a united and
patriotic spirit in passing legislation to confirm and
amplify this use of the Executive power as the fountain
head of authority. The most notable of these acts of
Congress was the Overman Act (approved May 20,
1918). The text is given in full in the Appendix of this
book[1] to show how completely the power of the President was recognized as the source of control over the
task of America. But we must realize that this act and

[1] Page 368.

all others were confirmatory, and endorsements of this use of the Executive power. The first instinctive use of the President's authority was the one right move—and the wartime legislation was the seal of approval, set by the representatives of the American people upon this best means of directing the manifold and novel agencies of our nation's effort in the World War.

With the beginning of the increase of transportation for troops, which has been described, our great plants for producing soldiers were in most successful operation. By this time, the training camps were fully equipped and were accomplishing results that were beyond all expectations. The stream of American troops was pouring from them in an increasing volume. And this movement had already made tests of the various stages of transportation, which proved that they would be able to carry through the movement on a larger scale.

The railroads of the country, under the Government control of the Railroad Administration, had become one great system with the transportation of troops and supplies the main object of its management. The Embarkation Service and the Inland Traffic Service were working together in allotting cars and routing the transportation. As has been stated, the facilities at the ports for receiving and embarking had been developed by the Embarkation Service, until they were prepared to take care of the great increase which was to come in the rush of troops overseas to meet the emergency.

The methods of transportation were very efficient. At the training camp, there would appear large numbers of cars on the miles of railroad sidings which were within the camp. Without warning, thousands of men would be entrained. The trains would disappear, with special way made for them by the Railroad Administration. And, at their destined port of embarkation, they would be swallowed up in the base from which they were to be embarked. Never was there a war with so few troops marching about and taking trains at the regular stations. People throughout the country saw trains loaded with troops passing through, and women waited at the stations to give them refreshments. But the great scope of the troop movement was not realized by the people.

Moreover, the troop movement was not estimated by the German agents in the United States. As to this, Ludendorff himself has left no doubt: "How many Americans had got across by April we did not know." And he has also made an admission which is an involuntary tribute to the skill with which this transportation was conducted: "But the rapidity with which they actually did arrive proved surprising." This is a measure of the failure of the whole elaborated German system of espionage. The fact was, the German agents were fussing about, gathering information according to instructions, but they were missing the one great thing. The very bigness and simplicity put it out of their ken. It was all impossible—according to German ideas!

The German agents also continued to score only failure in their other efforts. As has been said, there was some sabotage, but it never attained the importance of accomplishing results that crippled or seriously delayed our industrial effort. The same was true of the German efforts to stir up discontent. The German spies were very persistent in this way, and made use of different societies and organizations. But there continued to be such a spirit of Americanism throughout our local communities that these agencies were powerless to do much harm. There actually was no need for the stern repressive measures usual in time of war. There were no executions, and very little imprisonment. Most of the cases were handled by sending the obnoxious person to an internment camp.

It was notable that the continued operation of the Selective Service Act made the country even more united, instead of sowing discontent. Shirkers and objectors were so few, in proportion, that they did not count in the great totals. There is no question of the fact that a united and thoroughly aroused American nation faced the crisis of 1918.

CHAPTER XXVI

IN FRANCE BEFORE THE GERMAN OFFENSIVE

IN FRANCE, the first months of 1918 were strenuous for General Pershing in pushing forward his great port and railroad projects for the reception of the future American Army. His personal letters to the Secretary of War, at this stage, gave a picture of the difficulties encountered, and of the dogged resolution to carry these projects through.

As was inevitable after the strain of the war, the French railroads which were included in the American areas of service of supply were "very badly demoralized." After stating these bad conditions in one of his letters to Secretary Baker, General Pershing wrote of his preference for keeping the American railroad men in charge, instead of turning the railroads over to the Engineer Corps of the Army. His judgment in favour of these civilian experts was well founded: "We now have experienced railroad men in charge of the Railway Transportation Department, and to my mind it would be next to fatal to give it over to Engineers to run. None of them has ever had experience in railroading, and all would have to learn the business from the ground up. I should not think of changing back to their management." In the same letter General Pershing wrote of the delays of the French officials in giving over the ports to American control: "I have recently again represented the situation plainly in a strong appeal to M. Clemenceau, and I believe we are in a fair way to get it straightened out. So the situation is improving and promises to still further improve."

These are extracts from a letter of January 17, 1917. In a confidential letter to Secretary Baker, of February 4, 1918, General Pershing was able to write: "Conditions at our ports are improving, and I am pushing the turnaround of transports with all possible speed. The Navy is giving us better service of late in convoying transports as requested. The shortage of railway cars is easing up, and will grow better as the number of repaired cars to be obtained from the Belgians increases." In a letter of February 24, 1918, he wrote of the urgent need of providing for "the prospective early increase in the number of vessels available for transport" and of the shortage of labor and material: "We must now push port work to the utmost. In this connection, the next most vital improvement necessary are the railroads, and I am sending in a condensed cable to-day covering that also. Both ports and railways, however, should go along together."

In March 1-3, 1917, detailed estimates were sent to the Secretary in person, as a "Report on port facilities and necessary measures which must be taken to obtain maximum capacity therefrom," with note, "Unnecessary to have outside board such as suggested to make survey on port situation, as available officers here have made and can make better survey with their fuller knowledge of local conditions."

General Pershing ended his letter to Secretary Baker

as follows: "In order to handle the port situation in France and unload ships with the maximum speed, it is therefore necessary to: (a) Arrange for an increase in train facilities as outlined above, including the repair of as many cars and engines here as possible, and keeping in mind the possibility of establishing a car manufacturing plant in France. (b) Arrange to have the necessary railway facilities constructed. (c) Arrange for the necessary storage facilities at the ports to care for the excess freight which cannot be immediately moved.

"Of these three, the first two must be mainly provided for by getting material and personnel from the United States, who can send cars, car-repairers, and locomotives with the necessary track material to France. The third can and will be arranged for by me in France.

"I have therefore sent you this day a cablegram (copy of which is appended hereto) stating the necessities that exist in men and material in order to meet the situation at the ports.

"While this report sets forth our needs generally speaking, and should form the basis of shipment from the States, yet nothing should delay the rapid shipment of troops, material, and supplies, to the full capacity of available shipping, and I shall add that we shall take care of and handle all that can be sent. The necessity of the military situation as set forth in the frequent cablegrams should be the governing factor. Every possible energy is being and will continue to be exerted here to expedite matters."

Nothing could be a more complete exposition than this correspondence, to show the unflagging zeal and executive energy which prepared the great bases and services of supply to assure the success of the operations of the future great American Army on the Western Front. The vast scope of these projects has been described, and these all-important works were being carried on at the time when opinion abroad was all against the possibility of any such future American Army.

This opinion, held by the leaders of the Entente Allies, remained an obstacle to the endeavors of the American Commander-in-Chief. Although, as has been told, the Entente Allies had been made to understand that the object of the United States was to provide an American Army on the battlefield, instead of replacements scattered among the Allied armies, yet the Allied leaders remained wedded to the replacement idea, and all sorts of modifications of this idea were still being urged upon the United States.

The Supreme War Council of the Entente Allies had been organized. The military advisers were: General Foch for France, General Wilson for Great Britain, General Cadorna for Italy, General Bliss for the United States. And here it should be stated of General Bliss that the only reason for his first inclination to accede to the proposition for scattering American troops among the armies of the Allies was a misunderstanding which made him think the idea was approved by General Pershing. But, after a consultation in Paris, General Pershing stated: "General Bliss agreed with me, and we appeared before Mr. Lloyd George in full accord." In his letter of February 24, 1918, to Secretary Baker, General Pershing wrote: "I want to say that General Bliss is a most excellent choice for the post he now holds, and that our relations are most harmonious and I feel sure must remain so. He is an able man, as square as a die, and loyal to the core. I do not think you could have found anyone to fill the place with greater credit to us all."

It was most natural that the leaders of the Entente Allies should hold to the idea that the best use of the American troops would be to fill up their ranks. By this time it was in the air that there would be an assault upon the Western Front, with the German armies made formidable by troops brought from the East. The Allied armies on the Western Front, depleted by the wastage of the unsuccessful Allied offensives, were beyond reinforcement by means of their own resources. At this extremity appeared the prospect of troops from America. To the Allied leaders this was like manna in the wilderness, and we can understand their feeling that this was the best and quickest way to make use of the new supply of manpower. They could not see that American recruits scattered among their forces would only become a part of the unsatisfactory conditions existing among the Allied armies, and that a new army was necessary. As they had no faith in this new army, it is no wonder that the desire to use American troops as recruits for their own forces remained persistent.

"During January, 1918, discussions were held with the British authorities that resulted in an agreement, which became known as the six-division plan and which provided for the transportation of six entire divisions in British tonnage, without interference with our own shipping program."[1] The British allotted this transporta-

---

[1] General Pershing.

tion on condition that these troops should serve with the British for a training period of ten weeks. But General Pershing had kept on steadily with his preparations for the organization of an American Army. The matter of an American sector on the Western Front was mentioned in his letter of February 24, 1918, to Secretary Baker: "In accordance with a tentative agreement made by General Pétain and myself, we shall in time have a sector of our own as soon as our divisions are able to act independently. It will probably begin where the First Division is now finishing its training, between St. Mihiel and Pont-à-Mousson, from which base we shall likely extend both to the west and east."

In his report, General Pershing described the progress of American organization as follows: "It was also certain that an early appearance of the larger American units on the front would be most beneficial to the morale of the Allies themselves. Accordingly the First Division, on January 19, 1918, took over a sector north of Toul; the Twenty-sixth Division went to the Soissons front early in February; the Forty-second Division entered the line near Lunéville, February 21, and the Second Division near Verdun, March 18. Meanwhile, the First Army Corps Headquarters, Maj. Gen. Hunter Liggett commanding, was organized at Neufchâteau on January 20, and the plan to create an independent American sector on the Lorraine front was taking shape. This was the situation when the great German offensive was launched on March 21, 1918." On that date, General Pershing stated, "approximately 300,000 American troops had reached France."

At that time, Secretary Baker was in France. He

has given this account of the circumstances of his going:

"General Pershing had repeatedly urged me to go to France. I understood that his desire to have me was for two reasons: first, that there would be a certain stimulation of interest among his people and among the Allied military commands in having the American Secretary of War visit the field of operation. The second part of General Pershing's desire to have me come over, therefore, was undoubtedly that I might see with my own eyes the physical situation as it was in France, covering the ports, lines of communication and transportation, accommodations for the soldiers, and so forth, and thus be able more intelligently to understand his problem and work out our response to his requests.

"From the time we entered the war until January, 1918, we at the War Department felt the necessity of preserving everything we were doing as secret as possible. We had no means of knowing the extent to which our activities were under observation and by one process and another reported to the Germans. I still think we were entirely right in the cloak of secrecy we threw over our preparation, but it had one unfortunate consequence, which was that our people were mystified and felt increasingly restive from a lack of definite information. This was particularly true of the members of the Senate and House of Representatives, and led to a more or less continuous barrage of criticism against the War Department in both bodies. In the Senate particularly this was true. All sorts of letters of complaint and criticism were sent to senators and by them read on the floor of the Senate, and thus got into the record and scattered by the newspapers of the country generally. I think you will recall how widespread this criticism was and how in December, 1917, the feeling was more or less general that the War Department had 'broken down' and that we were doing nothing. By January, 1918, however, the situation had at last changed, and we felt that our progress was such that a public statement with regard to it could be made, both to satisfy home sentiment and as notice to the Germans that we were prepared to act in force. I, therefore, requested the Senate committee on Military Affairs to give me a public hearing in a large place so that we might have a big audience of senators, representatives, newspaper men, and the general public, and it was before this meeting of the committee that I made an address entitled 'What We Are Doing to Make War.' The effect of this speech, which was printed in full in newspapers all over the country, was immediate. Our own people were distinctly reassured, and the criticism from then on had to do with particular individuals and incidents, and no longer alleged any lack of general adequacy on the part of the War Department. When this happier sort of home sentiment had been created, I for the first time and at last felt free to go overseas, although I had long been aware that such a visit on my part would be very helpful to me, and perhaps stimulating to our men overseas in showing them that those in charge of things at home were interested and concerned about their welfare.

"It seemed to me of the highest importance that my visit should not be long; that it should be devoted intensively to study of conditions, and that it should not be interrupted by a round of official courtesies and ceremonial observances. I, therefore, asked the State Department through our ambassadors abroad to notify the governments overseas that my visit was as far as possible to be regarded as unofficial, and the overseas governments very generously acceded to my wishes, and beyond very simple courtesy calls on the President of the Republic in France and the King of England in London, I was not expected to devote any time to anything except the errand which took me. This, of course, also prevented my visit being a distraction and an embarrassment to the busy civilian and military men of the Allied armies, who all had their hands full and ought not to have been distracted by official courtesies.

"My particular objects in going abroad were as follows. I wanted to see with my own eyes as completely as possible the following things:

"1. The condition of our ports where we were already having difficulty in getting ships unloaded because of the accumulation on the docks and the difficulty of evacuating those supplies into the interior.

"2. Transportation systems from docks to the warehouses, and thence to the system of supply from the central warehouses to the front.

"3. Provisions for hospitalization, and the conditions surrounding the sick and wounded, the nurses and doctors.

"4. The actual conditions at the front under which the men had to live and fight.

"5. The operation of the war camp services of a recreational character.

"6. And by actual contact to discover the morale of the men and their needs.

"7. To see the actual condition and morale of the colored troops overseas, as to which conflicting reports had reached me in Washington.

"8. To confer face to face with General Pershing about any problems which were arising in the matter of coördinating his headquarters with Washington.

"9. To discover, if I could, the trouble with the mail service."

Accordingly, Secretary Baker sailed secretly from New York on U.S.S. *Seattle*, February 27, 1918, and arrived at Brest in France March 10. He was met the next morning at the Paris railroad station by General Pershing and General Bliss, and at once began his tour of inspection. Secretary Baker has written the following impression of the situation on the eve of the great German offensive:

"Although I went immediately from Brest to Paris, I stayed there but a day or two and then went to Bordeaux and began my inspection at the docks where our cargo transports were unloading. In effect, I followed our men and supplies from the sea to the front-line trenches and saw every type of installation which had been made in France. No adequate description can be given in a few words of what had been done. The distinctive thing about it, however, was that it looked like the building up of a new America on French soil, so completely were our installations and our processes American. It was as though we had extended ourselves into France. American unloading apparatus; American rails, locomotives, and cars; American telephone and telegraph lines and instruments; American forms of housing construction; and American institutions to prevent or reclaim waste. We even had a large American candy factory and great central American bakeries. It was at once clear that the foundation laid was susceptible of almost indefinite extension and expansion and that provision had been made for any army we could transport overseas."

CHAPTER XXVII

THE FIRST ASSAULT OF THE GREAT GERMAN OFFENSIVE OF 1918

SUDDENLY, on March 21, 1918, the storm broke upon the Western Front—and, then and there, all ideas of "stabilized" trench warfare were swept out of existence. It was not alone the numerical superiority of the Germans which smashed through the Allied defence, but it was the success of the new German system of tactics, which proved to be an overwhelming surprise for the Entente Allies. As has been stated, the strategy of both the British and French had been molded by their operations of 1916 and 1917, and they had grown to believe that all fighting on the Western Front would be of this pattern.

The French and British commands had expected German attacks on the Western Front, as the Germans gathered their forces and made their preparations almost openly, but the Allies measured the strength of their own defenses by the difficulties they themselves had experienced against similar defenses of the enemy. They did not imagine that new methods of attack would be devised by the Germans. Hindenburg has written: "If our western adversaries failed to obtain results in the battles of 1915 to 1917, it must be ascribed to a certain unimaginativeness in their generalship. The necessary superiority in men, war material, and ammunition, was certainly not lacking, nor can it be suggested that the quality of the enemy troops would not have been high enough to satisfy the demands of a more vigorous and ingenious generalship."

The fact was, the strategy of the Entente Allies, in all their attempted offensives on the Western Front when the Allied armies were superior in numbers, had never progressed beyond piecemeal attacks. These had won only small results—and at the expense of losses so prohibitive that each of these Allied offensives had dwindled away to nothing. Instead of imputing these failures to faulty tactics in attack, the Allied commanders had become imbued with an exaggerated idea of the strength of intrenched positions, in full belief that, since they were not able to carry the German positions, it followed that the Germans would not be able to carry the Allied positions.

The new German system of attack, the "Hutier manœuvre," had been carefully rehearsed for months. Many divisions were to be placed about the region of intended attack, with their movements and transportation carefully worked out, so that they would converge upon the objective in successive instalments. This meant that, not only would there be the usual attacking divisions brought into position the night before, but also there would be successive groups of divisions, at a distance, ready to march against the selected point of attack.

Following this plan, the preparations of the German Command for the first blow of the offensive of 1918 were made with great skill and thoroughness. The chosen area of attack was in the region of St. Quentin, a part of the British line held by the British Fifth Army under General Gough. Of course, the problem of the Allies was very difficult, in preparing to defend their long line against the concentration for the expected German offensive. But on this sector of the British line the prevailing overconfidence in the strength of intrenched defences was in evidence. "Three defensive belts"[1] had been constructed, but there were no deep defensive positions behind them. Evidently there was no suspicion that the Germans would use new methods of attack which would be too strong for the defensive zones of fire which had been devised.

In this new German plan of attack there was not to be the usual warning of a preliminary bombardment. But a great strength of artillery had been prepared, with high explosive and mustard gas shells, and a large part of this artillery was ready to be moved forward with the attack. So carefully had the movements of all these German forces been covered that their presence was not suspected by the British Command. Even when they were advancing for the attack, they were able to approach the British lines undiscovered.[2] In the early mists of the morning the great assault began on a front of about fifty miles.[3]

There were bombardments of intense violence, with

---

[1] Sir Douglas Haig's Despatches.

[2] "And the Germans were actually in some parts within a few yards of our front line before anyone knew of their approach."—Lloyd George.

[3] "Favoured by a thick fog, which hid from our artillery and machine guns the S O S signals sent up by our outpost line, and in numbers which made loss of direction impossible, the attacking German infantry forced their way into our foremost defensive zone."—Sir Douglas Haig's Despatches.

the use of great quantities of gas shells, and smoke screens were also used. The artillery was switched to a barrage, and the streams of infantry advanced. These unexpected and overwhelming attacks made gains at once. The British positions were penetrated, and the German drive continued with such increasing strength, as the successive forces of the Germans poured in, that the whole British defence was broken west of St. Quentin. This break in the British line was so different from anything that had been foreseen that it not only dislocated the British Fifth Army but brought about so disastrous and crippling[1] a retreat that the Fifth Army ceased to exist as an army.

"Within eight days the enemy had completely crossed the old Somme battlefield and had swept everything before him to a depth of 56 kilometres."[2] The Germans could claim 90,000 prisoners and 1,300 guns, taken from the British. These were very heavy losses, but they were not the most serious result for the Allied armies. There was another element in the situation which did much more harm. For, as the shattered British Fifth Army retreated toward the west, it left defenseless an increasingly long sector south of Noyon, curving north beyond Montdidier, and it was at once necessary that this dangerous opening should be defended by the French.[3] With extraordinary rapidity and efficiency

---

[1] "Crippling one of our great armies."—Lloyd George.

[2] General Pershing.

[3] "As a result of a meeting held in the afternoon of the 23, arrangements were made for the French to take over as rapidly as possible the front held by the Fifth Army south of Péronne, and for the concentration of a strong force of French divisions on the southern portion of the battle front."—Sir Douglas Haig's Despatches.

French troops were rushed to this region, and the almost impossible task was accomplished of repairing the defense. This was the most dangerous phase of the situation for the Entente Allies. At one blow the Germans had smashed in a gap which must be stopped by practically exhausting the available reserves of the Allied armies. As General Pershing expressed it. "The offensive made such inroads upon French and British reserves that defeat stared them in the face unless the new American troops should prove more immediately available than even the most optimistic had dared to hope."

The German victory had been amazing—beyond their expectation, as was shown by the exultation of the German military leaders at the time. Ludendorff's postwar pessimism has made him slur this battle, as he has others. But the Germans knew they had won great results.

This serious reverse for the Allied armies, and the situation which had been so quickly created, had been an object lesson in the weakness of divided commands. And, at last, the first steps were taken to do away with this greatest drawback for the operations of the Allied armies. At the height of this Battle of Picardy, after the French had been obliged to take over the defenses left open by the retreat of the British Fifth Army, there was a hurried conference at Doullens (March 26, 1918), and the following was adopted: "General Foch is charged by the British and French Governments to coördinate the action of the Allied armies on the Western Front. He will consult for this purpose with the commanders-in-chief who are to furnish him all the information necessary.

(Signed) CLEMENCEAU.
"MILNER."

This was a most grudging and partial concession, but it was the first step—and it was eventually to lead to the desirable goal of a united command.

These main facts, as to the eventful last days of March, 1918, must be appreciated, in order to understand the instant change that had been brought about in the military situation of the World War—especially in regard to the American military reinforcement for the Western Front. Even then the whole truth did not stand revealed. That was to be brought out by the ensuing events of the World War. But, as if by the wave of a wand, a new twofold situation had been created: first, that the only possibility of a counter attack against the victorious Germans lay in an American military reinforcement; secondly, that this American reinforcement would be better prepared for battle than had been thought.

This first condition was brought about by the fact that the Allied reserves had been used to repair the broken defense. From this time on, the best the Entente Allies could hope, from their own resources, would be to fill up the ranks of this existing defense. Any force for a counter attack must come from the United States Army—and this at once gave the American reinforcement on the Western Front a new decisive importance. The second condition was the result of the change in warfare on the Western Front, caused by the new German system of tactics. When the Germans surged through the British intrenched positions, they brought the fighting into the open. From this time, the use of hasty intrenchments was to be in conjunction with the tactics of open warfare, in accordance with our American doctrines. This was a vindication of our methods of military training, and of the American policy of insisting upon adherence to our own system of training American troops for open warfare, instead of allowing ourselves to be swayed by the Entente Allies. It was a notable event of the World War, that, at the very time the American Army was to be thrown into battle, the fighting of the World War changed to the very system of tactics for which this American Army had been trained. It is needless to point out that this change to our own system of fighting was to make the American Expeditionary Forces more efficient on the battlefield.

CHAPTER XXVIII

THE EMERGENCY CAUSED BY THE FIRST GERMAN ASSAULT

AFTER this fearful object lesson of German military superiority on the Western Front, the curtain was rent aside and the imminent crisis was revealed. This sudden revelation of the menace was in itself an urgent call for American assistance. The response was immediate. General Pershing has stated: "The grave crisis precipitated by the first German offensive caused me to make a hurried visit to General Foch's headquarters at Bombon, during which all our combatant forces were placed at his disposal. The acceptance of this offer meant the dispersion of our troops along the Allied front and a consequent delay in building up a distinctive American force in Lorraine, but the serious situation of the Allies demanded this divergence from our plans." In these manly words General Pershing has expressed the unselfish postponement of our own cherished aims in order to give the greatest possible help to the Allies at their extremity.

In fact, throughout this emergency, American troops were freely given to the British and French armies. This must be understood by the reader, but it must also be realized that General Pershing and the Secretary of War never abandoned their plan for an American Army. There was no uncertainty, as to this last, in the agreements with the British and French for the use of American troops in their armies. These allotments of our troops were always made with the explicit condition that the ultimate use of American troops was to be as an American Army. There can be no doubt of this, after the record has been read.

General Pershing has stated that, on March 27, the Military Representatives with the Supreme War Council prepared a joint note (No. 18) which contained the following: "The battle which is developing at the present moment in France, and which can extend to the other theatres of operations, may very quickly place the Allied Armies in a serious situation from the point of view of effectives, and the Military Representatives are from this moment of opinion that the above-detailed condition[1] can no longer be maintained, and they consider as a general proposition that the new situation requires new decisions.

"The Military Representatives are of opinion that it is highly desirable that the American Government should assist the Allied Armies as soon as possible by permitting in principle the temporary service of American units in Allied Army corps and divisions. Such reinforcements must, however, be obtained from other units than those American divisions which are now operating with the French, and the units so temporarily employed must eventually be returned to the American Army.

---

[1] Joint note No. 12, of January, 1918, (a) "That the strength of the British and French troops in France are continuously kept up to their present strength and that they receive the expected reinforcements of not less than two American divisions per month."

"The Military Representatives are of the opinion that, from the present time, in execution of the foregoing, and until otherwise directed by the Supreme War Council, only American infantry, and machine-gun units, organized as that Government may decide, be brought to France, and that all agreements or conventions hitherto made in conflict with this decision be modified accordingly."

The terms of this joint note were at once considered at a conference of Secretary Baker, General Pershing, and General Bliss, the American Military Representative with the Supreme War Council. As the result of this conference, the Secretary of War recommended to the President that this joint note No. 18 should be approved, with the following understanding:

"The purpose of the American Government is to render the fullest coöperation and aid, and therefore the recommendation of the Military Representatives with regard to the preferential transportation of American infantry and machine-gun units in the present emergency is approved. Such units, when transported, will be under the direction of the Commander-in-Chief of the American Expeditionary Forces, and will be assigned by him in his discretion. He will use these and all other military forces of the United States under his command in such manner as to render the greatest military assistance, keeping in mind always the determination of this Government to have its various military forces collected, as speedily as their training and the military situation permit, into an independent American Army, acting in concert with the armies of Great Britain and France, and all arrangements made by him for their temporary training and service will be made with that end in view."

Thus clearly was set forth our unswerving adherence to our one military plan of creating an American Army on the Western Front. And it was most fortunate for the cause of the Entente Allies that this idea was still held. The ensuing events of the war showed, beyond a doubt, that the scheme of the Allied leaders, for reinforcing their armies by means of American troops, would not have been adequate to win the successful result which was attained by carrying through the American plan. Yet this agreement with the Entente Allies made a most liberal provision for the use of American troops in the Allied armies, and, on April 2, the War Department cabled that "preferential transportation would be given to American infantry and machine-gun units during the existing emergency."

When General Pershing described this emergency, and wrote that the attacking German Army "was by far the most formidable force the world had ever seen," he had added: "In fighting men and guns it had a great superiority, but this was of less importance than the advantage in morale, in experience, in training for mobile warfare, and in unity of command." In regard to this last, our Administration and General Pershing were strongly in favor of a united command. After the first step in this direction had been taken, President Wilson had transmitted the following message to General Foch (March 30, 1918): "May I not convey to you my sincere congratulations on your new authority? Such unity of command is a most hopeful augury of ultimate success. We are following with profound interest the bold and brilliant action of your forces. WOODROW WILSON."

As has been stated, the first step toward this unity of command had been inadequate and unsatisfactory. But American influence was of great help in bringing about an actual supreme command. This whole question of Foch's command has been misstated so often that it is well to give the following account from the official record.

On April 3, 1918, a conference was held at Beauvais. There were present the British and French prime ministers, Lloyd George and Clemenceau, General Foch, Marshal Haig, General Pétain, General Wilson, General Bliss, General Pershing. Clemenceau, presiding, said: "We have come together to settle a very simple question regarding the functions of General Foch. I think we are all in agreement as to the coördination of Allied action. But there is some difference in the understanding of General Foch's powers as conferred upon him at the Doullens conference of March 26th. General Foch will explain his difficulties."

General Foch, after stating that his powers were limited to the coördination of action between the Allies, said: "They were conferred while the action was on. The power to coördinate has been construed to be limited to the time the Allies are in action. That was March 26th at Doullens. Now we are at April 3d. Now that the two armies are no longer in action but have stopped and are facing each other, there is nothing to coördinate. There should be authority to prepare for action and direct it. So that we are right back where we were before and nothing can be done until an action starts again."

Lloyd George recapitulated the difficulties of the last three years, and stated: "General Foch is now empowered to coördinate the action of the Allied armies, but this does not go far enough as he has no authority to control except by conferring with the respective commanders-in-chief. He wants authority to prepare for action. I think the resolution made at Doullens should be modified so that we may have a better understanding." Lloyd George then asked for American opinion.

General Pershing spoke in no uncertain terms: "The principle of unity of command is undoubtedly the correct one for the Allies to follow. I do not believe it possible to have unity of action without a supreme commander. We have already had experience enough in trying to coördinate the operations of the Allied armies without success. There never has been real unity of action. Such coördination between two or three armies is impossible, no matter who the commanders-in-chief may be. Each commander-in-chief is interested in his own army, and cannot get the other commander's point of view nor grasp the problem as a whole. I am in favor of a supreme commander and believe that the success of the Allied cause depends upon it. I think the necessary action should be taken by this council at once. I am in favor of conferring the supreme command upon General Foch."

Lloyd George said: "I agree fully with General Pershing. That is well put." After very little more consultation, a proposed resolution was put into form, but this referred only to the British and French armies. Very properly General Pershing interposed: "I think this resolution should include the American Army. The arrangement is to be in force, as I understand it, from now on, and the American Army will soon be ready to function as such and should be included as an entity, like the British and French armies."

General Pétain said: "There is no American Army yet as such, as its units are either in training or are amalgamated with the British and French." At this objection of the French Commander-in-Chief, which reflected the reluctance of the military leaders of the Entente Allies to admit the possibility of an American Army, General Pershing stated the policy of the American Government: "There may not be an American Army in force functioning now, but there soon will be, and I want this resolution to apply to it when it becomes a fact. The American Government is represented here at this conference and in the war, and any action as to the supreme command that includes the British and French armies should also include the American Army."

This timely assertion of our purpose was convincing, and the resolution was adopted in the following form: "General Foch is charged by the British, French, and American Governments to coördinate the action of the Allied armies on the Western Front. For this purpose there are conferred upon him all the powers necessary for its effective realization. To this end, the British, French, and American Governments confide to General Foch the strategic direction of military operations.

"The Commanders-in-Chief of the British, French, and American Armies will exercise to the fullest extent the tactical direction of their armies. Each Commander-in-Chief will have the right to appeal to his Government, if, in his opinion, his army is placed in danger by any instruction received from General Foch."

The resolution in this form was signed by all present, and there was an exchange of signed copies before the conference adjourned. It was evident that, even at this conference of April 3d, there was still a cautious spirit of treaty making between the British and French. But, in spite of the guarded phrases of the resolution, the result was a supreme command for General Foch, and this was effective on the Western Front throughout the rest of the war.

It was also important that the American plan, for an independent American Army, had been recognized and put on record at the Beauvais conference in the resolution of April 3, 1918. It is true that, for the leaders of the Entente Allies, the matter of securing American troops, as replacements in their divisions, remained the limit of what they could see of help from the United States. But, for the American Commander-in-Chief and the Secretary of War, it was a different thing—and, in our relations with the Entente Allies, our military affairs had been put on a basis which was destined to bring about the desired result.

Secretary Baker has written the following, in regard to the situation in France which was established just before he left for home, as the Secretary of War returned to the United States a few days after the Beauvais conference. Nothing could have been more fortunate than the time of his first visit to the American Expeditionary Forces, as he was there at the very time of the emergency, and was able to show to the leaders of the Entente Allies that the American Administration was unreservedly backing the American Commander-in-Chief and stood with him in asserting our military policies.

"I was in France during the latter part of March and very earnestly discussed with General Bliss at Versailles and in Paris the problem of unified command for the Allied forces. The military representatives of the Supreme War Council had some time before recommended the creation of an army of manœuvre to be placed under the command of General Foch and to some extent to operate under the independent direction of the Supreme War Council. The object of such an army was that it should be held back of the lines and brought into immediate action as soon as the point of the German drive became apparent. It was, of course, impossible to tell at what point in the line the German operation would be undertaken.

"This recommendation of the Supreme War Council was accepted in principle by the British and French, but was not carried out. Both General Pétain and General Haig apparently believed it unwise to detach divisions from their armies. As a substitute for this plan, Generals Haig and Pétain, at a conference, agreed to support each other in sustaining the blow of the German attack wherever it should fall. In discussing the matter with me, General Bliss was very positive in his belief in the wisdom of the plan adopted by the Supreme War Council, although he said, 'In my opinion it does not go far enough. If I had my way about it, I would create the position of Commander-in-Chief of the Allied forces and put General Foch in command.' Shortly after this the German drive took place and the Doullens conference was hastily assembled on the 26th of March, when the Germans were threatening and rapidly approaching Amiens. The next day I learned of the action taken at Doullens and discussed it with both General Pershing and General Bliss. We agreed that it was wholly inadequate. On the 27th or 28th of March I had a conference with M. Clemenceau. He brought up the action of the Doullens conference and asked me my opinion about it. I told him that I had discussed the matter with General Bliss and General Pershing, and that it was their opinion —which I shared—that the action was wholly inadequate and an ineffective substitute for a unified command. I further told him that President Wilson had long been for unified command, but realized that the size of the American army in France up to that time would not justify his insistence in a matter in which French and British sensibilities had to be considered, but that in the present emergency every other consideration ought to stand aside and that I felt sure President Wilson would earnestly support that view.

"At one of my conferences with General Pershing and General Bliss I prepared a cablegram in cipher to President Wilson recommending that he cable separately to Mr. Lloyd George and M. Clemenceau urging unified command in view of the situation, which at that time could not have been worse. When I returned to the United States later I found that President Wilson had sent separate cablegrams to Mr. Lloyd George and M. Clemenceau two days before I cabled him on the subject so that when the Beauvais conference was held on April 3 General Pershing's positive recommendation and views had the personal support of President Wilson, as well as the unanimous backing of the military representatives of the Supreme War Council.

"The circumstances of the offer of our troops to Marshal Foch in the emergency were as follows. General Pershing, General Bliss, and I had held a conference in Paris upon the general question of brigading the American troops with the British and French. From that conference General Pershing went immediately to Marshal Foch's headquarters and tendered him without restriction the fullest use of all American forces to meet the emergency. This action was taken by General Pershing spontaneously, but was wholly within his discretionary power, and there was, of course, no reason why the matter should be discussed with me. I have always assumed that General Pershing made up his mind to make the offer on his way to Marshal Foch's headquarters. The decision on General Pershing's part was a manifestation of the quality of daring which characterized him in emergencies. The offer was, of course, the right thing to do from every point of view."

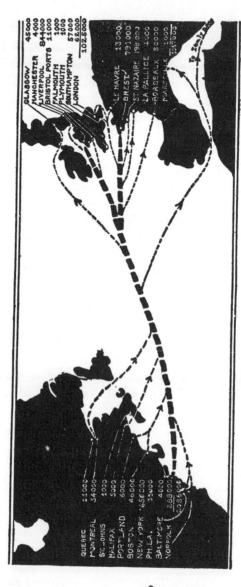

GLASGOW 45000
MANCHESTER 4000
LIVERPOOL 844000
BRISTOL PORTS 11000
FALMOUTH 1000
PLYMOUTH 1000
SOUTHAMPTON 57000
LONDON 62000
1025000

LE HAVRE 13000
BREST 791000
ST. NAZAIRE 198000
LA PALLICE 4000
BORDEAUX 50000
MARSEILLES 1000
1057000

To Italy

QUEBEC 11000
MONTREAL 34000
ST. JOHNS 1000
HALIFAX 5000
PORTLAND 6000
BOSTON 46000
NEW YORK 656000
PHILA. 35000
BALTIMORE 4000
NORFOLK 268000
2035000

THE BRIDGE TO FRANCE

Showing the totals of American troops sailing from American ports and landing at ports overseas in the greatest transportation operation of all history

258

CHAPTER XXIX

RUSHING AMERICAN TROOPS TO FRANCE

THE approaching crisis of the World War was now revealed beyond any misunderstanding. The "race" was on—and it was a race such as the world had never seen. The whole issue hung on the question whether American troops could be rushed to France in time to stem the tide of the great German offensive.

The first disastrous defeat had at once brought home to the British the realization that transportation of American troops was more important than any other use of shipping. "The losses had been heavy and the British were unable to replace them entirely. They were, therefore, making extraordinary efforts to increase the shipping available for our troops."[1] The Report of the British War Cabinet (1918) has stated the result: "At the same time, however, orders were given by the War Cabinet at the beginning of April that every effort was to be made to convey American troops to this country in the largest possible numbers. In order to effect this, every available ship suitable for the conveyance of troops was taken from every trade route in the world and diverted to the North Atlantic. The number of additional ships put into the service between the 31st March and the end of August was 124. By this means

---

[1]General Pershing, Report.

an average of over 150,000 American troops per month were conveyed on British ships and 10,000 per month on Italian ships (which were placed at the disposal of the British Government by the Italian Government)."

"Until May, 1918, almost all of our troops were embarked in our own Naval transports."[1] But, at last, the full resources of British shipping were being used, and the monthly totals of American troops sent overseas leapt to astonishing figures, as 84,889 had been taken across in March; 118,642 in April. In May, in consequence of the agreements with Great Britain, the number of American troops transported reached the unprecedented total of 245,945, and General Pershing could report: "Following the agreements as to British shipping, our troops came so rapidly that by the end of May we had a force of 600,000 in France." In order to keep in mind the facts as to this gigantic movement of American troops, which grew to such a flood in the ensuing months of the war, the following monthly totals should be stated here: June, 278,864; July, 306,350; August, 286,974; September, 257,457; October, 180,326. This meant that a million and a half American troops were rushed to Europe in the six months of the crisis of the World War,[2] and thus the United States accomplished her main object in the World War, and won the race by providing the decisive military reinforcement in France.[3]

It also should be noted that, in accordance with the

---

[1] Admiral Gleaves, *A History of the Transport Service.*

[2] "These hordes of American troops on the continent which turned the balance against us on the Western Front in 1918.—"Admiral Tirpitz.

[3] "America thus became the decisive power in the war."—Ludendorff.

agreements for priority of infantry and machine gun units which have been described, the first great rush of American troops provided a maximum strength of fighting men. The general policy as to the American troops overseas, agreed upon with the Entente Allies, had tended toward this direction from the beginning. By these give-and-take arrangements, field guns, animals, airplanes, etc., were to be provided at first by the Allies in exchange for raw material, in order that the whole effort of the United States might be concentrated upon the production of fighting men. But the new agreements went far beyond this, and the troopships were being used for the transportation of armed men, with only their equipment. This was a phase of the situation which the Germans could not understand. From their point of view, a division must be transported with all the impedimenta of its full organization for the field. The chagrined Ludendorff described "bringing over the American masses, crammed tight in transports, to France. The men carried only their personal equipments. . . . The whole operation was a *tour de force*, uncommonly effective for a short time, but impossible to maintain for a long period. Had the war lasted longer a reaction must have followed. . . . Ruthlessness and energy once again brought success." In their first disappointment at German defeat, the German leaders broke out with frank complaints, which showed their states of mind—and these statements can never be recalled. Their bewildered surprise at the success of the American military effort has been put on record. The very fact that Ludendorff should thus describe the transportation of American troops was an involuntary tribute, of which the significance cannot be mistaken. Something was happening that was outside of all German formulas—an utter failure of German calculations. Hence the "ruthlessness"!

In fact, the success of this great movement of troops overseas was marking the final failure of the ruthless German campaign of unrestricted U-boat warfare. At the time when this unexpected transportation of American troops was gathering way, the Germans were still persisting in their U-boat campaign. But, as their main grand strategy had been shifted to their great offensive of 1918 on the Western Front, the mission of the U-boats in 1918 must be held to consist of coöperation and assistance for this new German main object in the war. Consequently, the value of the U-boats to the Germans in 1918 must be measured by the results attained in preventing reinforcements and supplies from reaching their enemies on the Western Front. Measured by this test, the German submarines were failing.

In this case, theirs was a double failure. First, the convoyed troopships were proving their ability to bring the great American military reinforcement overseas, in defiance of the U-boats. Secondly, the U-boats were no longer destroying shipping beyond replacement—and this last meant that the Germans no longer threatened to cut off sea-borne supplies from the Entente Allies.

The Report of the British War Cabinet (1918) has thus recorded the stage when replacements of shipping balanced losses: "About the middle of 1918, mainly owing to the shipbuilding effort of the United States, the world's output of new tonnage equalled the rate of loss." This implied the passing of the peak of peril for the Entente Allies. It was true that the tonnage position of the Entente Allies abroad grew even worse. "The new ships from the United States shipbuilding yards were all required to meet the growing demands of the United States Army,"[1] and there was also the drain upon Allied tonnage to provide transportation for American troops and supplies, as has been stated. But all this was putting shipping to the best possible use for the cause of the Entente Allies, and was entirely to their advantage.

By this time the operation of the convoy system was like clockwork. As Admiral Sims expressed it, "The Admiralty in London was thus the central nervous system of a complicated but perfectly working organism which reached the remotest corners of the world." Admiral Sims has also written of shipping, that "now for the first time it was arranged in hard and fast routes and dispatched in accordance with schedules as fixed as those of a great railroad." He has added: "This comparison holds good of its operation after it had entered the infested zones. Indeed the very terminology of our railroads was used. . . . The whole gigantic enterprise flowed with a precision and a regularity which I think it is hardly likely that any other transportation system has ever achieved." In fact, Sir Eric Geddes, the new First Lord of the British Admiralty, who had done so much for this convoy system, was a trained engineer.

The troopships provided by Great Britain were controlled by this great British convoy system. They were operated by their owners, and their relation to the

[1]British War Cabinet. Report, 1918.

United States Government was that of chartered ships. But all were brought up to the United States Navy standards of health and safety. "Many of these vessels had been cargo carriers, and much of the work of refitting was done at New York under the direction of the Port of Embarkation."[1] "The Port of Embarkation spent $4,000,000 for life-saving equipment alone, either to supplement that already carried on British ships or to replace equipment which our officers condemned. The new equipment was sold to the British shipowners at cost."[2]

The diagram on page 258 shows at a glance the totals and distributions of the transportation of American troops overseas. It will be noted that New York was the great port of embarkation, and, with the subsidiary port of Norfolk, sent out over 1,900,000 of the two million American soldiers. Of the receiving ports abroad, Brest, with St. Nazaire, received the bulk of our troops sent direct to France. Of those sent to Great Britain first, to be relayed to France later, it is shown that Liverpool received the bulk. Of course, these last were, for the most part, from the British convoys of troopships.

The American troopships of the Cruiser and Transport Force remained a separate convoy system under United States Navy control. This American fleet of transports had been increased far beyond the total of the seized German shipping, which at the first had been its main reliance. At the time of the Armistice, 45 American troopships had been put into service with the

---

[1]Crowell and Wilson, *The Road to France.*
[2]*Ibid.*

Cruiser and Transport Force. These had been secured by the United States taking over every steamship that could be pressed into the service.[1]

Of these, only two were owned by the Shipping Board, the fine oil burners, *Orizaba* and *Siboney* (late *Oriente*). The rest were taken over from various sources, by requisition and charter or by downright purchase. Of course, many were taken over from the International Mercantile Marine and its subsidiaries. Notable among these were the *Finland* and *Kroonland* of the Red Star Line, and the sister ships *Manchuria* and *Mongolia* of the Atlantic Transport Company. Each of these last two had a carrying capacity of about 5,000 troops. Especial mention should be made of two very valuable transports, the *Northern Pacific* and *Great Northern*, secured from the Great Northern Steamship Company. These were new oil burners of twenty and twenty-one knots respectively. "They proved to be the best ships in the transport service—better even than the German ships, built primarily for troop transportation."[2] Three of our troopships were steamships commandeered from the Dutch, which had been taken over by the United States, as explained. Four steamships were assigned as troopships by the French Government, and these were grouped with the United States Navy convoys, as were ships assigned by the Italian Government. The French Government also assigned to the Cruiser and Transport Force a division of three cruisers under Rear Admiral

---

[1] "By November, 1918, the Army had brought into its own service about all the suitable passenger boats that the world could supply."—Crowell and Wilson, *The Road to France.*

[2] Crowell and Wilson, *The Road to France.*

Grout,[1] and these served as a welcome reinforcement in escorting the American convoys.

Admiral Gleaves and the officers under his command were tireless in improving the efficiency of the operation of the ships of the Cruiser and Transport Force. Everything was done to keep the ships at their best for the arduous task of voyage after voyage, rushed at top speed and with no delays in port. Crew repair parties were at work on them day and night. Actual major repairs, which would mean docking, were fought off as well as possible. "It was anything to keep the ships going."[2] All this was fearfully hard on the ships, and they were badly used up at the end. But they were successfully "kept going," and not one vessel broke down under the strain. By constant study of methods for getting the most out of the ships, the turnarounds of the round trip voyages were shortened to an incredible extent, and in this respect the troopships of the Cruiser and Transport Force "outdid any other ships placed at our disposal, and by a wide margin."[3] "The average turnaround of a British ship in the American troop service was 84.4 days, or nearly three months. The average American turnaround was 36.3 days, or slightly more than one month."[4]

A great help in producing this result of a much shortened round trip for the American troopship was the study given to the matter of coaling. In the preceding

---

[1] *Gloire* (flag), *Marseillaise*, *Du Petit Thouars*. This last cruiser was sunk in the Bay of Biscay.

[2] Crowell and Wilson, *The Road to France*.

[3] *Ibid.*

[4] *Ibid.*

hard winter, coaling had been a difficult problem. It had even come to a point where Admiral Gleaves recruited a working party from the Navy crews in port and, on his own initiative, commandeered the coaling equipment of the contractors in order to get a transport to sea without delay. "Thereafter, the Force itself continued to operate the coaling equipment in New York."[1] But the greatest advance in this direction was by increasing the bunker capacity of the troopships so that the necessity for recoaling was reduced. The Navy changed over the adjacent cargo holds into bunker space and connected them with the firing rooms. By this expedient a great deal of time was saved in each round trip.

For the largest transport of all, the *Leviathan*, this could not be done, but, as she could carry more troops than anything else afloat, the British were glad to make a special arrangement for her to load 1,200 tons of Welsh coal each time she reached her debarkation point. After delays on her first two voyages at Liverpool, on account of the tides, Admiral Gleaves recommended that this great troopship should be sent into Brest, where there was deep water at all tides. Thereafter, her trips were made to Brest, with her allotted coal there ready for her by agreement. After this, the turnaround of the *Leviathan* averaged the unprecedented short round trip of twenty-six days.[2] As will be seen from the table on page 109, the *Leviathan* alone transported overseas 96,804 American troops. On account of her high speed,

[1]Crowell and Wilson, *The Road to France.*

[2]". . . An increase of 30,000 men in her annual carrying capacity."— Crowell and Wilson, *The Road to France.*

this mighty ship usually travelled alone or in company
with the *Great Northern* or the *Northern Pacific*. These
new American steamships were the only troopships
that were able to maintain speed adequate to accomplish a trip with the *Leviathan*. These two American
steamships had another advantage, which made them
of great value as troopships. Both were oil burners and
could be fuelled for the round trip on each voyage.
Consequently, these two ships held the records for
short turnarounds over all other troopships.

It was not only by means of ability to make more
frequent trips overseas that the efficiency of the American troopships was increased. In addition, the actual
troop-carrying capacity of the American transports was
increased, and thus there was a double gain in efficiency.
Admiral Gleaves and his officers made intensive studies
of the means to increase the accommodations for troops
in each ship. All the normal space for passengers had
been utilized for berths. Yet, by clearing additional
space, from ripping out passages and cabins, and using
even mess halls, many more berths were installed. A
great gain was also made by utilizing head room to make
the standee berths in additional tiers. By these means the
carrying capacity of the American troopships was increased some 25 per cent. Admiral Gleaves even went
farther than this. He proposed that the troopships
should carry 50 per cent. above their total berth ac-
commodation, the men to sleep in shifts, each watch
occupying the berths for twelve hours. This plan was
adopted on nine of the best American transports,[1] and

---

[1] *Agamemnon, Mt. Vernon, Great Northern, Northern Pacific, Von Steuben,
America, George Washington, Orizaba, Siboney.*

was successful until the influenza epidemic in the fall put an end to overloading. But it has been estimated that "the intensive loadings of transports had landed in France 100,000 extra troops."[1] It will be evident from this that Ludendorff's horrified description, "bringing over the American masses, crammed tight in transports, to France," was in truth, all unintentionally, a high compliment to the efficiency of the Cruiser and Transport Force of the United States Navy.

[1]Crowell and Wilson, *The Road to France.*

CHAPTER XXX

THE CRISIS OF THE WORLD WAR

THE second assault of the German offensive was delivered on April 9, 1918—again on a British front. This attack was in the region of La Bassée and Armentières. Like the first, it was a successful surprise and penetrated the British defense. General Haig reported: "Favored by a thick mist which made observation impossible, the enemy succeeded in forcing his way into the Allied positions in the neighborhood of Neuve Chapelle" (Battle of the Lys). Again, as in the fighting of March, the Germans in ten days won a broad salient, extending from south of Ypres to Lens, and "Passchendaele Ridge, the capture of which had cost so dearly in 1917, was evacuated by the British."[1]

In this second British defeat there was a repetition of the bad feature of the former situation—the necessity for sending French troops to reinforce the British defense.[2] This second proof of German superiority, and the additional drain upon Allied troops, very naturally had the result of making the leaders of the Allied armies all the more anxious for increased numbers of American

---

[1]General Pershing.

[2]"I had represented the state of affairs to Gen. Foch, Commander-in-Chief of the Allied Forces. . . . Gen. Foch had complied with my requests without delay. Certain French forces were moved to the north. . . ." Sir Douglas Haig's Despatches.

troops to recruit the strength of their divisions. And they became more persistent in their contention that this was the one means by which the United States could give the best help in the war.

General Pershing went to London on April 21 to discuss this question, and the Secretary of War upon his return to the United States (April 16, 1918), found that Lord Reading "was pressing upon the President the earnest wish of Lloyd George to have a definite agreement entered into by the United States to the effect that infantry and machine-gun personnel at a rate of 120,000 per month should be shipped for four months to the exclusion of all other personnel." This is quoted from a letter written by Secretary Baker to General Pershing. And, true to his resolution of not hampering the American Commander-in-chief, Secretary Baker, in regard to the request for "some assurance to the British Government in the matter of the assignment of infantry and machine-gun personnel," wrote to General Pershing the following assurance: "I declined to discuss the question and told them that they had better cable Sir Henry Wilson to get into communication with you on the subject, as the whole determination of the subject rests in your sound discretion."

In London (April 24, 1918) General Pershing had confirmed the agreement for the shipment of these troops "during May for training and service with the British army in France up to six divisions." He had also agreed to extend this policy "if, when the program outlined is completed, the military situation makes advisable the further shipment of infantry, etc." But he had made a part of this agreement the stipulation: "That it is contemplated American divisions and corps when trained and organized shall be utilized under the American Commander-in-Chief in an American group."

Upon General Pershing's return to Paris, as he expressed it, "the entire question of the amalgamation of Americans with the French and British was reopened." In the early days of May this question was debated at sessions of the Supreme War Council, and General Pershing met the requests of the British and French with great liberality. But it was necessary for him to take a resolute stand in order to maintain our principle that the eventual use of American troops must be as an American Army. The representatives of the British and French were anxious to have the policy of amalgamating American troops with the Allied armies go on for months—with the question of an American Army consequently postponed. Lloyd George "suggested that September or October would be time for the United States Army to come in as an army."[1] From their point of view, as expressed by General Foch, "the greater the figure of American troops able to take their place at short notice in the trenches, the nearer and more decisive the success of the Allies would be." They were at such an extremity for recruits that they could only think of that aspect of the situation. General Foch stated that the number of British divisions "so severely handled that they could not be reconstituted" was ten. But, as is now universally admitted, the American plan was actually the best means of providing the full benefit of the American reinforcement, and General Pershing

---

[1] General Pershing.

knew this well. As he stated at this conference, "The morale of the American troops depended upon their fighting under their own flag."

"General Pershing said that he spoke for the United States Government and for himself when he said that they looked forward to the time when the United States would have its own Army. He must insist on its being recognized."[1] General Pershing's argument prevailed— and again it should be emphasized that the events proved his contention to be right. As will be evident from the following agreement, the American Commander-in-Chief made a most liberal response to the requests of the Allies for special shipments of troops in the emergency.[2] But he also had gained his point in "committing the Council to an independent American Army." The first paragraph of the agreement left no room for doubt in this regard—and it may be considered the final record on this important question: "It is the opinion of the Supreme War Council that, in order to carry the war to a successful conclusion, an American Army should be formed as early as possible under its own flag. In order to meet the present emergency, it is agreed that American troops should be brought to France as rapidly as Allied transportation facilities will permit, and that, as far as consistent with the necessity of building up an American Army, preference will be given to infantry and machine-gun units for training and service with

---

[1]Procès-Verbal, Meeting of Supreme War Council, May 1, 1918.

[2]The British War Cabinet Report of 1918 has given the following official recognition to this spirit shown in the emergency: "During this crisis, however, invaluable assistance had been rendered by America, who, disregarding all petty considerations of national *amour propre* had consented to allow American units to be brigaded in British and French formations."

French and British Armies; with the understanding that such infantry and machine-gun units are to be withdrawn and united with its own artillery troops into divisions and corps at the direction of the American Commander-in-Chief after consultation with the Commander-in-Chief of the Allied Armies in France."

The agreement as to the preferential shipments in the month of May was again confirmed to the extent of the six divisions, and "any excess tonnage shall be devoted to bringing over such other troops as may be determined by the American Commander-in-Chief." It was further agreed that this program should be continued for June, on condition that the British Government should furnish transportation, for 130,000 in May, for 150,000 in June, as a minimum, "and that troops sent over in June should be allocated for training and service as the American Commander-in-Chief may determine." It was also agreed that, if the British should be able to transport more than 150,000 in June, this excess should be infantry and machine-gun units, and that there was to be in June "a new review of the situation to determine further action."

All this was far removed from the proposed policy of the Allied leaders to amalgamate our American troops with the British and French armies, and consequently General Pershing could then keep on with his projects for an independent American Army, in spite of the temporary diversion of American troops. These projects have been described, and the forethought shown was soon to be vindicated by the proof, that preparations for organization, administration, and subsistence were much further advanced than the Allies realized, and, consequently, an American Army was also much nearer a reality.

At the time of the first attack, in March, "four combat divisions, equivalent in strength to eight French or British divisions, were available,"[1] aside from troops with the French and in Services of Supply, and three divisions were arriving. By the end of May there were 600,000 American troops in France, and "our Second Corps, under Major General George W. Read, had been organized for the command of the ten divisions with the British, which were held back in training areas or assigned to second-line defenses."[2]

It was providential that the American Expeditionary Forces were thus taking form, for the disasters to the Allied armies had continued, and had gone beyond any situation that could be remedied by merely reinforcing the Allied armies. The third assault of the great German offensive was against the French armies (Third Battle of the Aisne, May 27, 1918) in the sector between Soissons and Rheims, where the French had thought their defenses very strong. Yet the same German tactics were repeated with the same successful results. The French defenses were broken, and the Germans surged over the supposedly impregnable Chemin-des-Dames, captured Soissons, and drove forward over thirty miles in four days to the Marne itself. The Germans had taken 40,000 prisoners and 400 guns, and they had won another great salient, of which Château-Thierry was the apex. Ten days afterward, on June 9, the Germans made another gain of importance south of Montdidier

[1] General Pershing, Report.
[2] *Ibid.*

and Noyon, extending their gains and straightening their line west of Soissons.

These defeats gave a staggering blow to the French, and it destroyed any feeling of security in their own defense. The German drive had easily broken through what were considered the strongest French intrenchments. It had smashed through a long way on the road to Paris—and the Germans were back on the Marne. This fact made a profound impression on French public opinion. General Pershing wrote: "On reaching the Marne that river was used as a defensive flank and the German advance was directed against Paris. During the first days of June something akin to a panic seized the city and it was estimated that 1,000,000 people left during the spring of 1918."

The military situation had grown very serious for General Foch's armies. Not only had the German offensive made gains at each assault, but, in addition to the enormous losses inflicted, each time there had been so great a dislocation of Allied forces that all the efforts of the new Commander-in-Chief had been needed to bolster the defense. This had prevented any thought of a counter offensive, and there had been no decisive check to the German advance, which actually threatened Paris. In addition to this obvious danger, these successive reverses for the Allied armies, with no power yet developed of stopping the Germans, had greatly affected the spirits of their troops, and there is no question of the fact that their morale was ebbing.

It was in this desperate situation that the American Expeditionary Forces gave their aid as American combat divisions, and this aid went beyond all expectations of the Allies. There is no doubt of the fact that "the prevailing opinion among the Allies was that American units were suitable only for the defensive, and that at all events they could be used to better advantage under Allied command."[1] But General Pershing and his officers knew their men. They had been in personal contact with the American personnel, and they had rightly estimated the spirit and intelligence shown in all ranks. Short as their instruction had been, it had proved to be the right training for fighting the new tactics of the Germans. This was the victory for the American doctrine of "the development of a self-reliant infantry by thorough drill in the use of the rifle and in the tactics of open warfare."[2]

That the opinion of the American Command was right had been already shown by the test of battle. On May 28, in the region of Montdidier, the American First Division, which had taken the place of two French divisions, had "captured the important observation stations on the heights of Cantigny with splendid dash,"[3] and had repulsed the violent counter attacks of the enemy, who were "determined at all cost to counteract the most excellent effect the American success had produced."[4] In the first days of June the same fighting qualities had been shown by the American Second Division in hot engagements, including the fiercely contested action at Belleau Wood. It was in this last action that the Marine Brigade of this division fought so well.

---

[1] General Pershing, Report.
[2] *Ibid.*
[3] *Ibid.*
[4] *Ibid.*

These tests had proved General Pershing's case. He
could write as a demonstrated statement of fact: "Up
to this time our units had been put in here and there
at critical points as emergency troops to stop the terrific
German advance. In every trial, whether on the defensive or offensive, they had proved themselves equal
to any troops in Europe." These object lessons were
changing the opinions of the Allies as to the value of
American troops. But, in the desperate situation, the
Allies were only too glad to grasp at any helping hand,
and, at last, they listened to General Pershing's urgent
recommendation to throw into the battle American
combat divisions under their own commanders, and
concentrated for a counter offensive.

This idea of striking back at the Germans, instead
of the defensive strategy of the Allies, had been in
General Pershing's mind. In a letter to Secretary Baker,
of June 18, 1918, he had written: "After checking the
German offensive, we must be prepared to strike as
soon as possible." And, in a later letter to the Secretary
of War, he wrote the following, which is a vivid picture
of this situation: "On June 23d, when M. Clemenceau
was at my headquarters for the conference, I had an
opportunity to speak about the use of our troops. I
told him that they were being wasted and that, instead
of the Allies being always on the defensive, an American
Army should be formed at once to strike an offensive
blow and turn the tide of the war. He was very much
impressed at such boldness, as he had heard only of
our men going into French divisions as platoons or at
the most as regiments."

Yet this very idea of an American Army on the

offensive was what was destined to happen, and the stage was already being set for the great drama. The Germans were preparing, almost openly, for their final drive, in complete confidence that they had so impaired the Allied armies that resistance would be impossible. In this belief, they gathered their troops against the Château-Thierry salient. But they had left out of their calculations the new factor in the situation, something so unexpected that it came as a surprise. Massed forces of American troops were to be thrown into this decisive battle, and these were to change the whole aspect of this battle.

The Germans were so overconfident that they allowed it to become evident the Château-Thierry salient would be the point of greatest danger. A group of American divisions was accordingly collected in this region. The late Colonel Kelton well described this situation: "It was no longer a question as to which division had completed training according to any alleged schedule; it was a dire emergency, and a question as to what troops of any class were most available for Château-Thierry—to help the French in a desperate attempt to save Paris."

There have been many crises in military history, but it would be hard to find one that has been made so definite a matter of record by the official testimony of the highest authorities. Since the war there have been attempts to draw a veil of gentle serenity over the scene. But the record can not be expunged, and it proved that the Allied Armies were in a situation that made necessary the American reinforcement. The following clearly defined the crisis of the World War, and there is no need of any addition or explanation.

"General Foch has presented to us a statement of the utmost gravity . . . as there is no possibility of the British and French increasing the numbers of their divisions . . . there is great danger of the war being lost unless the numerical inferiority of the Allies can be remedied as rapidly as possible by the advent of American troops. . . . We are satisfied that General Foch . . . is not overestimating the needs of the case. . . .

> "D. LLOYD GEORGE.
> "CLEMENCEAU.
> "ORLANDO.

"Versailles Conference, June 12, 1918."

"We recognize that the combatant troops to be dispatched in July may have to include troops which have had insufficient training, but we consider the present emergency such as to justify a temporary and exceptionable departure by the United States. . . .

> "FOCH.
> "MILNER
> "PERSHING.

"Agreement, June 5, 1918."

CHAPTER XXXI

THE TURN OF THE TIDE

AS HAD been anticipated, the Germans planned a new drive for the middle of July, and the salient of Château-Thierry was the storm centre of the battle. This assault was the most dangerous of the war, as it was the final concentrated effort of the full military strength of Germany. The Germans had retained the offensive for four months, and they had badly shattered the French and British armies. They were supremely confident of the result, and were convinced that this battle would bring a decisive victory for the German Empire. This confidence of the German leaders had spread throughout their armies. As General Pershing expressed it, "The enemy had encouraged his soldiers to believe that the July 15 attack would conclude the war with Germany."

The German military plan was to make attacks through the Château-Thierry salient to the south and east, with the twofold object of extending their gains to the south and by the drive to the east broadening the salient below Rheims, to pinch off that city as the Germans were also to attack east of Rheims. If this plan had succeeded, Rheims would have been untenable, and the Germans would have controlled a wide terrain for operations threatening Paris. General Foch's statement that there was "a great danger of the war being lost" was a true statement of the case.

The strength of the American military reinforcement gathered to avert this danger, aside from the American troops which were with the British and French armies in other sectors,[1] has been stated by General Pershing as follows: "On July 15, the date of the last German offensive, the First, Second, Third, and Twenty-Sixth Divisions were on the Château-Thierry front, with the Fourth and Twenty-Eighth in support. . . . The Forty-Second Division was in support of the French east of Rheims." These American divisions in the zone of the great German assault were the equivalent of fourteen French or British divisions, and they were American fighting units under the command of their own officers in the ensuing action.

This German assault was delivered on July 15, 1918, with all the strength of their long preparation behind it. It was on a wide front, as the attacks east of Rheims extended as far as the Argonne. But the main attack was in the region of Château-Thierry, as had been expected. The German drive against this salient toward the southeast, below Rheims, won some measure of success. There were gains through the French positions, and an advance was made across the Marne in the southeast. But at the points of the main attacks to the south and southwest, where the Americans were con-

---

[1] "On the Alsace-Lorraine front we had five divisions in line with the French. Five were with the British Army, three having elements in the line. In our training areas four divisions were assembled and four were in the process of arrival."—General Pershing, Report.

centrated, the Germans were held without gains of any
account, and they were unable to push across the Marne
at Château-Thierry.

The German gains east of Château-Thierry had been
"effected against the French immediately to the right
of our Third Division. The following quotation from
the report of the commanding general of the Third
Division gave the result of the fighting on his front:
'Although the rush of the German troops overwhelmed
some of the front-line positions, causing the infantry
and machine-gun companies to suffer in some cases a
50 per cent. loss, no German soldier crossed the road
from Fossoy to Crezancy, except as a prisoner of war,
and by noon of the following day [July 16] there were
no Germans in the foreground of the Third Division
sector except the dead.'"[1]

General Pershing has added the following: "On this
occasion a single regiment of the Third Division wrote
one of the most brilliant pages in our military annals.
It prevented the crossing at certain points on its front,
while on either flank the Germans who had gained a
footing pressed forward. Our men, firing in three directions, met the German attacks with counter attacks at
critical points and succeeded in throwing two German
divisions into complete confusion, capturing 600 prisoners." This American regiment was the 38th Infantry,
commanded by Colonel U. G. McAlexander, who had
the intuition to prepare strong flank positions for defense, in case the French on his right were forced to
retire. For days of hard fighting this regiment alone

---

[1]General Pershing, Report.

blocked the Surmelin Valley, and, when the offensive came, in spite of its fearful losses, this regiment saluted its dead and moved forward.[1]

After the Second Battle of the Marne had continued for three days, with successful resistance to the German attack, General Foch was at last convinced that he possessed the much needed additional strength that would permit him to launch the counter attack against the Germans. This, as has been stated, was the desire of General Pershing's heart. He wrote: "Seizing this opportunity to support my conviction, every division with any sort of training was made available for use in a counter offensive."

"General Pétain's initial plan for the counter attack involved the entire western front of the Marne salient. The First and Second American Divisions, with the First French Morocco Division between them, were employed as the spearhead of the main attack, driving directly eastward through the most sensitive portion of the German lines, to the heights south of Soissons. The advance began on July 18, without the usual warning of a preliminary bombardment, and these three divisions at a single bound broke through the enemy's infantry defenses and overran his artillery, cutting or interrupting the German communications leading into the salient. A general withdrawal from the Marne was immediately begun by the enemy, who still fought stubbornly to prevent disaster. . . . The result of this counter offensive was of decisive importance. Due to the magnificent dash and power displayed on the field of Soissons

---

[1] "Let us cherish close within our hearts the memory of our fallen comrades, salute them, then forward."—Order of Colonel McAlexander.

by our First and Second Divisions the tide of war was definitely turned in favor of the Allies."[1]

The other American divisions bore a good part in this offensive, which the Germans were unable to check, and the Germans fell back until, "on August 6, the operation for the reduction of the Marne salient terminated. In the hard fighting from July 18 to August 6 the Germans were not only halted in their advance but were driven back from the Marne to the Vesle and committed wholly to the defensive. The force of American arms had been brought to bear in time to enable the last offensive of the enemy to be crushed."[2]

The foregoing is a bald account of the decisive events of the turn of the tide of war, but these events do not express a fraction of the moral effect produced by the enforced retreat of the Germans, after four months of uninterrupted victorious advance. The rebound of the Allies from the depths of depression to exultation was immediate, "for in those three days the morale of all the Allies had been born anew."[3] Equally marked was the effect upon the Germans of this startling overturn. The transition of the Germans from the elation of victory to the despondency of defeat followed at once. Nothing that could be written would express this great change as forcibly as the statement given out by the broken German Chancellor Hertling a few days before his death. "At the beginning of July, 1918, I was con-

[1]General Pershing, Report. In view of recent optimistic opinions, it would be well to quote the following from Sir Douglas Haig's Despatches (of 1918); "The complete success of the Allied counter-attack on the 18th July near Soissons marked the turning-point in the year's campaign."

[2]General Pershing, Report.

[3]Colonel R. H. C. Kelton, General Staff, U. S. A.

vinced, I confess it, that before the first of September our adversaries would send us peace proposals. . . . We expected grave events in Paris for the end of July. That was on the 15th. On the 18th even the most optimistic among us knew that all was lost. The history of the world was played out in three days."

Of course, after this, there was no more question of the quality of American troops on the field of battle. In fact, the victory on the field of battle had been to the same extent a triumph for the military ideas which General Pershing had so consistently advocated. It had been a hard struggle for the American Commander-in-Chief. For few realize how strong the opposition had been to his doctrines, and how all the Allied leaders persisted in using every argument and influence against his plea for the tactics of open warfare.[1] This never could have prevailed if it had not been for the unfailing support of Secretary Baker, and consequently of the Administration.

It is stirring to read, in General Pershing's letter to the Secretary of War at the time of the victory, the following unmistakable evidence of his well earned exultation, and of the unusual relations existing between a general and a war minister (July 28, 1918): "As it turned out, all these troops were engaged, with results you already know. The participation of our troops made this offensive possible, and, in fact, the brunt of it fell to them. Our divisions in this advance completely

---

[1] "General Pershing's decision for open-field warfare in face of the most violent opposition on the part of all the Allied leaders, who, it seems, could understand nothing but the trench warfare of attrition."—Major J. W. Woodbridge, *The Giants of the Marne.*

outstepped the French and had to slow down their speed occasionally for them to catch up. . . . I have had to insist strongly, in the face of determined opposition, to get our troops out of leading strings. You know the French and British have always advanced the idea that we should not form divisions until our men had three or four months with them. We have found, however, that only a short time was necessary to learn all they know, as it is confined to trench warfare almost entirely, and I have insisted on open-warfare training. To get this training, it has been necessary to unite our men under their own commanders, which is now being done rapidly.

". . . Orders have now been given by the French that all of our troops in sectors with the French would be placed under our own officers and that American division commanders would be given command of their own sectors. This has come about since my insistence forced the French to agree to the formation of an American Field Army. At a conference called by General Foch last Wednesday, the 24th instant, plans for assuming the offensive this year were discussed, as well as tentative plans for 1919. This is the first time the American Army has been recognized as a participant, as such, alongside the Allies. I shall give you from time to time an outline of what our plans are, but hope you will soon be here so that I may discuss them with you. . . . May I again express my warm appreciation of your confidence, and say also how gratifying it is to me to enjoy the personal relations that exist between us. Will you please convey to the President my best compliments and the Army's faith in his leadership."

In his report General Pershing stated: "The counter-offensive against the Marne salient in July and against the Amiens salient in August had gained such an advantage that it was apparent that the emergency, which justified the dispersion of our divisions, had passed. The moment was propitious for assembling our divisions. Scattered as they were along the Allied front, their supply had become very difficult. From every point of view the immediate organization of an independent American force was indicated. The formation of the Army in the Château-Thierry region and its early transfer to the sector of the Woevre, which was to extend from Nomeny, east of the Moselle, to north of St. Mihiel, was therefore decided upon by Marshal Foch and myself on August 9, and the details were arranged with Gen. Pétain later on the same day."

This meant the beginning of a different phase of the American military effort.

CHAPTER XXXII

THE FIRST AMERICAN ARMY

WHEN General Foch at last acquiesced in the decision for the formation of an independent American Army, on August 9, 1918, our Administration was already committing itself to a course which implied an army of large numbers. In June a joint telegram had been sent by General Foch and General Pershing to President Wilson advocating a program for the future that would "insure the existence in France, together with its necessary replacement troops, of an Army 46 divisions strong in October, 64 in January (1919), 80 in April (1919), and 100 in July (1919)".

On July 6, 1918, Secretary Baker had written in reply to General Pershing, assuring him that, "if any exertion on our part or any sacrifice can speed the successful termination, even by a single day, we should make it." The Secretary of War then stated: "We are, therefore, now having studies made to show the things necessary to be done for three possible programs, one involving 60, one 80, and one 100 divisions by the first of July, 1919. As soon as these programs are worked out, we will, in consultation with the War Industries Board, determine how far manufacturing facilities, already in existence or possible to be created, can supply the necessary material, and the assistance we shall have in the way of heavy artillery and transportation from the British and French."

He promised to take up the questions of this program with the British and French governments and "to arrange for concerted action among us which will lead to the increase in our effort which you and General Foch recommend." Secretary Baker had at once taken measures to send increased numbers of American troops to France. He wrote in this letter: "In the meantime, I have asked the British Government to continue the troopships, which they have had in our service during June, through July and August, and have told them frankly that we are considering an enlargement of our program which may require, for a time at least, the uninterrupted service of all the ships we have been using. If we are able in July and August to match the performance of June, it will mean another half million men in France, as the June embarkation figures show slightly more than 279,000 men."

This mark, which was set by Secretary Baker, was, in actual fact, overtopped by the totals of American troops sent to France in these critical months of 1918, and the promised reinforcement of half a million men was exceeded. As has been stated, in July and August 592,324 American soldiers were transported overseas. These astonishing totals were followed up by 257,457 sent over in September. The result was, the newly organized American Army on the Western Front was rapidly growing to numbers that exceeded the most sanguine expectations.

In the same letter Secretary Baker gave an explanation of this, which is in a nutshell a good account of the increased efficiency of the American training camps, which had been developed from the lessons of operating them: "The plan inaugurated by General March of having replacement divisions in this country from which deficiencies could be supplied, without robbing other divisions and disorganizing them, seems to me to solve the problem, and the divisions which come to you in August and September, will, I am sure, show highly beneficial results from this policy. In the meantime, we have discovered two things about training in this country which apparently nobody knew or thought of before we went into the war: first, that while it may take nine months or a year to train raw recruits into soldiers in peace time, when there is no inspiration from the existing struggle, it takes no such length of time now when the great dramatic battles are being fought and men are eager to qualify themselves to participate in them. We are certainly able to get more training into men now in three months than would be possible in nine months of peace-time training. And, second, we have learned that to keep men too long in training camps in this country makes them go stale and probably does as much harm, by the spirit of impatience and restlessness aroused, as it does good by the longer drilling. . . . The finishing touches, in any event, will have to be given in France, and I think you will find that men who have had four months training here are pretty nearly ready for use in association with your veteran and experienced troops, and that no prolonged period of European training, for infantry at least, will be found necessary. This makes the problem very simple from the point of view of the draft and the training camps."

All this, so utterly at variance with European military ideas, was in fact, as has been stated, the experience of our Civil War over again.

It was most timely that these means were being used, as the matter of replacements was one of the greatest difficulties for the American Expeditionary Forces. On July 25 General Pershing wrote to Secretary Baker: "To add to our difficulties there has been a shortage of replacements in men, as we have had to throw all available troops into the lines to stop the German advance. So that we have not even had any troops to spare for work to help out the rear, making it appear that we are unnecessarily falling behind in unloading ships. I have cabled a request for service of the rear troops to be sent at once and hope they will not be delayed. We have a lot to do to catch up and get our ports and lines of communication in shape to meet the heavy demands that are to be made upon them." From this it will be evident that the flood of American troops increased in volume at the very time when there was urgent need.

The difficulties in attempting to keep pace with these "heavy demands" had been very great—and were destined to be greater. Yet, shortly after the organization of the First American Army, General Pershing, in a warning against too much caution in carrying out the enlarged program, even if "without having our own tonnage in sight for their food supply," was able to cable this argument for his project (August 17, 1918):

"I ask consideration of the fact that instead of having 300,000 men here now as previously calculated, we have nearly one million and a half and they have been transported to France, handled by rail and fed during active operations without special inconvenience."

General Pershing has given this account of the organization of the First American Army: "Arrangements were concluded for the successive relief of American divisions, and the organization of the First American Army under my personal command was announced on August 10, with La Ferte-sous-Jouarre as headquarters. The Army nominally assumed control of a portion of the Vesle front, although at the same time directions were given for its secret concentration in the St. Mihiel sector."

At the conference at Bombon of all the commanders-in-chief, for the purpose of considering future operations, all had agreed that the Allied and American troops were to maintain the offensive. It was determined that this offensive should be carried out by operations along the whole Western Front, and that the first use of the Americans would be in the reduction of the St. Mihiel salient. While the American divisions were being assembled, the Allied armies continued the offensive by attacks in Picardy, beginning August 8, and these also won back much terrain which had been lost to the Germans in the great German offensive. These continued successes against the Germans led to the belief "that the limited offensive, which was to prepare for the campaign of 1919, might be carried further before the end of the year."[1]

On August 30, 1918, "a further discussion with

[1]General Pershing, Report,

Marshal Foch was held at my headquarters at Ligny-en-Barrois."[1] General Foch proposed a series of offensives which would again utilize the American divisions with the Allied armies. This was a surprise for General Pershing. As he expressed it, "The plan suggested for the American participation in these operations was not acceptable to me because it would require the immediate separation of the recently formed First American Army into several groups, mainly to assist the French armies. This was directly contrary to the principle of forming a distinct American Army, for which my contention had been insistent. An enormous amount of preparation had already been made in construction of roads, railroads, regulating stations, and other installations looking to the use of our armies on a particular front. The inherent disinclination of our troops to serve under Allied commanders would have grown and American morale would have suffered. My position was stated quite clearly, that the strategical employment of the First Army as a unit would be undertaken where desired, but its disruption to carry out these proposals would not be entertained."

The determined stand of General Pershing put an end to this ill-advised plan, and the matter was settled by another conference, held at General Foch's headquarters, where General Pétain was also present (September 2, 1918). General Pershing has stated: "After discussion the question of employing the American Army as a unit was conceded. The essentials of the strategical decision previously arrived at provided that the advantageous situation of the Allies should be

---

[1]General Pershing, Report.

exploited to the utmost by vigorously continuing the general battle and extending it to the Meuse. All the Allied armies were to be employed in a converging action. The British armies supported by the left of the French armies, were to pursue the attack in the direction of Cambrai; the centre of the French armies, west of Rheims, would continue the actions already begun, to drive the enemy beyond the Aisne; and the American Army, supported by the right of the French armies, would direct its attack on Sedan and Mezières.

"It should be recorded that, although this general offensive was fully outlined at the conference, no one present expressed the opinion that the final victory would be won in 1918. In fact, it was believed by the French High Command that the Meuse-Argonne attack could not be pushed much beyond Montfaucon before the arrival of winter would force a cessation of operations. The choice between the two sectors, that east of the Aisne including the Argonne Forest, or the Champagne sector was left to me. In my opinion, no other Allied troops had the morale or the offensive spirit to overcome successfully the difficulties to be met in the Meuse-Argonne sector, and our plans and installations had been prepared for an expansion of operations in that direction. So the Meuse-Argonne front was chosen. The entire sector of 150 kilometres of front, extending from Port-sur-Seille, east of the Moselle, west to include the Argonne Forest, was accordingly placed under my command, including all French divisions then in that zone. The First American Army was to proceed with the St. Mihiel operation, after which the operation between the Meuse and the western edge of the Argonne

Forest was to be prepared and launched not later than September 25."

There also had been another scheme in August for diverting the American troops to different uses, but General Foch's plan was the last of anything of the kind. Of course we know now that the various attempts of the leaders of the Entente Allies to change the consistent plan of war of the American Commander-in-Chief and the Secretary of War were misdirected. But it should be again emphasized that the mistaken attitude of the Allies was the natural result of the conditions on the Western Front. Their leaders had been so long contending with the problems there, without arriving at any successful solution, that these conditions had shaped their ideas. It had become the fashion to speak of this trench warfare as "stabilized." The same word might be used to describe the military ideas of the Allied leaders, and it is no wonder they were unable to believe that the ideas of newcomers would be better.

The last pregnant paragraphs of General Pershing, in describing this conference of September 2, were most significant. General Pershing's faith in the morale and offensive power of his American Army had been so great that he had deliberately chosen the most difficult operation of all, the Meuse-Argonne offensive. Although as General Pershing stated, no one could foresee anything of the kind at the time, yet this American offensive was destined to pass beyond the limit set by the Allied leaders, Montfaucon, as if it were not there, and to penetrate to a Sedan which was to end the war in 1918 by a German collapse, in contrast to the victorious Sedan of the War of 1870.

After fully gaining his contention for the right use of the First American Army, General Pershing went about his preparations for the attack on St. Mihiel. While these preparations were being made, Secretary Baker arrived for his second visit in France. As before, he came at the urgent desire of General Pershing, who had repeatedly written that the presence of the Secretary of War would be helpful. In August he had written: "Again I earnestly urge that you make an early visit here, as I feel that your presence at the ports, where I should ask you to talk to the men, and a general visit among the troops would brace them up tremendously and have an exceedingly good effect. Not that their morale is not high, for it is high, but at the same time, every soldier wants to feel that those in authority are behind him, supporting him to the limit; that they appreciate his sacrifices. He likes to feel this and occasionally to be told what a splendid man he is."

Secretary Baker has given the following interesting and personal account of what he saw at the front in France:

"My second trip to France during the war was in response to General Pershing's suggestion, and also and particularly to take up with the Inter-Allied Maritime Council the question of the allotment of further cargo tonnage. When I set out I did not know that the St. Mihiel operation was planned for a definite date. On my arrival at Brest I was met by Colonel De Chambrun, a French officer attached to General Pershing's headquarters, who told me that General Pershing desired me to come to his headquarters at the front, immediately and without stopping in Paris or elsewhere.

Accordingly, I arrived the day before the St. Mihiel battle opened, and was present throughout that battle.

"On September 13th I accompanied Generals Pershing and Pétain to St. Mihiel and witnessed the joy of a civil population delivered from an occupation which had lasted four years, during which time not a single newspaper or letter from the outside world had been permitted to reach an inhabitant of the city. All the young men in St. Mihiel had been carried off by the retreating German army, but the old men, women, and children danced in the public square to patriotic tunes, played by a military band, French flags were dug up from beneath cellar floors, and bits of bright ribbon gave a festive appearance to the sombre clothes with which the Germans had dressed the civil population during the occupation. The great compounds full of German prisoners and the immense stores of captured material indicated the size of the American success. As guns ceased firing in the St. Mihiel battle, they were immediately moved to positions assigned them in the Meuse-Argonne operation, which also opened before I left, so that the continuous battle which lasted to the end of the war raged throughout the entire time I was in France on my second visit.

"After the Battle of St. Mihiel I went to London, conferred with the Inter-Allied Maritime Transport Council, and secured quite definite assurance of large additions to the American cargo tonnage. I was accordingly able to cable to General March that the transportation of troops could continue unchecked. As a consequence, we were actually loading men on the transports in New York on the day the Armistice was signed.

"The night before the Battle of St. Mihiel I asked General Pershing whether there was anything I could do to help. He replied, 'Pray for a fog in the morning.' Just what potency he thought the prayers of the Secretary of War might have I do not know, but when daylight broke, during the preliminary bombardment, a blanket of fog protected our soldiers until they had passed beyond the defences of the enemy, and were in pursuit in open country. It then lifted and disclosed the long lines of German prisoners being conducted to our rear. The Battle of St. Mihiel was the most tremendous spectacle I have ever seen. Even a layman could understand the perfection with which the operation was executed, and the completeness of its success."

CHAPTER XXXIII

THE NAVAL FORCES SUPPORTING THE ARMY

WHILE the American reinforcement in France was taking the form of an independent American Army, the activities on the seas, which alone made this army possible, were on a scale never before imagined in warfare.

As London was the centre of the great convoy system, with which were interlocked all the activities of our own naval forces abroad, it was the only right move to have the headquarters of the United States Navy located in London, in constant touch with the British Admiralty. There Admiral Sims, as Commander of the United States Naval Forces Operating in European Waters, had established a strong administrative staff, of which the late Rear Admiral Nathan C. Twining was the efficient Chief of Staff. As the numbers of American naval units overseas increased, the policy was still continued of securing a united command by putting these American forces on active duty under the local British commanding officers, except that the great patrol area of the Brest American bases continued to be an independent American command. But all these American naval forces overseas remained under American control for maintenance, as was the case with the first contingents sent across.

For this reason, as the American naval forces overseas grew to large numbers, with detachments at Queenstown, Brest, Gibraltar, the Mediterranean area, and the Azores, with detachments with the Grand Fleet, and on other duties over the wide seas, including eventually even northern Russia, the American Headquarters was a busy place, and its activities extended in many different directions.

These detachments of the United States Navy, as well as Admiral Gleaves' Cruiser and Transport Force, were made more efficient by refuelling with oil at sea. This had been developed into a system that maintained a reliable service both winter and summer. Under the Office of Operations, and with the greatest secrecy, the positions of the tankers were plotted out to meet the different units which were to be refuelled. Broadly speaking, 30° Longitude had been designated as a boundary line. When they had passed to eastward of this line, the different naval details passed into the control of the American Headquarters in London, with Operations directing the policy and prescribing the point where 30° Longitude should be passed. That is, from the United States to 30° Longitude the details were under Admiral Mayo, or Admiral Gleaves. After passing to the east of 30° Longitude, they came under the control of Admiral Sims. In the same way, on trips westward they passed out of Admiral Sims' control on crossing 30° Longitude. This made a very practical basis for the constant long-distance activities of the United States Navy, and it worked out well in actual use.

The British War Cabinet Report (1918) has stated, of this stage of the war, that the British Navy and the

United States Navy "coöperated on terms of close alliance and high efficiency in maintaining the sea communication of the Allies and in transporting from the United States to European battlefields the rapidly growing armies which the American people provided." For the main British Naval force, activities were "necessarily lacking in incident. But, nevertheless, the Grand Fleet was the essential support of all the work carried out by the naval forces of the Allies in all the seas."[1] The attendant destroyers and light forces were still kept in close company with the British Battle Fleet.

The British Dover Patrol, under Rear Admiral Keyes in 1918, continued to protect the great volume of transportation between Great Britain and France. The net barriers in the Channel could not be maintained through the winter months, and in 1918 "the Straits were eventually closed by broad minefields extending from the British to the French coast."[2] This was a preliminary to putting into execution the American scheme for closing the northern exits by the great system of mine barrages for which preparations were being made.[3]

On the part of the Germans, Admiral Scheer has stated: "The winter months brought no change in the activities of the Fleet, which were directed towards supporting the U-boat campaign." There was but one departure from this program, a raid against the Scandinavian convoys in April, 1918. Admiral Scheer has put it on record that this was the last operation at a distance from the German bases undertaken by the

[1]British War Cabinet Report, 1918.
[2]*Ibid.*
[3]The Great Northern Barrage, *The Naval History of the World War.*

German Battle Fleet. Consequently, from this time and for the duration of the war, we must think of the High Sea Fleet as solely occupied in its mission of forwarding the U-boat campaign by keeping a wide area clear for the egress and entrance of the U-boats. But, as before, the British did not estimate this change of German naval strategy, and continued to keep all the forces of the Grand Fleet at a distance, on watch for an incursion into the North Sea which never came.

On the American side of the Atlantic, careful preparations had been made to guard against U-boat attacks, which were regarded as inevitable sooner or later. Of course the main task must be to safeguard the egress of the convoys. If the Germans had been able to interrupt these by operations of their U-boats in the Western Atlantic, it would have saved the whole situation for Germany. But it should be stated at once that the German attempts with their submarines off the American coasts never brought about the slightest delay in the rush of troops to France. Much less was there even the threat of an interruption.

Precautions for the safety of the convoys were unremitting. There was never any relaxation of vigilance throughout the many months in which there were no signs of the presence of U-boats. The channels of sailing were as carefully swept, and the convoys as vigilantly guarded by anti-submarine forces, as if there had been frequent U-boat attacks. The decision had been wisely made not to allow this escort duty on our side of the Atlantic to prevent any great number of destroyers from going overseas, and very few destroyers were retained for this service in the Western Atlantic. But the watch over the convoys was all the more painstaking from the very fact that it had to be carried on without them. It was here that the new submarine chasers were of value, and a large force of these craft was especially trained for this purpose. The energetic and adaptable young men who made up the personnel of this Naval force performed a most arduous duty, as their activities extended from Halifax to Key West, and few realize what an experience of wind and weather this involved.

Upon our declaration of war, the Coast Guard had become a part of the Naval Establishment for war duty, in accordance with an act of Congress of 1916. Its cruising cutters had been given more powerful guns, and a number of them were sent overseas. The rest rendered most valuable service in this great undertaking of patrolling the Western Atlantic. They were well adapted to our waters and were an important part of the system of cruisers and mother ships which supported the anti-submarine small craft.

The first appearance of German U-boats in the Western Atlantic was heralded by sudden attacks on shipping off the Delaware Capes. Two coastwise schooners were sunk on May 25, 1918, and there were sinkings in the first days of June, most of them on June 2, when seven vessels were sunk. These were coastwise craft, mainly schooners, with the steamship *Carolina* of 5,000 tons, the most important loss. There were renewed attacks in July, especially off Cape Cod, and again in August. On August 10 no less than nine coastwise schooners were sunk from 50 to 60 miles off Nantucket. "The appearance of enemy submarines in these waters necessitated the putting into effect of the convoy system for coastwise shipping and for the protection of individual ships engaged in the coastwise trade."[1]

"To forestall enemy submarine operations in the Gulf and Caribbean, a force was established called the American Patrol Force, and its headquarters was in the vicinity of Key West. . . . As was foreseen, the protection of the oil supplies from the Gulf to our own coast and then abroad was quite vital to the success of the general campaign, and these supplies the patrol detachment was prepared to safeguard by adopting at once the convoy system the instant they were threatened."[2]

Consequently, the German U-boat attacks never won success beyond these depredations against coastwise and incoming individual vessels. The U-boats never came near threatening the regular convoys, which were thus protected by sweeping their channels clear of the mines which the Germans spread, and guarded by escorting patrols of anti-submarine craft. These last were constantly hunting the U-boats with listening devices and depth bombs.

"On the whole the operations of the German submarines against our coast can be spoken of as one of the minor incidents of the war. . . ."[3] That these futile U-boat attacks can be thus dismissed, is evident from the fact that transportation of troops, instead of being diminished, leapt to the great totals, which have been given, in the very months of these attacks. Only one American fighting ship was lost off our coast, the ar-

[1]Report of Secretary of the Navy, December, 1918.
[2]*Ibid.*
[3]*Ibid.*

mored cruiser *San Diego* of the Cruiser and Transport Force. She was sunk by a mine off Fire Island on July 19, 1918, with the loss of six lives, three of these from the explosion.

Not only did these German raids with the U-boats against the American coast fail to produce any impression that would make us retain naval forces on this side of the Atlantic, but the Germans thus failed absolutely in what must be considered their one necessary object in these U-boat attacks—to break the chain of communications which was bringing and sustaining the American reinforcement that meant ruin to the confident military plans of the Germans. The American Expeditionary Forces remained successfully "based on the American Continent." The full measure of German failure was the fact that not one American troopship carrying our men to France was torpedoed. And this meant German failure, not only in American waters, but also in the other stages of transportation to the final destination at the ports of disembarkation overseas.

It would be well here to describe the losses in this service, in order to show beyond any question their small effect upon the great volume of American troops which at this stage of the World War poured into France without hindrance from the enemy. In addition to the *San Diego*, the only fighting ship of any size lost by the United States Navy, our Navy lost the destroyer *Jacob Jones*, the armed converted yacht *Alcedo*, the collier *Cyclops*, and the Coast Guard cutter *Tampa*, taken over by the Navy.

The *Jacob Jones* was torpedoed December 6, 1917,

when on her way alone from off Brest to Queenstown.[1] The *Alcedo* was one of the American armed yachts in French waters, and she was sunk by a U-boat while acting as convoy escort off the coast of France, November 5, 1917. The loss of the collier *Cyclops* was another of the many mysteries of the seas. She had reported at Barbados March 4, 1918, for coal, and left for Baltimore. She was never heard from again. The *Tampa* was one of the six Coast Guard cutters overseas which performed valuable services in the force of the United States Navy based at Gibraltar for escort and protection of convoys. She was acting as escort for a convoy from Gibraltar when she was destroyed in the Bristol Channel on the night of September 26, 1918. "Vessels following heard an explosion, but when they reached the vicinity there were only bits of floating wreckage to show where the ship had gone down. Not one of the 111 officers and men of her crew was rescued. . . ."[2]

The foreign transports, carrying American troops overseas, did not escape losses on their voyages to Europe. The most notable loss from enemy attack was the *Tuscania* (14,348 tons), a chartered Cunard liner under the British convoy system. She was torpedoed off the Irish coast on February 5, 1918, with the loss of 166 missing. The British chartered transport *Moldavia* was also sunk, with the loss of 56 lives. The unbroken record of immunity of the American troopships on their voyages to Europe was not maintained on their homeward voyages. Three of these American transports, *Antilles, President Lincoln, Covington*, were sunk on

---

[1]The American destroyer *Cassin* was torpedoed, but reached port.
[2]Report of Secretary of the Navy, December, 1918.

their way back to American ports, with loss of life in each case. The *Mount Vernon* (late German liner *Kronprinzessen Cecile*) and the *Finland* were torpedoed on homeward voyages, but each reached port and was repaired for service. The British chartered steamship *Dvinsk* was torpedoed and sunk on a homeward voyage.

These losses, compared with the great numbers of troopships which were plying between the United States and Europe to deliver the American reinforcement on the battlefield in France, show most strikingly that the Germans were not accomplishing any appreciable results, so far as concerned preventing this reinforcement from being thrown against their armies on the Western Front. In fact, the battle in France was actually being won on the seas. The wonderful record of the United States Navy in delivering our soldiers in France without losses tells the whole story.

CHAPTER XXXIV

THE CONTINUATION OF THE OFFENSIVE

THE task of gathering the forces of the First American Army for the attack on the St. Mihiel salient was "extremely difficult."[1] The American troops were disposed at different points along the Western Front. There were enough of them, but the difficulty was "to assemble combat divisions and service troops and undertake a major operation within the short period available and with staffs so recently organized."[2] Of the three Army Corps headquarters, which were to take part in the St. Mihiel operation, the First was on the Vesle, the Fourth at Toul, the Fifth not yet completely organized. This was a severe test of the projects of transportation, service of supply, and staff organization, which General Pershing had inaugurated far in advance, and they stood the test, for by these means the First American Army was assembled with an efficiency that left no doubt of the success of the operation.

The total of American troops engaged in this battle showed how rapidly things had progressed. There were 430,000 of the First American Army, and 70,000 French troops were attached to it. These French forces were placed by General Pétain under the personal command of General Pershing, "as they would be closely related

[1] General Pershing.
[2] *Ibid.*

to the attack of the First American Army."[1] Then was
to follow the test in battle of the newly organized First
American Army, in an engagement which demanded a
high degree of coördination, and consequently efficient
staff work.

St. Mihiel had been in the possession of the Germans
since September, 1914. It had always been a bad spot
in the battle line, as it was a projecting spur which
"threatened the entire region between Verdun and
Nancy, and interrupted the main rail line from Paris
to the east."[2] Besides this, its reduction was desirable,
because "it covered the most sensitive section of the
enemy's position on the Western Front, namely the
Mezières-Sedan-Metz Railroad and the Briey Iron
Basin."[3] The strength of the place had baffled the efforts
of the French. The Germans had used every means to
add to the defense provided by the natural difficulties
of the terrain. In this 1918 campaign, the Germans
were not determined to offer any such strong resistance
as in the past, as they were withdrawing along their
front. But to reduce this salient was a hard task set
for the new American Army.

On the night of September 11, the troops of General
Pershing's command were put into position for simultaneous attacks on the faces of the St. Mihiel salient.
On September 12, after four hours of violent artillery
fire to prepare for the advance, the assault took place
as planned. General Pershing has stated: "The operation was carried out with entire precision. . . . The

[1]General Pershing.
[2]General Pershing, Report.
[3]*Ibid.*

rapidity with which our divisions advanced overwhelmed the enemy, and all objectives were reached by
the afternoon of September 13. . . . We captured nearly
16,000 prisoners, 443 guns, and large stores of material
and supplies. The energy and swiftness with which the
operation was carried out enabled us to smother opposition to such an extent that we suffered less than
7,000 casualties during the actual period of advance.
During the next two days the right of our line west of
the Moselle River was advanced beyond the line of objectives laid down in the original orders. . . . Our divisions concluded the attack with such small losses and
in such high spirits that without the usual rest they were
immediately available for employment in heavy fighting
in a new theatre of operations."

These American troops were to be used in the projected great Meuse-Argonne offensive, which was to begin
only eleven days after the completion of the St. Mihiel
operation. Consequently, the positions won from
the Germans were put in condition for defense by the
smallest possible force, and the transfer of American
troops to the new scene of operations began at once.

As a result of the series of offensive operations, which
began with the decisive counter attack of July 18, not
only had all danger for Paris disappeared, but the
Germans had been driven from the positions that interfered with the lateral communications of Foch's armies.
Pursuing the policy of the continued offensive, which
had been agreed upon, General Foch was making preparations for an advance along the whole front from
Verdun to the North Sea in the last week of September,
1918.

The physical results of these victories had been very great, but the moral effect was greater than could be measured by any losses of men and terrain. Defeat was impairing the whole structure of the German Imperial Government. For the leaders of that autocratic government the blow had literally seemed to be a stroke from the blue.

At last the one thing had happened which was outside all the calculations of the Germans—and they could no longer be blind to the unexpected fact that the reinforcement of the American Army was actually present on the battlefield. The effect upon the Germans of this stunning revelation has been graphically described by General Pershing: "An American Army was an accomplished fact. No form of propaganda could overcome the depressing effect on the morale of the enemy of this demonstration of our ability to organize a large American force and drive it successfully through his defenses." General Pershing has also emphasized the result of the American doctrines for training, which have been described: "It gave our troops implicit confidence in their superiority and raised their morale to the highest pitch. For the first time wire entanglements ceased to be regarded as impassable barriers and open warfare training, which had been so urgently insisted upon, proved to be the correct doctrine."

The Germans could no longer delude themselves, in view of the radical change in the military situation. The German armies were no longer on the offensive, but were being pushed back by their reinforced enemies. And behind these repulsed German armies a sense of defeat was spreading back through the German people.

More than this, the shock of German defeat in France was quickly causing the carefully cemented edifice of the Central Powers to fall apart in ruins. As long as the Germans were winning, they held their allies together—but at the touch of defeat the coalition was collapsing. Austria-Hungary, Turkey, and Bulgaria had suffered more severely from the war than had Germany. The war had come home more closely to their peoples. There had been more actual privation. In fact, throughout these countries there were almost famine conditions in the last year of the war. Their peoples were utterly tired of the war and longed for peace.

While Germany was still winning victories in the first half of 1918, these causes of demoralization were only working under the surface, and the prestige of a victorious Germany still remained a strong dominating power in every region. A proof of this was the surrender of Rumania to the Central Powers in May, 1918. Under the same stimulus of these German victories, the Austro-Hungarian armies had also been induced to take the offensive against the Italians in June, 1918. These events were proof of the domination over its allies which the German Empire still exerted in 1918. There is no doubt that the German Empire would have been able to maintain this domination, and to keep these allies on the battlefield, if the German armies had remained victorious on the Western Front. But, after the turn of the tide had become evident, they dropped away without much resistance.

The beginning of the general collapse, due to German defeat, came in September, 1918, when Bulgaria was quickly put out of the war. The Salonica Army, which had been established and maintained by sea power, completed its successful guardianship of that region, and justified all efforts in maintaining it, by accomplishing the result of striking down this ally of Germany.

The Bulgarian surrender meant that communication with the Turks had been broken off, and Mittel Europa had been destroyed. The Turks were ready to follow suit, as all the efforts of the pro-German party could not induce them to stand by a defeated Germany. Austria-Hungary was also looking askance at the German Imperial Government, and the different jarring elements in the Dual Empire were breaking out in open dissatisfaction. Consequently, when the reinforced enemies of the German Empire were preparing for the final great series of battles on the Western Front, these battles were also destined to decide the war in the East, as all the rest of the elaborated structure of the Central Powers was ready to fall like a house of cards at the touch of German defeat on the Western Front. All this was the consequence of the turn of the tide of war—which was truthfully described by the dying German Chancellor in the heartfelt sentence, which has been quoted: "The history of the world was played out in three days."

CHAPTER XXXV

IT WAS natural that one of the first results of the change of the situation for the Germans, from victory to defeat, was a reaction against the German Naval Staff, which had promised to win the war by means of the U-boats. The German Naval Staff thus stood convicted, in the eyes of the German people, not only of failure to win the war with the U-boats, but also of failure to prevent the arrival of the American reinforcement on the Western Front, which had turned the tide of battle.

So strong was this reaction that there was an overturn in the German Navy, and Admiral Cappelle retired from his post as Secretary of State of the Imperial Ministry of Marine. Admiral Scheer was made Chief of the Admiralty Staff (August 11, 1918), and Admiral Hipper succeeded to the command of the High Sea Fleet.

In view of these changes in the German Navy, there was a very natural suspicion among the Allied and American authorities that there would be also a change in German naval tactics, and a use of the warships of the High Sea Fleet to attempt to upset the situation on the seas. Special precautions were taken by the United States Navy against any such change of tactics.

The main danger was held to be the possibility of raids by German battle cruisers to attack the troop convoys.[1] To guard against this, a division of three American battleships,[2] under the command of Rear Admiral T. S. Rodgers, was sent overseas, and based on Berehaven, Ireland. "The enemy raiders never appeared. This division made two trips into the Channel, escorting convoys when enemy submarines were reported in the vicinity."[3]

The reason for the lack of any such attempt is now an established matter of fact, and all speculation on this subject can be ended by knowing that the Germans never had any such intention at this time. The attitude of the German naval leaders was then characteristic of the German trend of mind in the World War. Their naval leaders were all so imbued with the doctrine of the U-boat, and so carried away by their own calculations, that, even at this stage in 1918, all their thoughts remained concentrated on plans for more extensive U-boat warfare. It followed that the new German Naval Secretary of State was the former head of the U-boat Office, Vice Admiral Mann-Tiechler, "in view of the fact that the chief task of this office now lay in furthering the construction of U-boats; and the building of reinforcements for the surface warships, which could no longer exercise any influence on the success of the war, was either given up or postponed, so that our entire

[1] "It was learned from Intelligence sources that for these reasons, if no other, the enemy contemplated an effort to send out battle cruisers to attack convoys, particularly troop convoys."—Office of Naval Intelligence, U. S. N.

[2] *Utah* (flag), arrived September 10, 1918; *Nevada*, arrived August 23, 1918; *Oklahoma*, arrived August 23, 1918.

[3] Office of Naval Intelligence, U. S. N.

capacity in shipbuilding was devoted to this one task."[1]

Admiral Scheer, on his new duty as Naval Chief of Staff, took his staff to General Headquarters in order to be in coördination with the Army Command in carrying out these plans for an increase of the U-boats. He has stated that, as a result of his arguments placed before Hindenburg and Ludendorff, "They both admitted that the main hope of a favorable end to the war lay in a successful offensive of the U-boats, and General Ludendorff promised, in spite of the great lack of personnel in the Army, to do his utmost to help to develop it further."

Admiral Scheer has also expressed beyond any mistaking the attitude of the whole German Navy as to the U-boats at this time: "We felt that we were responsible for the attainment of such an end to the war as had been promised to the German people, and that we could achieve it by these means alone. The Fleet was animated by one sole idea—we must and will succeed." Nothing can be more explicit than this, and we must look upon German naval strategy as still tied to the U-boat campaign, with the German Battle Fleet still allotted to its sole task of forwarding the U-boat campaign. If we think in these terms, which are the only deductions in accord with the facts, there is no difficulty in understanding the naval situation in Germany at this stage, when the rapid dissolution of the whole German structure was approaching. All the efforts of the German leaders were being concentrated on securing a greater output of U-boats.

There can be no possibility of mistaking this state of

[1] Admiral Scheer, *Germany's High Sea Fleet.*

mind. The Germans were again dealing in formulas of their own, with no conception of anything outside. It is strange to read that the program "for the next few months," with a grandiose increase in 1919, was being ratified by the visit of the German Emperor only two days before the enemy launched the great series of attacks which were destined to break down all German resistance. Consequently, it is established that the German naval leaders, although they knew that Germany was losing the war, yet could not believe that the end would come so soon, and they were absorbed in naval plans which could not produce any result before the downfall of Germany. Admiral Scheer has left no doubt of this by his own admission: "If I had foreseen the rapid development of events I would have preferred remaining with the Fleet rather than organizing the conduct of war at sea, for my plans never reached fulfilment." As a result of all this, there was no danger of a change to the offensive on the part of the warships of the German Battle Fleet before the total defeat of Germany put anything of the kind out of the question. Consequently, the convoys of troops and supplies remained free from the expected raids of German warships throughout the short remainder of the war.

In the wide areas of warfare on the seas, of course the outstanding feature was the great volume of American troops and their maintenance poured into the very heart of things in France. As to this fatal thrust against Germany, it must always be reiterated that British shipping made possible an American reinforcement of double the numbers we would have been able to deliver in France by means of our own transports. The fact that great numbers of British ships were thus being used must be kept in mind, in order to understand the broad movements of shipping in this final situation on the seas.

At this stage, over all the seas, the vast fleets of warships, transports, and cargo carriers were successfully working in concert for the one object of winning this war, which had grown to such unexpected proportions. From all over the world the convoys were bringing support and maintenance. The guardianship and protection of these large numbers of ships, as has been described, had brought about an urgent call for armed ships of all kinds and sizes, to an extent undreamt before. It is true that the distant seas had been swept clear of hostile naval forces, but, on the other hand, naval tasks had been greatly multiplied in the waters of the Atlantic and in the Mediterranean—and the reader must picture the momentous activity in these seas, which reached its culmination in the last months of the World War.

In regard to the Atlantic, this narrative has described the development of naval operations new to history— devoid to the end of the set actions of former wars. And yet, from Gibraltar to Iceland, these last months of the war saw a constant harassing naval activity that made the old days appear like a calm, in comparison with this modern storm. In these waterways of the Atlantic, the necessities of the crisis of the World War demanded that large numbers of ships should be concentrated, on their voyages to and from the central area adjacent to the battlefield of the gigantic struggle which was then deciding the fate of the war. And these crowding ships were obliged to play their parts in a drama of attack and defense created by the two most dangerous weapons of naval warfare, the submarine and the mine. The development of these weapons had called into being a multiplicity of naval forces, and the final act presented scenes of feverish activity on the seas which have not been generally realized. Yet they must be understood, in order to appreciate new adventures on the seas utterly outside of all former experiences in naval warfare.

What an extraordinary variety of conditions must be depicted to show the situation on the seas in the last months of the World War! On land, this war, carried on by means of all the resources of nations, had called into unexpected services hosts of men from civil life that dwarfed all the regular armies of the world. On the seas, it was even a stranger story. The numbers of men, outside the regular navies, who were called into the war on the seas were enormous—and these men were suddenly confronted with novel and exacting tasks, far beyond even the developments of the military tactics of the World War. It is strange reading to compare former ideas of European warfare with the actualities of the World War. As has been said in regard to other phases of the World War, the only comparison might be with the American Civil War, in which great numbers of men outside the regular Navy faced novel tasks on the seas.

This final situation of the World War, on the seas, should here be passed in review. Consider first the tasks that had come into being from the use of mines. The tentative experiments at the beginning of the war, in scattering a few mines on the waters, had grown into the vast systems of minefields, with the constant use by both sides of great quantities of mines, in defense and in offensives against the enemy. Both sides were constantly occupied in minelaying and minesweeping. Day and night, in all sorts of craft, these mine forces, recruited for the most part outside of the regular navies, were at work on their dangerous service. These mine forces grew to proportions that were navies in themselves. And they deserve their own epics of daring adventure.

But it is safe to say that the submarines, directly and indirectly, brought more men into hazardous service on the seas than any other factor in naval warfare. The fearful risks for those who served in the submarines have not been generally understood. The proportion of U-boats lost was very great,[1] and the horrible fate of the crew of a sunken submarine needs no description.

Of the men whose service on the seas called them to contend with the submarines the numbers had gone still farther beyond the former ideas of navies. In addition to the various naval forces engaged in anti-submarine warfare, we must include the great numbers of ships which were obliged to face the dangers of U-boat attacks, in their services as transports and cargo carriers. These ships were perforce participants in submarine warfare. It was not alone the ships protecting the convoys that must contend with the U-boats. Every ship must be prepared to fight or manœuvre. Many of them, as has been stated, were armed. Of American ships alone, about 500 carried guns for protection against U-boats. This meant some 1,000 guns and 10,000 young Americans as gun crews. But not only the gun crews

_____
[1] The Germans have stated their losses of U-boats as over 45 per cent.

but all the crews must be counted as taking part in submarine warfare. It will at once be apparent that the numbers of men involved in this new and hazardous naval warfare had grown to totals that were amazing.

It was altogether a tremendous picture spread over the seas and made bizarre by the camouflage coloring which had been widely adopted by the last months of the war. What would a deep-water sailor of the old type have thought, if he had been dropped into the midst of the parti-colored ships of 1918? Concealment camouflage had been practically given up, and the British had led the way in daring designs of stripes and blocks of colour to deceive as to sizes and courses of ships. An immense amount of ingenuity was shown in the use of designs and "dazzle" coloring on all kinds of ships—and this was typical of the startling changes of warfare on the seas. If the reader will think of this vast and varied panorama, the last scenes of the World War on the seas will take their true form.

As has been explained, the careful protection afforded by the convoy system had preserved the transports carrying American troops overseas from losses inflicted by the enemy that would bring about any appreciable percentage of interruption or delay. The one danger that actually threatened the success of this undertaking was from an unexpected source. It came from the sudden outbreak of influenza in America in September and October of 1918. "Thirty-eight troopships carried nearly 130,000 men across the ocean during the epidemic. . . . It is conservative to estimate that the influenza at sea cost, altogether, 2,000 lives. Many of the victims were buried at sea. . . . Judging by the statistics of the epidemic at the established camps, it is probable that if the troops had been held in quarantine more of them would have died than actually did die on the way across the ocean."[1] Both at the camps and on the transports heroic efforts were made to stem the disease. On the transports, the War Department decreased the number of troops loaded on each ship by 10 per cent. Consequently, this epidemic had a much greater effect upon the transportation of American troops than all the efforts of the enemy.

The desperate call for cargo carriers brought all kinds of craft into use. In the last months of the war, the American Cross-Channel Fleet was hard pressed to meet the enormously increased demands of the American Expeditionary Forces for coal from Great Britain. The efficiency of this fleet was greatly increased by the organization of the American Naval base at Cardiff early in September, 1918, by Rear Admiral Philip Andrews, and it was a most valuable source of supply for the American Army in the last months of the war.

In regard to all the cargo carriers, theirs was a service which cannot be rated too highly, and, in this far flung picture of the naval warfare of the World War, their place should be kept before the reader's eye. As has been stated, the ships of any speed were being used as transports, and the defense of speed was denied to the cargo carriers. There was no romance in their service, and the general public has hardly ever heard of them. But their crews were "heroes unsung"[2] in very truth. Their adventures, their dangers, and their fights—for

---

[1]Crowell and Wilson, *The Road to France.*

[2]*Ibid.*

they fought like heroes indeed—should be recorded. "No branch of naval service lived in greater danger or called for hardihood, resolution, and judgment in a higher degree. . . . The men knew that, as things went, the odds were against them; that they could expect no quarter. Yet they stood at their posts and faced the foe gallantly on unequal terms; and sometimes they emerged from the encounters in triumph."[1]

The United States cargo carriers had many fights with U-boats, and often were successful in saving their ships by their own gunfire. The American tanker *Sea Shell*, in the Mediterranean, must be given the credit of putting out an attacking U-boat by gunfire. The *J. L. Luckenbach* stood off a U-boat for four hours, until rescued in a badly battered condition by the destroyer *Nicholson*. The *Navajo* and *Nyanza* won commendation for successfully resisting U-boats, and the *Chincha* and *Paulsboro* beat off attacking U-boats. In the cases of the *Norlena* and *Borrinquin*, the crews had started to abandon ship after hits by torpedoes, but returned and drove off the U-boats by gunfire.

The crews of the cargo carriers showed equal courage in defeat. The *Campana* fought for four hours, and the *Moreni* for two hours, before being sunk by U-boat attacks. The most serious loss of life for the N. O. T. S. came from the loss of the *Ticonderoga* (late German steamer *Camilla Rickners*). She had fallen behind her convoy, from lack of speed owing to poor coal and was attacked by a U-boat in the early morning of September 30, 1918. After the *Ticonderoga* had been badly cut up by gunfire with many killed and wounded,

---

[1]Crowell and Wilson, *The Road to France.*

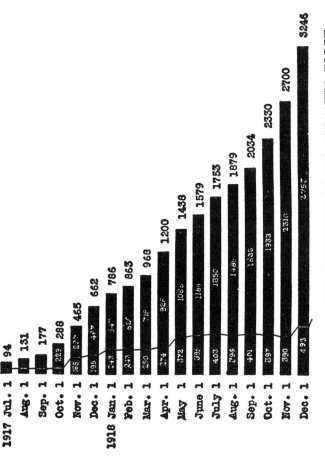

THE GROWTH OF THE AMERICAN TRANS–ATLANTIC FLEET
(Given in thousands of deadweight tons)

she was sunk by a torpedo. Of 240 on board only 25 were saved, most of them wounded, and only "after four days of incredible hardship."[1] These are but examples of the hazardous adventures of those who manned the American cargo carriers, and it will be evident that these men had accepted the call to a service that implied great sacrifice of life.

With these dangers common to all, not only must all the American elements on the seas be considered one great American naval force working for the one great object, but we must also realize how intimately bound together were the American naval and military forces in this vast joint operation, The preceding narrative has shown how closely interlocked were the Army and Navy in the administration and control of operations. This close association ramified through all ranks. Soldiers and sailors grew to know one another, as they were working together to forward the great joint offensive, "based on the American Continent" and striking at the very vitals of Germany. Perhaps there has never been so close an association of an army and a navy—certainly never on anything approaching the scale of this decisive joint operation of the World War. And, when studying the service rendered by the American Army in the final battles on the Western Front, we must always think of the successful result as attained by means of this close coördination of effort on sea as well as on land.

---

[1] Admiral Gleaves, *A History of the Transport Force.*

CHAPTER XXXVI

THE AMERICAN EXPEDITIONARY FORCES OF 1918

AT THIS stage, when the preparations were being made for the final grapple with the enemy on the Western Front, the time had come when the effort of America must be considered as at last translated into its final terms of a military reinforcement for the Entente Allies. And all the manifold activities which have been described, industrial, naval, military—on land and on sea—must be judged solely by the value of this one product, the American Army on the battlefield. All else was outside the question. This military value of the American Expeditionary Forces must be the one measure of success or failure. Judged by this rigid test, the only standard that can be applied, there is now no doubt of the fact that the effort of the American nation was successful.

As has been stated before, this successful result was no matter for complacency or boasting. It is true that we improvised an army—and improvisation of forces must be the resource of a nation in war, now that wars have gone beyond the eras when they were fought out by the regular forces. But it was a sorry showing for a great and progressive nation that not only all its forces but all its ideas had to be improvised. In regard to the vast unknown of the changed World War we were like babes in the wood, and it was hard work to find our way out. This is a true statement of the case, and it leaves no room for conceit in ourselves.

On the other hand, there was no excuse for the unreasoning clamor of faultfinding which flooded this country just after the end of the World War. The Wall of Lamentations at Jerusalem was a cheerful meeting place compared with America in those days. The timely outbreak of General Dawes did more to clear the air than anything else. The profane association of the harmless name of Maria with the infernal regions was a picturesque touch, which drew the attention of our people to the statement of a man who knew what he was talking about, and who proclaimed the nonsense of the wails which filled the air. Our people now know that something unusual was accomplished, and that the facts of that accomplishment should be given, just as much without undue depreciation as without undue claims for perfection.

The many processes, industrial, military, and naval, which were necessary to produce the American Army on the Western Front have been traced, as well as the great projects in France for its transportation, maintenance, and staff organization, which assured these important factors in advance. The result of all this, the American Army itself, should be described, before telling the story of its final and decisive operations in the field.

In the first place, as to command and staff, extending through its corps and divisions, the American Army was better equipped than had been thought possible. This was due to the condition that its carefully chosen officers of the Regular Army, in spite of the fact that their service had been with so small a force, soon proved that they were able to play their parts with the greatly increased numbers of the World War. The credit for this state of things, which stood the trying test of field service, must be largely given to the postgraduate courses of the Leavenworth Schools[1] and of the War College. By these means Army officers of active mind had been given the opportunity to study problems of command and staff, for armies on a large scale. Of course, the scope of these studies had been stimulated and broadened after the World War began in 1914. But, on the other hand, the doctrines of these schools had remained sound and not conventionalized by the prevailing European ideas. This was shown by the adherence to the tactics for open warfare, which fortunately had become the basis of our tactics and training. The result was, the officers who took these courses were not stuck fast in any ruts, but received a sound preparation for the wide range of new responsibilities in the enlarged American Army overseas. The good influence of these courses can be traced throughout the American Expeditionary Forces, as almost all those who were given high commands and important staff duties had taken these courses. For this reason, our American officers were not only better qualified for their new duties, but they were also well grounded in sound doctrines, which enabled them to associate with the British and French, and to receive the benefit of their experience without sharing the convictions of the Allies that the lessons of all warfare were bounded by the trenches.

---

[1] The General Service Schools, Fort Leavenworth.

Above all things, we must realize that these doctrines had the special effect of giving the American officers a valuable preparation for the campaign of 1918, when the Germans took the war out of the trenches, and, as has been explained, the operations of the World War changed to the use of the very tactics which were the groundwork of the American military doctrines.

The influence of these doctrines extended down through all ranks. All the personnel of the American Army had been imbued with these ideas. The new recruits, officers and men, had absorbed them in their training and in their contact with those who had been in the service. And one thing should be kept in mind in regard to the American Expeditionary Forces— lessons were not alone taught in the training camps. The whole Army was one great school and remained so throughout its operations in the field. Its personnel must fight and learn the lessons of its school at the same time. The call was too hurried for completing their instruction. The new officers and men were leavened by their contact with experienced soldiers, but there was not time to think only of training. In the matter of training, therefore, the American Army in France was never a finished product. But providentially its school was the right one —and its training, although never complete, was the right training. We must always think of the American Expeditionary Forces in these terms, as fighting in various stages of training.

As Secretary Baker had written, it had been found that American soldiers required a shorter period of training than had been thought necessary before the actual test. It was also proved that in service they kept on and learned their lessons with quick adaptability. This adaptability of the American soldier was too notable to be denied. It was due to the unusually intelligent personnel of the American Army, already eager with patriotic zeal, and stimulated to the utmost by the surroundings of the war. As General Pershing wrote, the first operations in the field had shown that we were on the right track, and the Americans consequently had great confidence in themselves from the beginning. All this gave them a high morale, and they had a fresh energy which, in action, made up for deficiencies in training and experience.

Yet, in attaining this quick result, there had been the seeming paradox that the American commanders had insisted on a longer course of training than had been suggested by the Allies. The Allied commanders, with their ideas limited to using the Americans as recruits in the Allied units, had thought that a course of training in the trenches would be sufficient for our soldiers. But the Americans had stood out against this, and invariably trained for open warfare. By so doing, the longer process had actually produced a quicker result, as was proved by the event—after open warfare had taken the place of stabilized trench warfare.

The foregoing accounted for the efficiency displayed by the new American levies. And all in the American Expeditionary Forces were, in this sense, new levies. For even the Regular Army divisions, which were first sent overseas, although built up on frameworks of experienced personnel, yet comprised so large a proportion of new officers and men that they could not be considered veteran units so far as training was concerned.

On the whole, the American Expeditionary Forces possessed a great advantage in personnel. But it must be stated that there were constant difficulties in keeping up with the demands for the numbers required. The calls for replacements were unending. As the American troops were hurried into action at the crisis, and this meant exhaustive service, the drain upon their units was very great, and there was a constant need of replacements for the nearly impossible task of keeping the active divisions in fighting strength. At times the supply of fighting men lagged far behind the requirements of the Army,[1] and it was a hard undertaking to maintain the efficient use of our troops on the battle line. The adoption of the policy of replacement camps was a help, but many divisions had to be broken up to supply replacements.[2] "Altogether seven divisions had to be skeletonized, leaving only one man per company and one officer per regiment to care for the records."[3] This matter of replacements remained the most difficult problem of our operations.

As can be seen from the above, there was no ideal situation as to getting the American Army into the battle. There were hosts of perplexities and difficulties to the end. Yet the net result was the unexpected American strength that was thrown on the battlefield at the crisis, and its greatest tribute was Ludendorff's utter surprise at its arrival. In the matter of actually

---

[1] "Combat divisions are short over 80,000 men."—Cable from General Pershing, October 3, 1918.

[2] There were two American divisions which each received over 30,000 replacements.

[3] General Pershing.

getting the American personnel into action, the record was remarkable, in spite of disappointments and shortcomings. Of the two million men in the American Expeditionary Forces, "1,390,000 saw active service at the front."[1] Aside from this impressive total of the number of Americans at the front, these figures made a good record for the high proportion of efficiency, out of the whole number of 2,084,000 soldiers sent overseas. Another significant fact proved how rapidly the American Army had developed as a factor on the Western Front: "From the middle of August until the end of the war the American divisions held during the greater part of the time a front longer than that held by the British."[2]

It must be reiterated that this great American personnel could not have been put into action and maintained at the front if it had not been for the advance projects of transportation and maintenance which have been described. In the matter of transportation, after arrival in France, General Pershing's advice to the War Department to leave the matter in the hands of American railroad men had been justified by results. The purchase of cars, locomotives, cranes, tugs, barges, etc., and the organization of the personnel of the Transportation Department of the Expeditionary Forces were under the Director General of Military Railways, Samuel M. Felton, who was president of the Chicago and Great Western Railroad. The military railway personnel in France, "made up almost entirely of men formerly employed by the railways of the United

[1] A Statistical Summary, General Staff U. S. A.
[2] *Ibid.*

States,"[1] amounted to nearly 60,000. "The immediate responsibility of the work in France was intrusted to Brigadier General W. W. Atterbury, formerly of the Pennsylvania Railroad, who was appointed Director General of Transportation, and who, with his able staff, has succeeded in transporting our troops and supplies over the 500 miles of railroad from seaboard to battle line with remarkable efficiency and dispatch."[2] In addition to the great movement of troops passing into France, through the bases which had been prepared, the following showed the proportions to which the volume of supplies had grown: "At the cessation of hostilities the Army was using 12 French ports with a permanent assignment of 70 berths, and was discharging supplies at the rate of 1,000,000 tons a month, a rate exceeding that maintained by the British during the period of their operations in France."[3]

These great totals showed the enormous tasks of the Services of Supply of the American Expeditionary Forces, which must distribute these vast volumes of necessities, by handling them at the base depots, the intermediate depots, and the advance depots. The personnel of the S. O. S. comprised the enormous total of 668,312 at the time of the Armistice, all soldiers except 23,772 civilian employees. Major General James G. Harbord was the Commanding General of the S. O. S. and ably directed its many difficult activities. For Colonel Ayres was able to report: "The Army in France always had enough food and clothing. . . . At no time

---

[1] Report, Secretary of War, 1918.
[2] *Ibid.*
[3] *Ibid.*

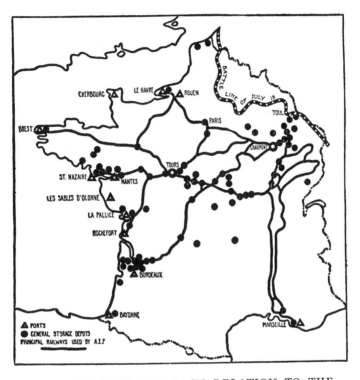

THE AMERICAN S. O. S. IN RELATION TO THE
BATTLE FRONT

was there a shortage of food in the Expeditionary Forces. Soldiers sometimes went hungry in this as in all wars, but the condition was local and temporary."[1]

As to weapons, the solution of the problem of rifles has been described, also the reciprocal agreement with the Entente Allies as to artillery. By these means the two greatest needs of the Army for weapons were supplied. There was also an agreement with the French to furnish machine guns to the divisions which first went overseas. After July 1, 1918, the American divisions embarking were equipped with light and heavy Browning guns. These American machine guns were very successful types. In pistols there was always a shortage. Troops in France likely to use them in close combat were supplied, but full equipment was never secured. In ammunition there was always a sufficient supply.

As to aviation, at first, when the American troops took over sectors on the battle front, they remained dependent upon the Allies for aircraft. The American program never produced enough planes for the needs of our Army. "The first aëroplanes received from home arrived in May (1918), and altogether we received 1,379 planes of the De Haviland type. The first American squadron completely equipped by American production, including aëroplanes, crossed the German lines on August 7, 1918. As to our aviators, many of whom trained with our Allies, it can be said that they had no superior in daring and fighting ability."[2] The chief contribution of the United States in aviation was the

---

[1] A Statistical Summary, General Staff U. S. A.
[2] General Pershing, Report.

standardized Liberty 12-cylinder motor, which was very practical and successful. Of these, at the time of the Armistice, 4,435 had been delivered to the American Expeditionary Forces and 1,025 to the Allies.

In the matter of providing quarters for the American Expeditionary Forces, an infinite variety of work was done by the Renting, Requisition, and Claims Service, which had been organized in March, 1918. This organization had charge of the complicated questions which arose when our forces were quartered over a strange country. It was created "to procure billeting areas, supervise the quartering of troops with an organization of zone and town majors, ...d to have charge of the renting, leasing, and requisitioning of all lands and buildings required by the American Expeditionary Forces." General Pershing has stated: "The efficient administration of this service had an excellent effect upon the people of the European countries concerned." As can be imagined, the problem of sanitation was always difficult in the primitive surroundings of most of the billeting areas. But the utmost effort was directed toward improved conditions, and remarkable results were achieved. The general good health of our armies "under conditions strange and adverse in many ways to our American experience and mode of life,"[1] was proof of these results.

In this regard, as in their other duties for the care of our soldiers, the physicians of the United States continued in France the same magnificent work that had marked an epoch in camp conditions at home. General Pershing has written: "The Army and the Medical De-

[1] General Pershing, Report.

partment were fortunate in obtaining the services of leading physicians, surgeons, and specialists in all branches of medicine from all parts of the United States, who brought the most skilful talent in the world to the relief of our sick and wounded. The Army Nurse Corps deserves more than passing comment. These women, working tirelessly and devotedly, shared the burden of the day to the fullest extent with the men, many of them submitting to all the dangers of the battle front." Every word of this tribute was deserved. For it is a mere statement of fact to say that never in history was an army so well taken care of by its physicians and surgeons.

The hospital service was worthy of all praise—"one of the largest and most difficult of the medical problems of the American Expeditionary Forces. That the needs were always met and that there was always a surplus of several thousand beds, were the results of great effort and the use of all possible expedients to make the utmost of resources available."[1] The service of evacuation of the sick and wounded was also very ably organized.

But, in addition to all the medical and sanitary care, the exceptional good health of the American Army must be credited to the good conduct of its personnel. As to venereal disease, "the control was successful to a degree never before attained in our armies, or in any other army. It has been truly remarkable when the environment in which our men lived is appreciated. . . . The low percentage was largely due to the fine character of men composing our armies."[2] This high standard of

[1]General Pershing, Report.
[2]*Ibid.*

conduct was greatly helped by the extension of the welfare work of the societies which had accomplished such good results for the morale of the American soldiers in the training camps. All these societies continued their activities overseas, with great zeal shown by their members in accepting the hardships of service in the war areas. The well deserved praise from Secretary Baker for the good work of these societies has been quoted in Chapter XVII. They surrounded the American soldiers with good influences, both in service and on leave, and kept the soldier in touch with home life and home entertainments. These societies also furnished religious workers to help the Board of Chaplains, of which Bishop Charles H. Brent was the head, and which had a widespread influence upon our soldiers. General Pershing has also given praise to this organization for religious work: "Chaplains, as never before, became the moral and spiritual leaders of their organizations, and established a high standard of active usefulness in religious work that made for patriotism, discipline, and unselfish devotion to duty."

Taken altogether, and appraised by the many severe tests of their quality, in camp, in transport, in their arduous duties overseas, the American Expeditionary Forces comprised an extraordinary body of men. Their origin and their evolution made for zealous effort, with the right control giving the right direction to their effort. The result was an impetus to greater efficiency than could have been thought possible before their deeds proved their merit. There was a spirit within, which even their arch enemy, Ludendorff, involuntarily recognized when he wrote that for the American soldiers the war became a "crusade." The absence of class distinctions in our nation was a great help toward coördination, and this was carried farther by the order of August 7, 1918, which discontinued the designations Regular Army, Reserve Corps, National Guard, National Army, and all the military forces of the nation were consolidated into the United States Army.

All this gave to the partly trained and hurriedly organized American Expeditionary Forces a morale and a self-confident striking power that rendered the American military reinforcement a formidable fighting force. This must be the verdict of impartial history.

CHAPTER XXXVII

ON SEPTEMBER, 26, 1918, the great final battles began on the Western Front, and soon there was fighting all along the line from Verdun to the sea. On the opening day General Foch began his assaults upon the Germans with an attack by the First American Army of General Pershing, on the sector from the Meuse to the western edge of the Argonne, and a simultaneous attack by the French in the Champagne. This offensive was followed on the next day by an attack by the British toward Cambrai. On successive days following, there were assaults in Flanders by the British and Belgians, and an attack in force toward St. Quentin. As will be evident, the American Army was an independent force in this series of offensives, acting in coöperation with the Allied armies, having its own objective in the wide general scheme of attack and under its own Commander-in-Chief.

It was another successful test of the value of the American organization, prepared in advance, that the First American Army was able to undertake two major operations in two different areas, when only "an interval of 14 days separated the initiation of the two attacks. During this short period the movement of the immense numbers of troops and the amount of supplies

involved in the Meuse-Argonne battle, over the few
roads available, and confined entirely to the hours of
darkness, was one of the most delicate and difficult
problems of the war."[1]

Of the fifteen American divisions concentrated for
the beginning of the Meuse-Argonne battle, seven had
been used at St. Mihiel, three were brought from the
Vosges, three from near Soissons, one from a training
area, and one from near Bar-le-Duc. "Practically all the
artillery, aviation, and other auxiliaries to be employed
in the new operations were committed to the St. Mihiel
attack, and therefore could not be moved until its success was assured. . . . That part of the American sector
from Fresnes-en-Woëvre, southeast of Verdun, to the
western edge of the Argonne Forest, while nominally
under my control, did not actively become a part of
my command until September 22, on which date my
headquarters were established at Souilly, southeast of
Verdun."[2] Under General Pershing's command on his
front were also three French Colonial divisions and three
French divisions, "holding the front north and east of
Verdun."[3]

General Pershing has also told of the following dis-
positions, which gave the Americans the advantage of
surprise: "At the moment of the opening of the Meuse-
Argonne battle, the enemy had ten divisions in line and
ten in reserve on the front between Fresnes-en-Woëvre
and the Argonne Forest, inclusive. He had undoubtedly
expected a continuation of our advance toward Metz.

[1]General Pershing, Report.
[2]Ibid.
[3]Ibid.

Successful ruses were carried out between the Meuse River and Lunéville to deceive him as to our intentions, and French troops were maintained as a screen along our front until the night before the battle, so that the actual attack was a tactical surprise."[1]

The first attack was led by nine divisions, and General Pershing has made the following statement of the auxiliaries employed: "About 2,700 guns, 189 small tanks, 142 manned by Americans, and 821 airplanes, 604 manned by Americans, were concentrated to support the attack of the infantry. We thus had a superiority in guns and aviation, and the enemy had no tanks."

With this superiority assured, in addition to the advantage of surprise, General Pershing was able to state: "During the first two days of the attack, before the enemy was able to bring up his reserves, our troops made steady progress through the network of defenses." It is most interesting to note that, although the Germans made tenacious efforts to hold Montfaucon, this point, which had been set by the opinion of the Entente Allies as the limit of the American advance, was captured at noon of the second day. Thus, on the second day, the Americans had passed their assigned stopping place for the winter!

General Pershing has summed up the first phase of this greatest of American battles as follows: "By the evening of the 28th a maximum advance of eleven kilometres had been achieved. . . . The right had made a splendid advance . . . but the extreme left was meeting strong resistance in the Argonne. The attack continued without interruption, meeting six new divisions which

[1]General Pershing, Report.

the enemy threw into first line before September 29. He developed a powerful machine gun defense supported by heavy artillery fire, and made frequent counter attacks with fresh troops. . . . We were no longer engaged in a manœuvre for the pinching out of a salient, but were necessarily committed, generally speaking, to a direct frontal attack against strong, hostile positions fully manned by a determined enemy."

These sentences are well worth study, as they touched on the essentials of this American continued operation, which made the American Army's part different from that of the Allied armies. In the first place, General Pershing had deliberately committed the American troops to this most difficult battle of all, the "direct frontal attacks" against the enemy's strongest positions, because, as he has stated, he felt that the American Army was the one force with the fresh energy and morale that would be able to carry through the assault, which was certain to be opposed by the utmost efforts of the enemy. The reason for the necessity of a desperate German defense against the American attack was the condition involved, that every advance of the American Army was an increasing menace to the main German railroad communications through Mezières and Sedan. There lay the key of the whole German military situation. The Germans could fall back on their right without disaster, but, if the American attacks penetrated, it meant the fall of everything.

The second element in the situation was the result of the first, and made the American attacks of double value to the Entente Allies. For, not only was every advance of the American Army a thrust into the very vitals of the German position on the Western Front, but the continued American assaults were all the time drawing away German troops to bolster the defence. General Pershing has stated: "From the moment the American offensive began until the Armistice, his defense was desperate and the flow of his divisions to our front was continuous." General Pershing's staff compiled data which proved that there was "an increase of 27 divisions on the American front during the battle."

These conditions gave the American operation a two-fold objective and mission, to penetrate the key of the German position and to consume in the battle the great number of enemy troops which had been drawn into the defense. In both these objects the American Expeditionary Forces were successful, and it is now evident that this operation was the greatest possible service which could be rendered to the Entente Allies.

There was another aspect of this Meuse-Argonne battle which should be understood, as it increased the effectiveness of the American thrust. The whole scheme of General Foch's offensive operations pivoted upon the region of Verdun. It was the reverse of the campaign of 1914, when the German right was advanced by a wide sweep through Belgium into France, with the whole great German offensive pivoting upon the same region of Verdun. In this last campaign of 1918, after the scale had been turned against the Germans and they had lost the offensive, the only recourse of the Germans was to fall back over the same ground, without yielding too much near the hinge of the pivoting point. It was there that the American Expeditionary Forces were attacking. As General Pershing stated, "The enemy must hold fast to this part of his lines or the withdrawal of his forces with four years' accumulation of plants and material would be dangerously imperilled." It followed that the pressure against the line of the great radius so near the hinge forced the whole line back. To quote again from General Pershing, "Our dogged offensive was wearing down the enemy who continued desperately to throw his best troops against us, thus weakening his line in front of our Allies and making their advance less difficult."

All this justified General Pershing in his choice of the most difficult task for the American Army. Its pressure was swinging back the whole wide arc of the radius. But its greater difficulties might be described as if they were the labors of a man who must push open a heavy, unyielding door by exerting his strength near the hinges, instead of being allowed to push against the easier swinging edge.

With the American Army always persisting in its efforts, without giving the Germans a chance to divert their forces elsewhere, the battle was continued in October, and the whole German line was swinging back in retirement from the territory the German armies had held for so long a time. Of course, this retirement was of greater distances at the outer edge of the swinging radius, and Belgium and northern France were being rapidly evacuated. "Continuous fighting was maintained along our entire battlefront, with especial success on the extreme left, where the capture of the greater part of the Argonne Forest was completed. The enemy contested every foot of ground on our front in order to make more rapid retirements further west and withdraw his forces from northern France before the interruption of his railroad communications through Sedan."[1]

Yet it is an extraordinary fact, and showing how persistent preconceived ideas can be, that even after this American offensive was well under way, and doing its invaluable service for the Entente Allies, there were still attempts to divert American troops to the Allied armies. Early in October Secretary Baker had been in England to attend a session of the Inter-Allied Maritime Council. While he was in England, he was asked to meet the British Prime Minister, who again strongly urged that American troops should be amalgamated with the British. He was very insistent in pressing this view, which the British leaders still held to be the best scheme for success in the war. But he made no impression upon Secretary Baker, who wrote to General Pershing: "I pointed out to him that the President and I had repeatedly both verbally and in writing insisted that the American Army as such was the thing we were trying to create. That we had no intention of feeding our soldiers into the French or British Army, and intended to have an American Army in exactly the same sense that Great Britain had a British Army and France a French Army."

In answer to Lloyd George's arguments, the American Secretary of War pointed out "that our occupation of a substantial portion of the line in Lorraine and our operation there had undoubtedly both cost the enemy heavily and required the German High Command to remove

[1] General Pershing, Report.

divisions from the British fronts thus rendering Sir Douglas Haig's operations easier by diminishing the forces opposed to him."

Of course, with the President, the Secretary of War, and the American Commander-in-Chief all standing unitedly together against any attempts to change the American plan of war, there was no chance of impairing our effort by diverting it into any other channel. But it would have been a tragedy, if the arguments of the leaders of the Allies had caused the American leaders to swerve from their course. It is a pathetic showing, to try to imagine the results that could have been attained by the method proposed by the leaders of the Allies, in comparison with what was actually being achieved by adhering to the American plan.

Aside from the damaging advances made by General Pershing's army, which kept on eating into the vital German position, the numbers of German troops drawn into the battle and consumed told the story. By the middle of October, General Pershing could report: "A maximum advance of 19 kilometres had been made since September 26 and the enemy had been forced to throw into the fight a total of 15 reserve divisions." At that time General Pershing had been confronted by the scarcity of replacements, as has been stated, and had been compelled to break up newly arrived divisions in the attempt to fill his ranks. Yet "at this time the First Army was holding a front of more than 120 kilometres: its strength exceeded 1,000,000 men."[1] With the rapid growth of the Army to this size it had become too

---

[1] General Pershing, Report. In all, there were 1,200,000 American troops used in the Meuse-Argonne operation.

large for a single command. The Second American Army was then constituted, under the command of Lieutenant General Robert L. Bullard, the command of the First Army was given to Lieutenant General Hunter Liggett, and General Pershing's advance headquarters for army group control was established at Ligny-en-Barrois (October 16, 1918).

General Pershing has stated, of this arduous and incessant series of combats: "While the high pressure of these dogged attacks was a great drain on our troops, it was calamitous to the enemy. . . . Once a division was engaged in the fight, it became practically impossible to effect its relief." As has been stated, he placed the total of these German divisions, which were thus involved in the battle and defeated, at forty-seven.

"The demands of incessant battle which had been maintained day by day for more than a month had compelled our divisions to fight to the limit of their capacity. Combat troops were held in line and pushed to the attack until deemed incapable of further effort because of casualties or exhaustion; artillery once engaged was seldom withdrawn and many batteries fought until practically all the animals were casualties and the guns were towed out of line. The American soldier had shown unrivalled fortitude in this continuous fighting during most inclement weather and under many disadvantages of position. Through experience the army had developed into a smooth-running machine, and there was a supreme confidence in our ability to carry through successfully. . . . Every member of the American Expeditionary Forces, from the front line to the base ports, was straining every nerve. Magnificent efforts were exerted by the entire Services of Supply to meet the enormous demands made on it. Obstacles which seemed insurmountable were overcome daily in expediting the movements of replacements, ammunition, and supplies to the front, and of sick and wounded to the rear. It was this spirit of determination animating every American soldier that made it impossible for the enemy to maintain the struggle until 1919."[1]

This last sentence from General Pershing's report described the ultimate result of the Meuse-Argonne operation—a result that was beyond all expectations, even of the confident American Commander-in-Chief. For not even General Pershing had dared to believe that the World War could be ended in 1918. Yet this ending was brought about, more than by any other influence, by the effect produced at Washington by General Pershing's first urgent plea that "we must come to their relief in this year, 1918." It was the stimulus of this call for our great army to be on the battlefield in 1918, and the constant adherence to this conception as our goal, and our one American plan of war, that must be given the credit for the unexpected strength of America on the battlefield, and the equally unexpected result of shortening the war.

General Pershing's claim, that the American military reinforcement actually shortened the war, is now considered a mere statement of fact. There have been optimistic statements lately, which can only be described as finding it easier to win the war in this year, 1927, than was the case when the leaders of the Entente Allies signed the record of their dire need in 1918. But even

---

[1]General Pershing, Report.

the most optimistic of these has admitted that it would have been a long protracted struggle without the American reinforcement, and conceded, as a self-evident fact, that the help of America brought about the quick ending of the World War.[1]

---

[1]On the occasion of the Convention of the American Legion in Paris (September, 1927), Marshal Foch made this unmistakable statement as to the decisive value of the American reinforcement in the World War:

"The American people can feel justifiably proud for having brought to bear such powerful aid at the decisive moment of the war and to have made victory possible by going straight into the conflict without hesitation and in accomplishing an end absolutely without parallel."

CHAPTER XXXVIII

AS A result of the combined assaults of the Allied and American armies, which began in the last days of September, 1918, the whole military defense of the Germans on the Western Front crumbled and was swept back in defeat. From this time, it became evident that the battered German armies were being compelled to retreat by the reinforced enemies of Germany. The extent of the reverses of the German armies was plainly defined for all to see by the milestones of terrain abandoned by them. These included areas where the Germans were supposed to be established for good, and consequently a revelation of utter defeat began to spread back through Germany. With this evidence before the eyes of the Germans, it was no longer possible for the German Imperial Government to conceal the extent of the disaster from the German people.

When the German people read the record of withdrawals in retreat, self-deception became impossible. In the swing backward of the wide radius of manœuvre, which has been explained, all the Allied armies were advancing, and of course the withdrawal of the German right had become a rapid retreat, because the outer arc of the circle was giving way over longer distances. The German people read that Lens and Armentieres had been evacuated on October 3, Cambrai on October 9, Laon and La Fère on October 14. On October 17, the Allies were in Lille, and they had advanced along the Belgian coast beyond Ostend and Zeebrugge, the two German submarine bases for which the costly battle of Flanders had been vainly fought in 1917. Farther south the advance had naturally been slower, but the Germans had retreated beyond St. Quentin, and the French, after crossing the Chemin-des-Dames, were advancing in the Champagne.

All these places were household words in Germany, as landmarks of victorious advance into enemy territory. The evacuation of all in rapid succession could only have one meaning, and this realization of defeat became a tidal wave of chagrin and depression throughout Germany. This absolute evidence of German disaster was the blow that threw down the weakened structure of the Central Powers. The end followed quickly for Austria-Hungary. The people were hungry and desperate. Disaffection and revolt broke out everywhere. These conditions spread to the armies on the Italian front. These Austro-Hungarian armies were also hungry and disaffected. Their morale was gone, and they were ready to break at the first assault. On October 24, the Italians attacked. The result was never in doubt. The formidable Austro-Hungarian armies, which had penetrated far into Italy, had become disorganized mobs. They offered no resistance to the enemy, and great numbers of them were captured. Austria-Hungary was in revolution, and completely eliminated as a factor in

the World War.[1] At the same time the Turks were also
eliminated, as, on October 30, 1918, an armistice was
signed, which amounted to an unconditional surrender.

In the meantime, Germany was also going down to
defeat, although there was no such military collapse of
her armies as in the case of her allies. The German
armies retained their organization and resisted to the
last, although, of course, their morale fell away in defeat. The demoralization of defeat was spreading
through all Germany and leading to revolution, but it is
an error to state that revolution brought about this
defeat of the German armies.[2] The revolution was a
result, not a cause, of German defeat.

As has been stated, if Ludendorff had been able to
gain the promised victory, the German people would
have stood by the German Imperial Government. But
the German people had held the Imperial Government
to this test, and, upon the failure of the German Supreme Command to win the war before the arrival of
the American reinforcement, the German people repu-
diated the German Imperial Government. The "race"
had been won by the Americans, and the German people
had lost all respect for the loser. Ludendorff's complaint
was: "By working on our democratic sentiments the
enemy propaganda succeeded in bringing our Government into discredit in Germany." But all the propaganda in the world would not have accomplished this
if the German armies had kept on winning. It was the

---

[1] Armistice requested October 27, 1918. This was signed November 3.
It was followed by the abdication of the Emperor, and Austria-Hungary
had become a number of separate States.

[2] "The stab in the back."

actual physical defeat of the German armies that brought about disaffection and revolution against the German Imperial Government.

The fact should again be stated, that the test of war was between the United States and the German Imperial Government. It was against this Imperial Government that the United States had gone to war, not against the German people. And this had been made so evident to the German people, in spite of every possible misrepresentation on the part of the leaders of the German Imperial Government, that no propaganda was necessary to proclaim to the German people the issue, which was plain to all the world, a war between the United States and the Imperial German Government.

As has been explained, the hold of the German Imperial Government upon the German people, at this stage, had derived its strength solely from the promise of military victory. When victory changed to an ebbing tide of defeat, the German Imperial Government lost its only hold upon the German people. Discontent became open revolt, and social revolution spread throughout Germany. This inevitable factor in the situation was bringing the end much sooner than was realized, either by the German leaders or by the leaders of the Entente Allies.

Of this last, there was unmistakable proof given by each side. As has been explained, the French High Command had not believed that the offensive could win the war before winter would force a cessation of operations. It is also a fact that on October 4, 1918, Marshal Foch had called the American Secretary of War to a conference as to the share of the United States in the campaign of 1919. "This was one day before the first German peace note and 38 days before the end of the war, but Marshal Foch was then calling upon America to make her great shipments of munitions and her supreme contribution of manpower for the campaign of the following year."[1]

On the part of the Germans, it had become evident, even to the most obsessed of the German militarists, that it was impossible to withstand the new strength of the Allied and American armies, and a note had been sent in the first week of October asking for an armistice. Yet it is indisputable that the German leaders still continued to pin their naval strategy to the U-boat campaign, and were actually then busy on a program which could only bring results in 1919! Admiral Scheer has stated: "None of us had the vaguest notion that the situation of the war on land was such that the cessation of all hostilities would soon be urged, and that in a few weeks the U-boat campaign would be abandoned." At a meeting on October 1, attended by representatives of both the Army and Navy, "everyone agreed that it would be possible to carry out the extended U-boat program, so long as the requisite number of workmen, amounting to 69,000 altogether, was forthcoming: these men were chiefly wanted in the shipyards."

In this same spirit the German leaders still clung to their U-boat strategy after the evacuation of the Bruges bases, and even through the negotiations which followed the first German request for an armistice. These negotiations were accompanied by further outbreaks of revolutionary discontent, and by the downfall of the German

[1] A Statistical Summary, General Staff, U. S. A.

Imperial Government founded upon militarism. President Wilson, who was the spokesman for the Entente Allies, had answered the first German note on October 8 by taking the firm stand: "No armistice negotiations so long as the German armies remain upon enemy soil." This was followed by President Wilson's note of October 14, containing the demand: "Cessation of U-boat hostilies against passenger ships and change of the form of Government in Germany." It was notable that this crucial demand upon Germany by our President was a consistent reiteration of the position of the United States in the World War. There could be no dealing with the discredited German Imperial Government of 1917 and 1918.

To this note of President Wilson there was a chastened reply from the Germans on October 21: "U-boats have received orders which exclude the torpedoing of passenger ships, and with regard to the form of Government: The responsibility of the Imperial Chancellor to the representatives of the people is being legally developed and made secure."

It was a fact, most significant of the German state of mind, that throughout these exchanges, the German Naval leaders had been only concerned in regard to the U-boat campaign—whether it was to be suspended or not. It was not until after this German note of October 21, with its practical surrender of unrestricted U-boat warfare, that the German Naval leaders turned to a change of navai strategy. Admiral Scheer has stated this as follows: "This decision as to the limitation of the U-boat campaign was very important because the further operative measures of the Navy Command depended upon it; the High Sea Fleet must again now obtain complete freedom of action." Here there can be no mistaking the record of German strategy at this stage. There was no thought of a change to the offensive use of the German Battle Fleet until the Germans were on the point of surrender—and then it was too late from any practical point of view.

The record of this very important element in the situation of the last months of the war has thus been established by the Germans themselves beyond any recall. The Germans have shown that they clung to their U-boat strategy to the last, and any danger of interruption of the vast movement of troops and supplies to France by means of the battle cruisers or battleships of the German High Sea Fleet can now be dismissed as out of the question. It is no wonder that there was much anxiety on this account, while the great movement was in operation, as it can be readily imagined that a raid of German capital ships against the troopship convoys might have done in a few hours incalculable harm. But it is not even worth while to speculate as to this, because it was outside the trend of the German mind, and consequently something that was not to be undertaken by the Germans.

It is almost equally useless to discuss the projected change of German naval strategy, undertaken at the last stage. Admiral Scheer, himself, has described this as an attempt to summon the German Battle Fleet "to exert its full powers at the eleventh hour." He should have called it "at the twelfth hour." For at that time the final hour had already struck for the German Empire.

This last-minute effort of the German Navy was to be "a plan directed against the English Channel."[1] Admiral Scheer has stated: "The Fleet was finally assembled for this enterprise in the outer roads of Wilhelmshaven on October 28." By this time there was no chance for any naval move that would avert the onrushing course of events. The whole militaristic structure of Germany had already fallen. After a stormy session in Berlin, Ludendorff, who had been the incarnation of the last phase of German militarism, had been forced to resign (October 26th). This meant the final fall of the Imperial régime that had staked its existence upon German victory in 1918.

The reaction against this régime, which was now also discredited in Germany, had spread through the German nation. Disorders broke out all over the country, and red flags began to appear in the German cities. How complete had been the overturn in Germany was best shown by the answer to another Wilson note (October 23), in which was repeated the demand for abolition of the Imperial Government: "The German Government has duly noted the reply of the President of the United States. The President is aware of the fundamental changes that have taken place and are still taking place in the German Constitution. The peace negotiations will be carried on by a Government of the people, in whose hands the decisive power actually and constitutionally lies. The military forces are also subject to it." Nothing more opposite to the former truculent German Imperial Government could be imagined—and this German note was an acknowledg-

[1] Admiral Scheer, *Germany's High Sea Fleet.*

ment of the victory of the stand taken by the United States in the World War.

The outbreak of revolution against the German Imperial Government had spread to the German Navy before it affected the organization of the German Army. This was a consequence of an unusual situation in the German Navy. As the German naval policy had been to build up and organize a Battle Fleet especially adapted for service in the areas of the North Sea about the German naval bases, this in itself implied the condition that the High Sea Fleet was much in port. Consequently, its crews were in touch with the German people. Naturally, when the realization of defeat came home to the German people, the Naval personnel shared this knowledge, and became infected by the prevailing spirit of revolt against the Imperial Government, which had promised German victory and then led the German Empire to defeat. As was the case with the German people, this disaffection of the Naval crews was a direct result of the overwhelming German defeat.

In both the cases of the German people and of the German Navy, it is blurring the issue to call the revolt against the Imperial Government the cause of German defeat. Particularly in the case of the German Navy, this recent excuse for defeat cannot stand the test of truth. The German leaders have shown unmistakably their own record of persisting in their naval strategy of concentrating their efforts wholly on their U-boat campaign until all was lost. Why should it be any surprise that they met mutiny at a sudden change to a last-minute plan for a desperate sortie of the Battle Fleet?

Admiral Scheer has stated: "Insubordination broke out when, on October 29, the Commander-in-Chief of the fleet was making preparations to weigh anchor for the planned attack. . . . Since October 29, when the first signs of dissatisfaction had become manifest, the movement had continued to spread, so that he did not think it possible to undertake an offensive with the Fleet." That was all there was to the matter. The artificial militaristic German Government had lost its hold, for the one reason that it had met final defeat on the battlefield, and all German resistance was at an end.

Under these circumstances, any last-minute naval plan for the German Battle Fleet is not worth consideration, for it could never have been carried out. But, even if it had been possible to induce the disillusioned German crews to make this sortie, it was too late to change the great result. Events had moved too rapidly, and there was nothing that could turn back the torrent which had overwhelmed the German Imperial Government. The phrase "a Government of the people" in the German note to President Wilson meant that the Imperial Government had acknowledged its downfall.

The war party had attempted to delay the departure of a German delegation to treat for an armistice, but Hindenburg himself declared there was no other course, and that any delay in obtaining peace would only do harm. This ended the last hope of prolonging resistance, and the final negotiations for an armistice were carried on by a new German Government, as the revolt had spread to Berlin, and on November 9, 1918, the German Emperor abdicated, taking refuge in Holland.

In the meantime, General Foch's armies had been

steadily pushing forward. The Americans had penetrated to Sedan, the vital centre of German railroad communication, and the military position of the German armies was hopeless for maintaining a successful war. It was poetic justice that Sedan should be turned to a name of defeat for the German Empire, and also that the British Army should be back in the region of Mons, from which their retreat had begun in 1914. Secretary Baker's personal note to General Pershing written November 8, when the last negotiations were carried on, reflected the thanksgiving of Americans: "I am writing this note in the tense hours during which the representatives of the German Government are supposed to be in consultation with General Foch. . . . Fortunately there has been so much heroism and endurance that one robs nobody else by claiming his own share. And so, with full credit to our gallant associates of England, France, and Italy, we Americans can have a full cup of happiness and pride from the effort our nation has made and the success which has crowned the chivalrous gallantry of our Army."

The Armistice was signed and became effective at 11:00 A. M., November 11, 1918—and the hostilities of the World War were ended.

All discussions as to what might have happened if the war had been prolonged are fruitless. But one fact should be stated. At the time, both the French and British commanders-in-chief put themselves on record as being absolutely satisfied with the result. General Foch's statement is clear, as to any question of a desire to keep on with the campaign, and General Haig was in complete accord in this matter. General Foch stated:

"But they had behind them the line of the Sarre, where we should have had to pause again. To have launched that attack would mean one victory the more, but that is all and we got by the Armistice everything we could have gained by the battle."[1]

Another point should be made clear. There is no truth in any idea that our troops were engaged longer than was necessary. General Foch felt that the German military leaders might shift at any favorable turn of affairs, and he urged his generals to keep up the pressure until the last. The Commander-in-Chief's orders were very insistent in this regard.[2] As soon as the Armistice was signed, word was sent to all units that it would be effective at eleven o'clock on the eleventh, and there were only isolated cases of troops, who had advanced beyond touch, fighting beyond that hour.

The Armistice ended the history of the American military reinforcement in the World War. On the day hostilities ended, the effort of the United States had accomplished its task. The demobilization of forces and the aftermath of the World War are outside the province of this work. And no sermon will be preached with this book as a text. The narrative of facts and events has told the story of the effort of a united nation—an effort which the changed conditions of the World War

---

[1]General Haig in his published despatch ("Sir Douglas Haig's Despatches") used almost the same words, showing that the British and French Commands agreed in this. "On the other hand, the Armistice in effect amounted to complete surrender by the enemy, and all that could have been gained by fighting came into our hands more speedily and at less cost."

[2]Telegram from General Foch, November 9, 1918, 9:00 P. M.: "It is important to coördinate and expedite our movements. I appeal to the energy and initiative of the commanders-in-chief and of their armies to make decisive the results obtained."

decreed must be threefold—industrial, military, naval. These three forces were welded together to produce our military reinforcement on the Western Front. This reinforcement could only be brought into being by the joint labor of all three, and this reinforcement cannot be understood or estimated unless we study its three-plied fabric.

THE END

APPENDIX

Section 2 of the Army Appropriation Act, Approved August 29, 1916, Creating the Council of National Defense.

Sec. 2. That a Council of National Defense is hereby established for the coördination of industries and resources for the national security and welfare, to consist of the Secretary of War, the Secretary of the Navy, the Secretary of the Interior, the Secretary of Agriculture, the Secretary of Commerce, and the Secretary of Labor.

That the Council of National Defense shall nominate to the President, and the President shall appoint, an advisory commission, consisting of not more than seven persons, each of whom shall have special knowledge of some industry, public utility, or the development of some natural resource, or be otherwise specially qualified, in the opinion of the council, for the performance of duties hereinafter provided. The members of the advisory commission shall serve without compensation, but shall be allowed actual expenses of travel and subsistence when attending meetings of the commission or engaged in investigations pertaining to its activities. The advisory commission shall hold such meetings as shall be called by the council or be provided by the rules and regulations adopted by the council for the conduct of its work.

That it shall be the duty of the Council of National Defense to supervise and direct investigations and make recommendations to the President and the heads of executive departments as to the location of railroads with reference to the frontier of the United States, so as to render possible expeditious concentration of troops and supplies to points of defense; the coördination of military, industrial, and commercial purposes in the location of extensive highways and branch lines of railroad; the utilization of waterways; the mobilization of military and naval resources for defense; the increase of domestic production of articles and materials essential to the support of armies and of the people during the interruption of foreign commerce; the development of seagoing transportation; data as to amounts, location, method, and means of production, and availability of military supplies; the giving of information to producers and manufacturers as to the class of supplies needed by the military and other services of the Government, the requirements relating thereto, and the creation of relations which will render possible in time of need the immediate concentration and utilization of the resources of the Nation.

That the Council of National Defense shall adopt rules and regulations for the conduct of its work, which rules and regulations shall be subject to the approval of the President, and shall provide for the work of the advisory commission, to the end that the special knowledge of such commission may be developed by suitable investigation, research, and inquiry and made available in conference and report for the use of the council; and the council may organize subordinate bodies for its assistance in special investigations, either by the employment of experts or by the creation of committees of specially qualified persons to serve without compensation, but to direct the investigations of experts so employed.

That the sum of $200,000 or so much thereof as may be necessary is hereby appropriated, out of any money in the Treasury not otherwise appropriated, to be immediately available for experimental work and investigations undertaken by the council, by the advisory commission, or subordinate bodies, for the employment of a director, expert and clerical expenses and supplies, and for the necessary expenses of members of the advisory commission or subordinate bodies going to and attending meetings of the commission or subordinate bodies. Reports shall be submitted by all subordinate bodies and by the advisory commission to the council, and from time to time the council shall report to the President or to the heads of executive departments upon special inquiries or subjects appropriate thereto, and an annual report to the Congress shall be submitted through the President, including as full a statement of the activities of the council and the agencies subordinate to it as is consistent with the public interest, including an itemized account of the expenditures made by the council or authorized by it, in as full detail as the public interest will permit: *Provided, however,* That when deemed proper the President may authorize, in amounts stipulated by him, unvouchered expenditures and report the gross sum so authorized not itemized.

The Overman Act
(Approved May 20, 1918)

AN ACT Authorizing the President to coördinate or consolidate executive bureaus, agencies, and offices, and for other purposes, in the interest of economy and the more efficient concentration of the Government.

Be it enacted by the Senate and House of Representatives of the United States of America in Congress assembled, That, for the National security and defense, for the successful prosecution of the war, for the support and maintenance of the Army and Navy, for the better utilization of resources and industries, and for the more effective exercise and more efficient administration by the President of his powers as Commander-in-Chief of the land and naval forces, the President is hereby authorized to make such redistribution of functions among executive agencies as he may deem necessary, including any functions, duties, and powers hitherto by law conferred upon any executive department, commission, bureau, agency, office, or officer, in such manner as in his judgment shall seem best fitted to carry out the purposes of this act, and to this end is authorized to make such regulations and to issue such orders as he may deem necessary, which regulations and orders shall be in writing and shall be filed with the head of the department affected and constitute a public record: *Provided*, That this act shall remain in force during the continuance of the present war and for six months after the termination of the war by the proclamation of the treaty of peace, or at such earlier time as the President may designate: *Provided further*, That the termination of this act shall not affect any act done or any right or obligation accruing or accrued pursuant to this act, and during the time that this act is in force: *Provided further*, That the authority by this act granted shall be exercised only in matters relating to the conduct of the present war.

Sec. 2. That in carrying out the purposes of this act the President is authorized to utilize, coördinate, or consolidate any executive or administrative commissions, bureaus, agencies, offices, or officers now existing by law, to transfer any duties or powers from one existing department, commission, bureau, agency, office, or officer to another, to transfer the personnel thereof or any part of it either by detail or assignment, together with the whole or any part of the records and public property belonging thereto.

Sec. 3. That the President is further authorized to establish an executive agency which may exercise such jurisdiction and control over the production of aëroplanes, aëroplane engines, and air-craft equipment as in his judgment may be advantageous; and, further, to transfer to such agency, for its use, all or any moneys heretofore appropriated for the production of aëroplanes, aëroplane engines, and aircraft equipment.

Sec. 4. That for the purpose of carrying out the provisions of this act, any moneys heretofore and hereafter appropriated for the use of any executive department, commission, bureau, agency, office, or officer shall be expended only for the purpose for which it was appropriated under the direction of such other agency as may be directed by the President hereunder to perform and execute said function.

Sec. 5. That should the President, in redistributing the functions among the executive agencies as provided in this act, conclude that any bureau should be abolished and it or their duties and functions conferred upon some other department or bureau or eliminated entirely, he shall report his conclusions to Congress with such recommendations as he may deem proper.

Sec. 6. That all laws or parts of laws conflicting with the provisions of this act are to the extent of such conflict suspended while this act is in force.

Upon the termination of this act all executive or administrative agencies, departments, commissions, bureaus, offices, or officers shall exercise the same functions, duties, and powers as heretofore or as hereafter by law may be provided, any authorization of the President under this act to the contrary notwithstanding.

INDEX

Advisory Commission, Council of National Defense, 38 ff. *see* Council of National Defense.

Æolus, troopship, 109.

Africa, South and East, 176.

Agriculture, Department of, creation of, 23.

Agamemnon, troopship, 109, 268.

Aide for Operations, U.S.N., 30.

Aircraft, 336, 337.

Aisne, 275.

Alaska, 50, 165.

Alcedo, converted yacht, lost, 306, 307.

Allen, destroyer, 88, 96.

Allenby, General, 199.

Allied Command, weakness of divided commands, 244; first steps for united command, 244, 245; conference at Beauvais, 251 ff.; united command assured, 251 ff.

Allied Maritime Transport Council, 172.

Alpine, John R., 118.

Alsace-Lorraine, 282.

Ambrose Channel Lightship, 87.

America, troopship, 109, 268.

American Army, *see* United States Army.

American Civil War, lessons of, 10, 17; influence of, 18, 19; influence on Secretary of War, 77; lessons as to training, 145, 146; lessons in tactics, 147; experience of, 192; naval precedent, 320.

American Expeditionary Forces, cast on large scale from the first, 76, 77, 80 ff.; first troops overseas, 84 ff.; preparations overseas,

119 ff.; rifles and artillery, 133 ff.; make-up of divisions of, 151, 152; cargo carriers for, 162; first disappointment of Entente Allies, 171; their mistaken estimate of, 172; organization of in advance, 178 ff.; the "race," 203, 204; problems of transportation, 204 ff.; N.O.T.S., 211 ff.; Cross-Channel Fleet, 217; situation before German offensive, 234 ff.; importance of, 245, 246; aid given in emergency, 247 ff.; totals sent overseas in emergency, 260 ff.; aid at the crisis, 277 ff.; the turn of the tide, 281 ff.; independent American Army, 288, 289 ff.; choice of Meuse-Argonne area, 295, 296; offensive operations, 309 ff.; description of, 327 ff.; ordnance, 336; aircraft, 336, 337; good influences overseas, 338 ff.; Meuse-Argonne, 341 ff.

American Government, *see* United States.

American Industries, their share in the American effort, 14, 15; influence upon American nation, 22 ff.; stimulated by war, 25, 26; represented in Council of National Defense, 37 ff.; associated with the war powers of the President, 41, 42; problems of material, 51 ff.; associated officially with Army and Navy, 55 ff.; General Munitions Board, 56 ff.; in touch with Services, 58; development of control of, 60 ff.; importance in American effort, 81, 82; share overseas, 120, 121; mobilization of, 126 ff.; War Industries Board, 139 ff.; importance of industries, 178, 179; influence of leaders of, 193, 194; in relation to shipping, 208, 209; development of industrial forces, 218 ff.; effect on, of Shipping Board, 222 ff.; benefit of Council of National Defense, 222.

American Lake, 71.

American Library Association, helpful work of, 151; continued overseas, 338.

American Merchant Marine, importance to Navy, 156, 157.

American Nation, development of, 16 ff.; united in every sense, 19, 20; debt to men of the Civil War, 20; loyalty of all elements, 20, 21; *see* United States.

American Navy, *see* United States Navy.

American Patrol Force (U. S. N.), constituted, 305.

American People, 16 ff., 27 ff.; *see* United States.

American Railway Association, 62, 71, 168.

American troops, *see* United States Army.

Amerika, 109.

Amiens, 256, 288.

Ammen, destroyer, 88, 96.

Angaria, right of, 210, 211.

Antigone, troopship, 109.

Antilles, troopship, 86, 96; cost, 307.

Aphrodite, converted yacht, 96.

Aquitania, troopship, 205.

Argonne, 282, 341.

Argonne Forest, 295, 342, 346.

Arizona, 6, 68.

Arkansas, battleship, 215.

Armentières, 270, 353.

Armistice, 362.

Army Nurse Corps, U.S.A., praise of, 338.

Army Transportation Service, U. S. A., 101; *see* Embarkation Service.

Atlantic, situation in, 319 ff.

Atlantic Fleet, U. S. N., *see* United States Navy.

Atterbury, W. W., Brig. Gen., 334.

Australia, 176.

Austria-Hungary, moral effect upon, of entrance of United States, 8; effect of German defeats, 313, 314; collapse of, 353.

Ayres, Colonel Leonard P., U.S.A., 45, 52, 126, 127, 133, 134; statement as to efficient supply of Army, 334, 335.

Azores, 91, 216, 301.

Baker, Newton D., Secretary of War, 36; Chairman of Council of National Defense, 39; magnitude of tasks, 39; action as to Selective Service Act, 47; as to Joffre's estimate of American Army, 51, 52; problems of material 52, 53, 54; use of leaders of industries, 53, 54; General Munitions Board, 55 ff.; as to early stages of war, 60; description of national uprising, 63, 64; as to Mexico, 70; as to Plattsburg camps, 72; selection of General Pershing, 77; influence of the Civil War, 77; as to first transportation overseas, 94, 95; relations with Pershing, 77 ff.; Cantonment Construction, 111, 115; as to rifles, 135 ff.; as to artillery, 139; as to training camp activities, 149 ff.; support given Pershing as to scattering American troops, 182 ff.; as to commanders overseas, 185 ff.; as to Chief of Staff, 191, 192; adoption of Shipping Control Committee, 209; in France, 234 ff.; as to emergency for Entente Allies, 254 ff.; support of Pershing, 271; enlarged programme, 289 ff.; as to camps and replacements, 290 ff.; second visit to France, 297 ff.; as to American Expeditionary Forces, 330; veto of last attempt to absorb American troops, 347, 348; note of congratulation to Pershing, 362.

Balfour, Arthur, in America, 11, 12; pessimism of, 112.

Baltic, 198, 213.

Baltimore, 307.

Barbadoes, 307.

Barbarossa, 109.

Barker, A. B., Captain, U.S.A., 58.

Bar-le-Duc, 342.

Barry, Thomas H., Maj. Gen., U.S.A., 188.

Baruch, Bernard M., 39, 59, 140, 141, 220.

Bassens, 122.

Bayonne, 122.

Beauvais, 251, 254, 256.

Belgian Army, attacks of, 341.

Belgium, evacuation of, 353.

Belknap, Charles, Commander, U. S. N., 212.

Bell, J. Franklin, Maj. Gen., U.S.A., 188.

Belleau Wood, 277.

Benson, W. S., Admiral, U. S. N., Chief of Naval operations, coöperation with Army, 160, 161; as to Emergency Fleet Corporation, 222, 223.

Berehaven, 316.

Berlin, 3, 5.

Bethman-Hollweg, German Imperial Chancellor, against the U-boat campaign, 1, 2.

Biddle, John, General, Chief of Staff, U. S. A., 161.

Birmingham, scout cruiser, 96.

Bliss, Tasker H., General, Chief of Staff, U. S. A., 136, coöperation with Navy, 161, 191; representative of United States in Supreme War Council, 232; Pershing's praise of, 232, 238, 249, 251; in favour of united command, 255, 256, 257.

Board of Chaplains, A. E. F., good influence of, 338.

Bolton, Chester C., 59.

Bombon, 293.

Bordeaux, 122, 238.

Borrinquin, N.O.T.S., 324.

Boston, 88.

Bowles, F. T., Rear Admiral, U. S. N., 223.

Brest, 93, 95, 122, 216, 238, 264, 267, 297, 301, 307.

Bridges, General, 187.

Briey, 121, 310.

Bristol Channel, 307.

British Army, to guard Channel ports, 121, 122; British officers in United States, 147; project to scatter American soldiers in, 182 ff.; disadvantage at beginning of 1918, 199 ff.; no chance for an offensive by, 201, 233; defeat in March, 1918, 240 ff.; reinforced by French, 243, 244; defeat in April, 1918, 270 ff.; plans for, 295 ff.; general offensive, 341 ff.

British Commission, in America, 11, 12.

British Fifth Army, disaster to, 241 ff.

British Grand Fleet, 99; mission in North Sea, 213, 214; American reinforcement for, 215, 302.

British Navy, 99; strategy of, 213 ff, 302 ff.

British War Cabinet, as to U-boats, 4; severity of terms to Rumania, 199; importance of Western Front, 199; strength of German tactics, 201; as to shipping at the emergency, 259, 260; recognition of generous spirit of America at the crisis, 273; tribute to coöperation of U. S. Navy, 301, 302.

Brookings, Robert S., 140, 141.

Browning machine guns, 336.

Bruges, 356.

Bulgaria, effect of German defeats upon, 313; collapse of, 313, 314.

Bullard, Robert L., Lieut. Gen. U. S. A., 349.

Burrows, destroyer, 88, 96.

Cadorna, General, Italian representative in Supreme War Council, 232.

Cambrai, 295, 341, 353.

Camouflage, on the seas, 323.

Campana, N.O.T.S., 324.

Camps and Cantonments, conception of, 73; locations of, 74; construction of, 111 ff.; totals of, 126, 127; training at, 143 ff.; high standards at, 148 ff.; increased numbers from, 206; process of transportation, 226, 227; German surprise at results, 227; replacements from, 291; repetition of experience of Civil War, 292; outbreak of influenza, 322, 323.

Canada, 176.

Cantigny, 277.

Cantonment, *see* Camps and Cantonments.

Cantonment Adjustment Commission, 118.

Cantonment Division (Q. M. C., U. S. A.), constituted, 112; duties, 112 ff.; consolidated with Construction Division (U. S. A.), 126.

Cape Cod, 304.

Capps, W. S., Rear Admiral, U. S. N. 59, 222, 223.

Cardiff, base, 323.

Cargo Carriers, heroic work of, 323 ff.

Cassin, destroyer, torpedoed, 307.

Central Powers, favourable position of, 1 ff.; moral effect upon of entrance of United States, 7, 8; shut off from sea, 25; strength of, 79; favourable situation at first of 1918, 197 ff., 233; great German

assault, 240 ff., 270 ff.; crisis of the war, 279, 280; unexpected defeat, 285 ff.; effects of German defeats, 341; disintegration of, 352 ff.; collapse of German Imperial Government, 355 ff.

Champagne, 295, 341, 353.

Channel, English, 302, 316, 359.

Channel Ports, 121, 122.

Charleston, cruiser, 96.

Châteauroux, 123.

Château-Thierry, apex of salient, 275, 279; attacks upon, 281 ff.

Chemin-des-Dames, loss of, 275, 276, 353.

Chincha, N.O.T.S., 324.

Christobel, converted yacht, 95.

Cincinnati, 109.

Civil War, *see* American Civil War.

Clarkson, Grosvenor, B., 170.

Clemenceau, French Premier, 230; first steps for united command, 245, 246; at Beauvais conference, 251 ff.; ignorance as to United States troops, 278; statement of crisis, 280.

Coast Guard (U. S.), 304; *see* United States Navy.

Coffin, Howard E., 39, 54, 55, 59.

Colby, Bainbridge, 222.

Columbus, 70.

Commerce, Department of, creation of, 23; Secretary of Commerce member of Council of National Defense, 36.

Commission on Training Camp Activities, efficient work of, 149 ff.

Conscription, *see* Selective Service Act.

Construction Division, U. S. A., 126, 127.

Corsair, converted yacht, 88, 96.

Convoy, American help for adoption of system, 13; first American Naval, 84 ff.; in relation to transports, 153 ff.; success of system, 157; American Naval convoy, 158,

159; American cargo carriers under British system of, 162; victory of, 175 ff., 263; successful operation of, 263 ff.; London centre of, 300; protection of, 302 ff.; last months on the seas, 315 ff.

Council of National Defense, creation of, 32; inadequate ideas of preparedness in 1915, 33 ff.; description of, 36 ff.; personnel of, 38, 39, 40; use of war powers of the President, 41, 42; problems of material for Army and Navy, 51 ff.; General Munitions Board of, 56 ff.; value of, 61 ff.; control developed, 62 ff.; cantonment construction, 111 ff.; mobilization of industries, 126 ff.; War Industries Board, 139 ff.; increased activities of, 163 ff.; influence throughout the American effort, 169; freedom from politics, 170; developments from, 219 ff., necessity for, 221, 222; text of Act creating, 365 ff.

Covington, troopship, 109; lost, 307.

Crezancy, 283.

Cross-Channel Fleet (U. S. N.), value of, 217, 323.

Crowder, E. H., General, Judge Advocate General, U. S. A., efficient administration of Selective Service Act, 47, 49; coördination with Emergency Fleet Corporation, 224.

Crozier, William, General, Chief of Ordnance, U. S. A., 56, 135, 136, 137.

Cruiser and Transport Force (U. S. N.), genesis of, 86, 87; first transportation overseas, 87 ff.; American transports of, 102 ff.; repairing German steamships, 104 ff.; number of troops transported by German steamships, 109; in relation to convoy system, 157 ff.; coördination with Army, 158 ff.; value of German steamships, 174;

embarkation bases for, 195, 196; troops transported in emergency, 259 ff.; efficiency of, 266 ff.; losses, 306 ff.; the culmination on the seas, 315 ff.

Cruse, Thomas, Brig. Gen., U. S. A., 58.

Cummings, destroyer, 92.

Cyclops, armed collier, 96; lost, 306, 307.

Czernin, Count, comment on Ludendorff, 202; on confidence of German Imperial Government, 203.

Dakotan, troopship, 86, 96.

Daniels, Josephus, Secretary of the Navy, preparedness for Navy, 30, 31; member Council of National Defense, 36; coördination with Army, 161, 162.

Dardanelles, 198, 199.

Dawes, Vice President, comment of, 328.

De Chambrun, Colonel, 297.

De Haviland, airplanes, 336.

De Kalb, transport, 85, 88, 91, 96, 109.

Delaware, battleship, 215.

Delaware Capes, 304.

Denmark, 217 .

Department of Science and Research Council of National Defense, 166.

Destroyer Force of the United States Atlantic Fleet, U. S. N., 84, 88.

District of Columbia, 49, 65, 69.

Donald, John A., 222.

Doullens, 244, 251, 252, 256.

Dover Patrol, British, 301.

Draft, ungrounded fear of, 46; *see* Selective Service Act.

Du Petit Thouars, French cruiser, 266.

Dvinsk, transport, lost, 308.

Eastern Department, U. S. A., 71.

Edward Luckenbach, troopship, 86, 93, 96.

El Occidente, troopship, 86, 96.
Elbe River, 125.
Embarkation Service, U. S. A., 160, 161; efficiency of, 161, expansion in advance at bases and camps, 195, 196, 205 ff.
Emergency Construction, Committee on, organized by General Munitions Board, 112; cantonment construction, 112 ff.
Emergency Fleet Corporation, *see* United States Emergency Fleet Corporation.
Enfield rifles, 133 ff., 145.
Engineer Corps, U. S. A., 125.
England, *see* Great Britain.
English Channel, 217.
Enlisted Reserve Corps, U. S. A., 35.
Entente Allies, unfavorable position of, 1 ff. discouragement of, 11; loss of Russia, 12, 14; greatest danger for, 14, 15, 16; war material for, 25; military failures of, 33, 34; bad situation of, reported by Pershing, 79 ff.; lack of information from; 97, 98; doubt as to American preparations overseas, 120; agreement as to artillery, 138, 139; a new situation for, 163; supplies for, 167; mistaken estimate of American military forces, 171 ff.; project to scatter American soldiers among the allied troops, 182 ff.; serious situation of at first of 1918, 197 ff.; renewed efforts to absorb American soldiers, 232, 233; serious defeats, 245; emergency for, 247 ff.; united command assured, 251 ff.; rush to assist them at emergency, 259 ff; the crisis, 270 ff.; revival of idea of absorbing American troops, 271 ff.; official statement of crisis, 279, 280; turn of the tide, 281 ff.

Fanning, destroyer, 88, 96.
Fayal, 91.

Federal Reserve Banks, creation of system of, 23; importance of, 23, 24; great services in finances of war, 45, 46.
Federal Shipping Act, 40.
Felton, Samuel M., 333.
Finland, troopship, 86, 96, 265; torpedoed, 308.
Fire Island, 306.
First American Army (U. S. A.), decided upon, 288; program for, 289 ff.; organization of, 293; objectives chosen, 294 ff.; plans for, 295 ff.; St. Mihiel, 309 ff.; Meuse-Argonne, 341 ff.
Fisher, H., Colonel, U. S. A., 58.
Flanders, British area of operations, 121; Battle of, 200.
Fletcher, F. F., Rear Admiral, U. S. N., 140.
Fletcher, William B., Rear Admiral, U. S. N., 95.
Florida, battleship, 215.
Flusser, destroyer, 96.
Foch, General, representative of France in Supreme War Council, 232; first steps for united command, 244, 245; American aid offered to, 247; command given to, 251 ff.; called upon to reinforce British, 270; serious situation of his armies, 276; official statement of crisis, 279, 280; "danger of the war being lost," 281; counter offensive, 284 ff.; consent to independent American Army, 288; contention as to its use, 293, 294; employment of independent American Army conceded, 294, 295; limit set at Mountfaucon, 295; plans for offensive, 295 ff.; general offensive, 341 ff.; tribute to American effort as decisive, 351, statement of satisfaction with end of campaign, 362, 363.
Food Administrator, 61, 62; *see* Herbert C. Hoover.

Food and Fuel Control Act, 62.
Fosdick, Raymond B., praise of his work, 150.
Fossoy, 283.
France, impending danger for, 11 ff.; military policy of, 33; bad situation reported by Pershing, 79 ff., first arrival of American troops in, 94, 95; American preparations in, 119 ff.; need of material for ordnance, 138; serious situation of, at beginning of 1918, 197 ff.; before the German offensive, 229 ff.; defeats and emergency, 240 ff., 247 ff.; the crisis, 270 ff.; official record of crisis, 280; turn of the tide, 281 ff.
Franklin, P. A. S., 209, 210.
Frayne, Hugh A., 140.
French Army, serious defeats, 79, 80; to guard Paris, 121; French officers in United States, 147; project to scatter American soldiers in, 182 ff.; disadvantage at beginning of 1918, 199 ff.; no chance for an offensive by, 201, 233; reinforcements for British Army, 243, 244, 271; defeat of May, 1918, 275, 276; depression, 276; turn of the tide, 281 ff., 295 ff.; general offensive, 341 ff.
French Commission, in America, 11, 12, 51.
Fresnes-en-Woëvre, 342.
Freytag-Loringhoven, regret at not learning lessons of Civil War, 10.
Friedrich Der Grosse, 109.
Fuel Administrator, 62; see Harry A. Garfield.
Fuller, George W., 115.

Garfield, Dr. Harry A., Fuel Administrator, 62; control of, 166, 167, 168; as to shipping, 208; evolution to drastic authority, 221.
Garlington, S. A., Brig. Gen., U. S. A., 118.

Geddes, Sir Eric, 263.
General Munitions Board, of Council of National Defense; origin of, 54, 55; creation of, 56; description of, 56 ff.; use of war powers of President, 57, 58; personnel of, 58, 59; importance of, 61; increased tasks, 80, 81; cantonment construction, 111 ff.; mobilization of industries, 129 ff.; superseded by War Industries Board, 139, 140.
George Washington, troopship, 109, 268.
Gerard, James W., American Ambassador to German Imperial Government, 4.
German Army, leaders acquiesced in U-boat campaign, 1; in relation to proposed American area in France, 121; overwhelming superiority on the Western Front at first of 1918, 200 ff., 233; victory of March, 1918, 240 ff.; superiority of, 250; continued victories, 270 ff.; the crisis, 279, 280; confidence of, 279, 281; turn of the tide, 281 ff.; defeats of, 309 ff.; driven back from France, 341 ff.; defeats cause of revolution, 355 ff.
German Battle Fleet (High Sea Fleet), 103; use of, to forward U-boat campaign, 213 ff., 302 ff.; continued confidence of Germans in U-boats, 316 ff.; abortive plan for offensive, 358 ff.; mutiny in, 360, 361.
German Empire, policies of Imperial Government, 1 ff.; at war with United States, 7; moral effect upon of entrance of United States, 8, 9; issue in, 9; see German Imperial Government.
German General Staff, errors as to United States, 9, 10, 144, 145.
German Imperial Government, decision to win by unrestricted U-

boat warfare, 1 ff.; aggressions against United States, 4 ff.; distinct from German people, 8, 9; mistake as to strength of United States, 9, 10; failure of spies and plots of, 19, 20, 21; surrenders in cases of *Lusitania* and *Sussex*, 27, 28, 29; effect upon United States of aggressions of, 29 ff.; the presage of the fall of, 43; error as to German steamships, 103, 104; overconfident at beginning of 1918, 197; domination by, 197 ff.; the "race" with the United States, 203, 204; failure of spy system in United States, 227, 228; the crisis, 279, 280; confidence of, 281, 282; unexpected defeat, 285, 286; effects of presence of American Army, 312 ff.; continued confidence in U-boats, 316 ff.; effects of German defeats, 341 ff.; loss of allies, 352 ff.; collapse and revolution, 355 ff.; downfall of, 359 ff.

German Navy, 85; strategy of, 213 ff., 302, 303; confidence in U-boats as main weapon, abortive attempt to change at last gasp, 358, 359; revolt in, 360, 361.

German people, distinct from German Imperial Government, 8, 9.

German steamships, used as American transports, 102 ff., 109; *see* Cruiser and Transport Force.

Germany, *see* German Empire.

Gherardi, W. R., Captain, U. S. N., 91.

Gibraltar, 216, 307, 319.

Gieves, 124.

Gifford, Walter S., Director of Council of National Defense, 40, 55.

Gleaves, Albert, Admiral, U. S. N., as to Joffre's underestimate, 52; designated Commander of Convoy Operations in the Atlantic, 84; first transportation overseas, 84

ff.; careful organization, 89 ff.; able conduct of, 94, 95; as to German overconfidence, 105; as to German steamships 105 ff.; praise of N. O. T. S., 207; as to troops transported by American transports, 260; efficient command of Cruiser and Transport Force, 266 ff.

Gloire, French cruiser, 266.

Godfrey, Dr. Hollis, 39.

Gompers, Samuel, 39, 118.

Gough, General, 242.

Grant, U. S., General, U. S. A., comment of, as to leaven from Regular officers, 146.

Great Britain, to be forced into peace by unrestricted U-boat warfare, 3; depression in, 12; military policy of, 33; delay in adopting conscription, 46; Ministry of Munitions, 56, 57; serious situation at beginning of 1918, 197 ff.; shipping provided by at emergency, 259 ff.

Great Lakes, 156, 217.

Great Northern, troopship, 265, 268.

Great Northern Barrage, 214, 215, 302.

Griffin, R. S., Rear Admiral, U. S. N., 104.

Grosser Kurfurst, 109.

Grout, Rear Admiral, 266.

Guthrie, Sir Cannop, 209.

Haig, General, confidence of, 12; comment on British defeat in March, 1918, 242, 243; at Beauvais Conference, 251; as to detaching troops, 255; as to French reinforcements, 270; "the turning point," 285; general offensive, 341 ff.; statement of satisfaction with ending of campaign, 363.

Halifax, 89, 304.

Hamburg, 109.

Hampton Roads, 212.

Hancock, J. H., Paymaster, U. S. N., 59.

Hancock, transport, 85, 96.

Harbord, James G., Maj. Gen., U. S. A., 334.

Harden, Maximilian, 203.

Harvard, converted yacht, 95.

Havana, troopship, 85, 91, 96.

Hawaii, 50, 165.

Henderson, transport, 85.

Hertling, German Chancellor, statement as to turn of the tide, 285, 286.

High Sea Fleet, *see* German Battle Fleet.

Hindenburg, General, statement of decision of German Imperial Government, 1, 2; confident America could not be a factor, 10; association with Ludendorff, 202; the "race," 203; adherence to belief in U-boats, 317; declared German Armies hopeless, 361.

Hines, Frank T., Maj. Gen., U. S. A., 160, 206.

Hoboken, N. J., 195.

Hodgson, F. G., Colonel, U. S. A., 58.

Hoff, A. B., Commander, U. S. N., 104.

Hoffer, J. E., Lt. Col., U. S. N., 58.

Hoffman, General, comment of, 2.

Hog Island, 224.

Holcomb, R. C., Surgeon, U. S. N., 59.

Holland, 361.

Holtzendorff, Admiral, Chief of German Naval Staff, Mem. of, 2, 3; mistake as to German steamships, 103, 104.

Hoover, Herbert C., Food Administrator; appointed by President, 61, 62; in association with War Industries Board, 141; nationwide work of, 166, 167; as to shipping, 208; evolution of drastic authority, 221.

Howe, L. McH., 59.

Hurley, Edward M., 222, 224.

Huron, troopship, 109.

Hutcheson, Grote, Maj. Gen., U. S. A., 161.

"Huttier manœuvre," 241.

Iceland, 319.

Industrial Preparedness, Committee on, 37, 40; *see* Naval Consulting Board.

Influenza, serious effect of outbreak of, 322, 323.

Inland Traffic Service, 226.

Inter-Allied Maritime Transport Council, 258.

International Mercantile Marine, 209, 265.

Interstate Commerce Commission, creation of, 23.

Ireland, North, 91.

Italy, no longer a factor for an offensive against the Central Powers, 198, 199; victory of, 353, 354.

J. L. Luckenbach, N. O. T. S., 324.

Jacob Jones, destroyer, lost, 306, 307.

Japan, 6, 7.

Jellicoe, Admiral, statement as to American destroyers necessary for convoy, 12, 13, 215.

Jerusalem, 199.

Jessop, E. P., Captain, U. S. N., 104.

Jewish Welfare Board, efficient work of, 151; overseas, 338.

Joffre, Marshal, in America, 11; in 1915, 33; mistaken estimate of American military effort, 51, 52; request for an American division overseas, 83, 84, 94; as to physique for command in field service, 187.

Jones, Hilary P., Rear Admiral, U. S. N., 161.

Kaiser Wilhelm I, 109.

Kanawha, armed collier, 93, 95, 96.

Kearney, T. A., Commander, U. S. N., 59.

Kelly, William, Major, U. S. A., 112.

Kelton, R. H. C., Colonel, U. S. A., 279, 285.
Key West, 304, 305.
Keyes, Rear Admiral, 302.
Kitchener, Lord, 33, 57.
Kléber, French cruiser, 94.
Knights of Columbus, *see* National Catholic War Council.
Koenig Wilhelm II, 109.
Koester, O. W., Captain, U. S.N., 104.
Krag-Jorgensen rifles, 145.
Kronprinz Wilhelm, 109.
Kronprinzessin Cecile, 109.
Kroonland, troopship, 265.

La Bassée, 270.
La Ferte-sous-Jouarre, 293.
Labor, control of, 63; agreement as to, 118.
Labor, Department of, creation of, 23; Secretary member of Council of National Defense, 36.
La Fère, 353.
Lake Arthur, steamship, 217.
Lake boats, from Great Lakes, 217.
Lambert's Point, 196.
Lamson, destroyer, 96.
Laon, 353.
La Pallice, 122.
Leavenworth Schools, good effect of, 329.
Le Havre, 122.
Leigh, R. H., Commander, U. S. N., 59.
Lemly, W. B., Lieut. Col., U. S. A., 59.
Lenape, troopship, 86, 96.
Lens, 270, 353.
Leviathan, troopship, 109, 267, 268.
Liberty Bonds. 43 ff.
Liberty Motor, for airplanes, 337.
Liggett, Hunter, Lieut. Gen., U. S. A., 234, 349.
Ligny-en-Barrois, 294, 349.
Lippmann, Walter, 118.
Littell, J. W., Colonel, U. S. A., 114, 115.

Liverpool, 267.
Lloyd George, David, British Premier, statement as to America, 10, 12; first Minister of Munitions, 57; with American generals, 232; as to British defeat, 243; at Beauvais conference, 251 ff., 256; as to American aid, 271, 272; official statement of crisis, 279, 280; last attempt to absorb American troops 347, 348.
London, centre of convoy operations, 300.
Lorraine, 121, 234, 247.
Lovett, Robert S., 140.
Ludendorff, General, unconscious tribute to spirit of United States, 7, 8; comment on America as "decisive power in the war," 17; statement of German numerical superiority, 200; grinding will of, 202, 203, 244, 260; as to transportation of American troops, 261, 262, 269; adherence to belief in U-boats, 317; involuntary praise of American soldiers, 339, 340; failure and complaint of 354, 355.
Lundoff, C. W., 112.
Lunéville, 234.
Lusitania, effect of sinking of, 27; result of American protest, 28, 31; crisis, 102.
Lys, Battle of the, 270.

Madawaska, troopship, 109.
Mallory, troopship, 86, 96.
Manchuria, troopship, 265.
Mann-Tichler, Vice Admiral, 316.
March, Peyton C., General; Chief of Staff, U. S. A., coöperation with the Navy, 161; appointment of, 192; great ability of, 192; scheme of replacements, 291.
Marine Corps, U. S., with U. S. A., 144, 277.
Marne, Germans again at, 275, 276;

Second Battle of, 282 ff.; Marne salient, 288.

Mars, hospital at, 124.

Marseillaise, French cruiser, 266.

Marseilles, 123.

Martha Washington, troopship, 109.

Martin, Dr. Franklin, 39, 59.

Maumee, oil tanker, 88.

Mauretania, troopship, 205.

McAdoo, William G., appointed Director General; *see* United States Railroad Administration.

McAlexander, U. G., Colonel, U. S. A., brave stand of his regiment, 283, 284; his order, 284.

McCall, destroyer, 96.

McCormick, Vance C., 211.

Medical Corps, U. S. A., efficiency of, 148, 149; able service overseas, 338, 339.

Mediterranean, 301; situation in, 319.

Mercury, troopship, 109.

Merritt, Camp, N. J., 195.

Mesopotamia, 76.

Metcalf, Leonard, 115.

Metz, 121, 310, 342.

Meuse, 295, 341.

Meuse-Argonne, chosen as area of American operations, 295; belief of High Command offensive could not progress beyond Montfaucon, 295; American faith in, 296; preparations for, 311; Battle of, 341 ff.; important results of 344 ff.

Mexican border, 5 ff., 68 ff.

Mexico, 5 ff., 68 ff.

Mexico, Gulf of, 305.

Mezières, 295, 310, 344.

Military Service Bill, British, delayed until 1916, 46.

Mills, Camp; enlargement of, 206.

Milner, Lord, 245, 280.

Ministry of Munitions, British, contrast with General Munitions Board, 56, 57, 219.

Ministry of Shipping, British, contrast with Shipping Control Committee, 219.

Mobilization of Industries Essential for Military Preparedness, Board on, 36.

Moldavia, transport, lost, 307.

Momus, troopship, 86, 96.

Mongolia, troopship, 265.

Mons, 362.

Montanan, troopship, 86, 96.

Montargis, 123.

Montdidier, 243, 275, 277.

Montfaucon, limit set for American advance, 295, 343.

Moreni, N. O. T. S., 324.

Morrison, Va., 196.

Moselle, 288, 295, 311.

Moselle Valley, 121.

Mount Vernon, troopship, 109, 268; torpedoed, 308.

Munitions Standards Board, 54, 55.

Nancy, 310.

Nantes, 122.

Nantucket, 304.

Napoleon, 17.

National Army, raised by Selective Service, 72, ff.; *see* United States Army.

National Catholic War Council (Knights of Columbus), efficient work of, 151; overseas, 353.

National Defense Act, 1916; product of tension with German Imperial Government, 32, 35; description of, 35, 36; amplified powers of President, 35, 36, 38, 41, 42, 58; as to National Guard, 69; as to Army, 72.

National Guard, in National Defense Act, 35; strength of, 67, 68; in Federal Service, 68; *see* United States Army.

National Research Council, 166.

Navajo, N. O. T. S., 324.

Naval Building Program of 1916, authorized, 32; cut down at Dis-

armament Conference, 32; suspended in 1917, 224.
Naval Chief of Staff, German, Mem. of, 2, 3; overconfidence of, 3; error as to German steamships, 103, 104.
Naval Consulting Board, U. S. N., creation of, 31; value of, 31, 37, 40, 54.
Naval Operations, U. S. N., Chief of, constituted, 30; coördination with Army, 160.
Naval Operations, U. S. N., Office of, transportation principal task of, 99, N. O. T. S., 212 ff.; control of areas, 301.
Naval Overseas Transportation Service (N. O. T. S., U. S. N.), under British convoy system, 162, 207; creation of, 211; good record of, 212, 213; difficult tasks of, 323; heroism of, 323 ff.; actions and losses, 325, 326.
Naval Reserve, U. S. N., 30.
Navy Department, U. S., warnings as to serious inroads of U-boats, 12; see United States Navy.
Neckar, 109.
Neufchâteau, 234.
Neuve Chapelle, 270.
Nevada, battleship, 316.
Nevers, 123.
New Mexico, 6, 68.
New York, 85, 88, 91, 95, 195, 206, 238, 267.
New York, battleship, 215.
New Zealand, 176.
Newport News, Va., 85, 196.
Nicholas, Grand Duke, 33.
Nicholson, destroyer, 324.
Nivelle, General, 79.
Noma, converted yacht, 95.
Nomeny, 288.
Norfolk, Va., 264.
Norlena, N. O. T. S., 324.
North Sea, 311, 360.
Northern Pacific, troopship, 265, 268.
Norway, 217.

Noyon, 243, 276.
Nyanza, N. O. T. S., 324.

Officers Reserve Corps, U. S. A., 35.
Oglethorpe, 71.
Oklahoma, battleship, 316.
Olmstead, F. L., 112.
Olympic, troopship, 205.
Orizaba, troopship, 265, 268.
Orkney Islands, 213.
Orlando, 280.
Orleans, 123.
Ostend, 353.
Overman Act, confirming war powers of President, 225, 226; text of, 368 ff.

Page, Walter H., American Ambassador to Great Britain, 120.
Page, Charles P., 222.
Palestine, 176.
Paris, 78, first American troops in, 94; French Army protecting, 121, 122, 172, 238, 255, 257, 272, threatened by German armies, 276; exodus from, 276; "to save Paris," 279, 281.
Parker, destroyer, 88, 96.
Passchendaele Ridge, 270.
Pastores, troopship, 85, 96.
Patrol Squadrons Operating in European Waters (U. S. N.), 95.
Pauillac, 122.
Paulsboro, N. O. T. S., 324.
Péronne, 243.
Pershing, John J., General, U. S. A., service in Mexico, 68 ff.; appointed Commander-in-Chief, 77; sent overseas, 77 ff.; far seeing information from, 78 ff.; relations with Administration, 76 ff.; preparations overseas, 119 ff.; as to rifles, 135 ff.; as to American base, 159; as to American reinforcement, 163, 164; foresight of, 172 ff.; organization in advance, 178 ff.; as to

scattering American soldiers among the Allies, 182 ff.; backed up by Secretary Baker, 183 ff.; selection of commanders overseas, 185 ff.; as to Chief of Staff, 191, 192; situation before German offensive, 229 ff.; invitation to Secretary Baker to come to France 235; aid to Foch at emergency, 247 ff.; at Beauvais conference, 251 ff.; at the emergency, 256 ff.; upholds his contention for an American Army, 271 ff.; advocacy of offensive, 278; the turn of the tide, 281 ff.; triumph of military ideas of, 286 ff.; independent American Army, 288; contention for its use, 293 ff.; choice of Meuse-Argonne area, 295, 296; invitation to Secretary Baker to come to France, 297 ff.; effect of presence of American Army, 312, 313; as to American Expeditionary Forces, 331 ff.; final campaign, 341 ff.

Pétain, General, tentative agreement with, 234; at Beauvais conference, 251 ff.; as to detaching troops, 255; counter offensive, 284 ff., independent American Army, 268, 294; general offensive, 341 ff.

Phillips, Asa E., 115.

Picardy, Battle of, 244, 293.

Pierce, Palmer E., Major, U. S. A., 55, 58.

Piez, Charles, 223.

Pig Point, Va., 196.

Plattsburg, training camps, 71, 72; Naval, 100.

Pocahontas, troopship, 109.

Pont-à-Mousson, 234.

Port-sur-Seille, 295.

Porto Rico, 50, 165.

Powhatan, troopship, 109.

President Grant, troopship, 109.

President Lincoln, troopship, 109; lost, 307.

Presidio, 71.

Preston, destroyer, 96.

Princess Matoika, 109.

Prinz Eitel Friedrich, 85, 109.

Prinzess Alice, 109.

Prinzess-Irene, 109

Prize Law, 29.

Pullman Company, 71.

Queenstown, 88, 92, 95, 301, 307.

Railroads' War Board, 62, 168; good effect of, 221.

Railways Military, American, effective work of men from American railroads, 324, 333.

Raw Materials, Minerals, and Metals, Committee on, 129, 131; *see* Council of National Defense.

Raymond, H. H., 209.

Read, George W., Major, U. S. A., 275.

Reading, Lord, 271.

Regular Army (U. S.), 35; strength of, 67, 68; Service in Mexico, 68 ff., 72 ff.; value of in training, 146; *see* United States Army.

Renting, Requisition, and Claims Service, A. E. F., 337.

Reserve Corps, U. S. A., 72; *see* United States Army.

Reserve Officers Training Camps, 35; *see* Plattsburg.

Rheims, 275, 281, 282.

Rhein, 109.

Robertson, General, British Chief of Staff, project for absorbing American troops, 182; support for General Pershing by the President and Secretary of War, 183; defects of scheme, 184, 185.

Rock Island Arsenal, 135, 139.

Rodman, Hugh, Rear Admiral U. S. N., 215.

Roe, destroyer, 96.

Root, Elihu, Secretary of War in 1902, 46.

Rosenwald, Julius, 39, 59.

Ross rifles, 145.
Rousseau, H. H., Rear Admiral, U. S. N., 59.
Rumania, 199; conquest of, 313.
Russia, collapse of, 2; lack of knowledge of this, 12; effects of loss of, 13, 32; helpless condition of, 197 ff.

Saar Basin, 121.
Sables-d'Olonne, 122.
Salmon, D., Chief Psychiatrist, 150.
Salonica, 176, 199; victory of Army of, 313, 314.
Salvation Army, good work of, 151; continued overseas, 338.
San Antonio, Texas, 71.
San Diego, armored cruiser, lost by mine, 306.
San Jacinto, troopship, 86, 96.
Saratoga, troopship, 85, 96.
Sarre, line of, 363.
Scapa, 103.
Scapa Flow, 103.
Scheer, Admiral, statement of capitulation of German Imperial Government in case of *Sussex*, 29; as to strategy of German Battle Fleet, 214, 302; Naval Chief of Staff, 317; persistent with U-boats, 317, 318; ignorant that defeat was so near, 356 ff.; account of mutiny, 361.
Schwab, Charles M., 223.
Scott, Frank A., 55, 56, 58, 136, 137, 140.
Scott, Hugh, General, U. S. A., Chief of Staff, 47, 135, 136, 191.
Sea Shell, tanker, 324.
Seattle, armored cruiser, 84, 86, 88, 91, 96, 238.
Second Armerican Army (A. E. F.), constituted, 349.
Sedan, 121, 295; contrast with Sedan of 1870, 296, 310, 344; importance of, 346, 347, 362.
Selective Service Act, signed by

President, 43; doubts as to conscription, 46; origin and enactment of, 47; description of, 47 ff.; totals of, 67, 68; National Army raised by, 73, 74; importance of, 76, 163; effect on nation, 164; cooperation with Emergency Fleet Corporation, 224; appeal to the whole nation, 228.
Services of Supply (A. E. F.), first preparations overseas, 81, 82; projects of, 121 ff.; organization of, in advance, 181, 182; great development of, 334 ff.; efficiency of, 349, 350.
Shanks, David C., Maj. Gen., U. S. A., 161, 206.
Shaw, Dr. Anna Howard, 164.
Shaw, destroyer, 88, 96.
Shipping Board; *see* United States Shipping Board.
Shipping Control Committee, constituted, 209; good effect of, 210; advantage from, 219; control of allotments of product of Emergency Fleet Corporation, 224.
Shipping, impairment of Allied, 100, 101; totals of American, 108; increase of American, 108, 110; need for, 120; convoy, 153 ff.; effect of against U-boats, 157; low estimate of Entente Allies, 172; vital to success, 174 ff.; gloomy views of Entente Allies as to, 175; utmost importance of American transportation, 176, 177; problems of transportation, 204 ff.; Shipping Control Committee, 209, 210; seizure of foreign shipping, 210, 211; development of Emergency Fleet Corportation, 222 ff.; totals of American, 223; revelation of the emergency, 259 ff.; improved situation owing to American shipbuilding, 262, 263; British transports, 290; protection of, 302 ff.; last months on the seas, 315 ff.

Sibert, William L., Maj. Gen., U. S. A., 188.
Siboney, troopship, 265, 268.
Simpson, F. F., 59.
Sims, William S., Admiral, U. S. N., information from, 12, 95; as to convoy, 263; Commander of the United States Naval Forces Operating in Europe, 300; division of authority, 301.
Soissons, 234, 275, 276, 284, 285, 342.
Spee, Admiral, 85.
Springfield Arsenal, 135.
Springfield rifle, 133 ff., 145.
Spy system, German, failure of, 20, 21; continued failure of, 227, 228.
Starrett, W. A., Major, U. S. R., 112.
Stevens, Raymond B., 222.
St. Johns, N. B., 89.
St. Louis, cruiser, 96.
St. Malo, 122.
St. Mihiel, 234, 288, 293, 297; Secretary Baker's account of, 297 ff.; American capture of, 309 ff., 342.
St. Nazaire, 93, 94, 122, 124, 264.
St. Quentin, 242, 243, 341, 353.
Stuart, Camp, 196.
Submarine chasers (U. S. N.), value of, 304; see United States Navy.
Submarines, German Imperial Government overconfident in regard to, 1 ff.; unrestricted U-boat warfare adopted, 2 ff.; serious inroads of, 11 ff.; U-boat campaign not crisis of World War, 13; American naval aid against, 13; surprise to Entente Allies, 98; American aid against, 99, 100; impairment of Allied shipping, 100, 101; effect of convoy upon, 157; gloomy views of Entente Allies as to, 175; defeat of, 175, 176; as to the fleets, 213 ff.; failure to stop American troops, 262 ff.; off American coast, 304, 305; American losses, 306, 307; failure of,

306, 307; continued German confidence in, 316 ff.; fearful losses of, 321; German Imperial government's surrender, 356 ff.
Sultana, converted yacht, 95.
Summers, L. L., 59.
Supplies, Committee on, of General Munitions Board, 129, 132.
Supreme War Council of the Entente Allies, organized, 232; appeal for American aid, 248, 249; plans of, 255; united command, 256, 257; question of absorbing American troops, 272, 273; recognition of American Army, 273, 274; official statement of crisis, 279, 280.
Surmelin Valley, 284.
Susquehanna, troopship, 109.
Sussex, Channel steamer, torpedoed, 27; surrender of German Imperial Government at ultimatum of United States, 28, 29; comment of Tirpitz, 29.

Tampa, Coast Guard, lost, 306, 307.
Tenadores, troopship, 85, 96.
Terry, destroyer, 96.
Texas, 6, 68.
Texas, battleship, 215.
Thirty-eighth Infantry, U. S. A., heroic action of, 283, 284.
Ticonderoga, N. O. T. S., 324, 325.
Tirpitz, Admiral, mistaken belief in rifts in American nation, 20; description of Sussex ultimatum, 28; chagrin at German surrender, 29; statement that American troops turned the balance, 260.
Toul, 234, 309.
Toulon, 123.
Tours, 123.
Training Camp Activities, Commission on, remarkable work of, 149, 150; Secretary Baker's praise of, 150.
Trans-Atlantic Fleet, American, growth of, 325.

Transportation and Communication, Committee on, Council of National Defense, 168.
Transportation Corps, U. S. A., 124.
Transports, first American, 84 ff.; need of, 97 ff.; German ships acquired, 102 ff.; transports for cargo, 108 ff.; troops carried by German steamships converted into American transports, 109; need for, 120; American divisions transported to France, 152, 153; relation to convoy, 155 ff.; operated by Navy, 158 ff.; cargo ships in British convoy system, 161; vital to success, 173 ff.; embarkation bases for, 195, 196; problems of, 204 ff.; first of British troopships, 204, 205; N. O. T. S., 211 ff.; the rush at the emergency, 259 ff.; British, 290; operations and losses, 305 ff.; last months on the seas, 315 ff.
Troopships; see Transports.
Turkey, effect of German defeats upon, 313, 314; surrender of, 354.
Tuscania, troopship, lost, 307.
Tuttle, M. C., 122.
Twining, Nathan C., Rear Admiral, U. S. N., 300.

U-boat; see Submarines.
Ukraine, 198.
Ultimatum, from United States to Germany, 28; surrender of Germany, 29.
United States of America, entrance into the World War, 1 ff.; acts of German Imperial Government against, 5, 6, 7, moral effect of entrance of, 8, 9; unexpected strength of, 10; object of, in World War, 11 ff.; supreme effort of, 14, 15; people of, 16 ff.; loyalty in, 19, 20; failure of German Imperial plots in, 20, 21; influence of industries, 22 ff.; effect of state of war upon, 27 ff.; effect of agressions of German Imperial Government, 29 ff.; assertion of rights, 29; awakening in 1916, 34 ff.; immediate action after declaration of war, 43 ff.; finance and manpower, 43 ff.; problems of material, 51 ff.; the nation at work, 60 ff.; scale of military effort, 76 ff.; the American problem, 98, 99; overseas, 119 ff.; mobilization of industries, 126 ff.; training its soldiers, 143 ff.; war activities, 163 ff.; underestimated by Entente Allies, 171, 172; military organization overseas, 178 ff.; at home, 190 ff.; war plan of, 190, 191; the "race" with the German Imperial Government, 203, 204; development of industrial forces, 218 ff.; failure of German spy system, 227, 228; aroused to meet crisis of 1918, 228; crisis revealed, 259 ff.; official record of need for American aid at crisis, 279, 280; German statement, 285, 286; effect of presence of American Army, 312, 313; Meuse-Argonne and its effect, 341 ff.; the "race" won, 354; its victory over the German Imperial Government, 359 ff.; its united threefold effort, 364.
United States Army, confidence of German leaders that it would not be a factor, 3; their mistake, 10, 11; rôle of, 14, 15; manpower provided by Selective Service Act, 46 ff.; Joffre's mistaken estimate of, 51, 52; problems of material, 51 ff.; General Munitions Board, 56 ff.; expansion of, 64, 65, 67, 68; service in Mexico, 68 ff.; increase of, 71 ff.; right estimate of American Expeditionary Forces, 80 ff.; first troops overseas, 84 ff.; preparations overseas, 119 ff.; coördination with General Muni-

tions Board, 129 ff.; rifles, 133 ff.; training American soldiers, 143 ff.; divisions of, 144; doctrines in tactics, 147, 148; make-up of divisions overseas, 151, 152; coordination with Navy, 158 ff.; organization in France, 178 ff.; doctrines of 184, 185; organization in America, 190 ff.; consistent war plan of, 190, 191; Chief of Staff, 191, 192; expansion of, 192 ff.; increased numbers going overseas, 206, 234; indication of doctrines, 245, 246; aid to Entente Allies in emergency, 247 ff.; rush of troops to France, 259 ff.; at the crisis, 274 ff., 281 ff.; First American Army, 289 ff.; independent American Army assured, 294 ff.; offensive operations, 309 ff.; final campaign, 341 ff.

United States Census Bureau, 165.

United States Emergency Fleet Corporation, creation of, 65; great development of, 222 ff.; coöperation with Selective Service Act, 224.

United States Navy, changed aims of, 12, 13; important rôle of, 14, 15; effect upon of aggressions of German Imperial Government, 29 ff.; Chief of Operations, 30; Naval Consulting Board, 31; Naval Building Program of 1916, 32; good faith of, 32; problems of material for, 54 ff.; expansion of, 65; importance of naval factor, 81, 82; first transportation overseas, 84 ff.; naval strategy necessarily dictated by military situation, 97, 98, 99; enormous size of, 99; changed tasks of, 99 ff.; German steamships repaired by, 103 ff.; definite control of American troopships, 107; coördination with General Munitions Board, 129 ff.; difficult tasks of, 155 ff.; relation

to convoy, 157 ff.; coördination with Army, 160 ff.; transportation overseas, 174 ff.; problems of transportation, 204 ff.; N. O. T. S., 211 ff.; stations overseas, 216, 217; Cross-Channel Fleet, 217; its share in American effort, 218; building program, 224, 225; troops transported in the emergency, 259 ff.; Naval forces supporting the Army, 300 ff.; losses, 306, 307, 308, effect of effort of, 308.

United States Railroad Administration, 169; good results from, 221; efficient transportation by, 226, 227.

United States Shipping Board, creation of, 40; active war board, 65, 104; requisition of American shipping, 110; absorbed Shipping Committee, Council of National Defense, 166; problems of transportation, 204 ff.; Shipping Control Committee, 209, 210; reorganized, 222 ff.; effect of building program, 262, 263.

Upton, Camp, L. I., 195; increase at, 206.

Utah, battleship, 316.

Vaterland, 103, 109.

Vedette, converted yacht, 95.

Verdun, 121, 234, 310, 311, 342, 345.

Versailles, 255, 280.

Vesle, 285, 293, 309.

Villa, Francisco, 68, 69, 70.

Viviani, M., with French Commission in America, 11.

Von Steuben, troopship, 109, 268.

Wadsworth, Fort, 71.

Wall of Lamentations, 328.

Wallace, Charles, Major, U. S. A., 58.

War Bond Bill, 43, 44.

War Camp Community Service, good work of, 151.

War College, U. S. A., benefits from, 329.

War Industries Board, evolved from General Munitions Board, 139 ff.; as to shipping, 208, 209; advantages from, 209, 210; reconstituted, 219 ff.; increased army program, 289.

Washington, D. C., 60, 80, 81, 84, 170, 182, 238.

Washington Disarmament Conference, 32.

Western Atlantic, 303, 304.

Western Department, U. S. A., 71.

Wilhelmshaven, 359.

Willard, Daniel, 39, 220.

Wilkes, destroyer, 88, 96.

Wilson, G. H., 104.

Wilson, Sir Henry, General, British representative in Supreme War Council, 232.

Wilson, Henry B., Rear Admiral, U. S. N., 95, 216, 271.

Wilson, Woodrow, President of the United States; distinction between the German Imperial Government and the German people, 5; statement of position of United States, 8; message of 1914, 29; call for program of national defense, 31, 33; amplified powers in National Defense Act, 35, 36; his description of Council of National Defense, 37, 38; executive powers, 41, 42, 43; action as to Selective Service Act, 47; executive powers of, 57, 58; appointment of Food Administrator, 61, 62; appointment of Fuel Administrator, 62;

executive authority to U. S. Shipping Board, 65; effects of war powers, 65, 66, 68, 140; central of American railroads, 168, 169; effectiveness of use of war powers of, 219; plenary powers to War Industries Board, 219 ff.; confirmation of war powers of, 225, 226; endorsement of united command, 250, 251, 256, 257; appreciation from Pershing, 287; support of Pershing, 348; insistence on repudiation of German Imperial Government, 359 ff

Woëvre, 288.

Woman's Committee, Council of National Defense, 62; importance of work, 164, 165; widespread service of American women, 164, 165, 166.

Wood, Leonard, Major General, U. S. A., originator of Plattsburg idea, 71, 72; physical disability of, 188, 189; notable services of, 189.

Woodbridge, J. W., Major, U. S. A., 286.

Wyoming, battleship, 215.

Young Men's Christian Association, efficient work of, 151; continued overseas, 338 ff.

Young Women's Christian Association, efficient work of, 151; continued overseas, 338 ff.

Ypres, 270.

Zeebrugge, 353.

Zimmermann, German Foreign Secretary, note to urge support of Mexico, 5, 6; cession of New Mexico, Texas, and Arizona promised, 6.